CAMBRIDGE STUDIES IN PHILOSOPHY

Supererogation

T0382625

CAMBRIDGE STUDIES IN PHILOSOPHY

General editor D. H. MELLOR

Advisory editors J. E. J. ALTHAM, SIMON BLACKBURN
DANIEL DENNETT, MARTIN HOLLIS, FRANK JACKSON
JONATHAN LEAR, T. J. SMILEY; BARRY STROUD

Supererogation
Its status in ethical theory

David Heyd

Lecturer in Philosophy
The Hebrew University of Jerusalem

Cambridge University Press

CAMBRIDGE
LONDON   NEW YORK   NEW ROCHELLE
MELBOURNE   SYDNEY

CAMBRIDGE UNIVERSITY PRESS
Cambridge, New York, Melbourne, Madrid, Cape Town, Singapore, São Paulo, Delhi

Cambridge University Press
The Edinburgh Building, Cambridge CB2 8RU, UK

Published in the United States of America by Cambridge University Press, New York

www.cambridge.org
Information on this title: www.cambridge.org/9780521109666

First published 1982
This digitally printed version 2009

A catalogue record for this publication is available from the British Library

Library of Congress Catalogue Card Number: 81–15476

ISBN 978-0-521-23935-6 hardback
ISBN 978-0-521-10966-6 paperback

Contents

Acknowledgments

This book is based on my doctoral dissertation submitted at the University of Oxford. I am especially indebted to Sir Stuart Hampshire and Mr G. J. Warnock whose critical comments and sympathetic reading of earlier drafts were a necessary stimulant in the process of forming my ideas on the relatively neglected topic of supererogation.

I also benefited from some very useful suggestions made by Mr J. O. Urmson and Mr D. Parfit. Urmson's own written work on the subject significantly influenced my ideas.

Mr J. L. Mackie read the whole typescript and clearly went beyond his duty in making so many valuable remarks – on both substance and style.

I also wish to express gratitude for another supererogatory act, the generous financial support given by the Hebrew University of Jerusalem and the British Friends of the Hebrew University, which made my stay in Oxford and the work on this book possible.

Chapter 3 is almost identical to my article 'Beyond the Call of Duty in Kant's Ethics', which was published in *Kant-Studien* **71** (1980). I should like to thank the editor for giving me permission to use this material.

Introduction

There is a lack of proportion between the importance ascribed to acts of supererogation in everyday life and the relative paucity of theoretical analysis of these acts in the history of ethics. While most people are usually highly impressed and moved by acts which go beyond the call of duty, only a few philosophers have tried to provide an ethical account of the concept of supererogation. This may be due to a theoretical or a moral bias against the classification of supererogation as a separate class of morally valuable acts.

This work suggests a theory of supererogation which will serve to analyse and justify the special status of these acts. Obviously, one of its principal aims is to show that supererogation is a distinct and determinate class of moral action deserving of special scrutiny, and that there are both theoretical and moral reasons for treating these acts as belonging to a separate category.

The Latin etymology of the term *supererogation* refers to the act of paying out more than is required or demanded. Historically, the use of this term has become confined to religious and moral contexts, meaning acts which go beyond the call of duty. Consequently, works of supererogation or supererogatory acts are now commonly understood to be those acts which a person does over and above his religious or moral duty, i.e. more than he ought to or has to do.

Now this very rough definition contains some of the more important features of the definiendum. First of all, supererogation is primarily attributed to *acts* or *actions* rather than to persons, traits of character, motives, intentions, or emotions. Secondly, these acts are *optional* or *non-obligatory*, that is – distinguished from those acts which fall under the heading of duty. Thirdly, they are *beyond* duty, fulfil *more* than is required, *over and above* what the agent is supposed or expected to do. This means that although they are distinguished from obligatory acts, they are not just a different moral category, but stand in a specific relationship (of transcendence, excellence or over-subscription) to obligatory action. Finally, this relationship implies that supererogatory acts have a special value; they are *morally good* and praiseworthy.

These features, derived from the initial description of supererogation as the class of acts which go beyond the call of duty, will be further analysed, developed and qualified in the following chapters. At this stage some examples of supererogation will suffice to elucidate the crude intuitive definition, and so will describe the subject of this study.

Perhaps the most typical cases of supererogation are the so-called 'saintly and heroic acts'. Leading an ascetic life, abstaining from pleasures normally enjoyed by most people, or sacrificing one's life in an act of martyrdom, are all regarded as saintly acts by some religions. Heroism is displayed by people who are willing to take great risks or to make a sacrifice in order to achieve a morally good end. This is exemplified by Captain Oates of the Arctic expedition sacrificing his life so as to secure his friends' survival, or the soldier who with his own body covers an exploding hand-grenade in order to protect his fellows. And of course some less extravagant acts involving risk or sacrifice also deserve to be called saintly and heroic.

Another type of supererogatory acts includes charity, generosity and giving, or more generally – acts of beneficence. Giving money to the poor, donating blood in a voluntary system, or otherwise helping people in trouble are all cases of beneficent action.

Then there are those acts of kindness and consideration. These, as we shall see, are borderline cases of supererogation. Still, they ought to be discussed under that title as they meet – in most cases – the conditions of supererogatory acts briefly mentioned above. Helping a stranger to find his way in town, or assisting an old woman to cross the road cannot be considered as saintly or heroic, nor as generous or beneficent. Yet they are supererogatory.

Forgiveness, mercy, and pardon form another group of acts that are typically supererogatory. Forgiving a person for the wrong he has done, instead of acting in a retaliatory manner (albeit justified) is one example. Acting mercifully towards someone who deserves punishment, or pardoning a criminal by remitting his sentence are other examples.

Finally, volunteering is another category of supererogation. Going on a dangerous mission in place of someone else whose duty it is, or selecting oneself to do a certain unpleasant job (where no criteria for selecting any particular individual in a group obtain) are by definition supererogatory acts. They may also be heroic, but they do not necessarily have to be so in order to be called supererogatory. The very act of volunteering means doing something over and above what is required. One cannot volunteer to pay one's debts, or feed one's children.

These are just a few examples of what is normally judged to be supererogatory action. These will be further analysed and characterized as paradigm cases and should not be regarded as an exhaustive list. Moreover, these examples partly serve as evidence for but also partly presuppose a theory of supererogation. That is, on the one hand, their very existence, and our intuition that they are different from other types of moral action, serve as a justification for the distinction between supererogation and duty; on the other hand, their special status and moral worth is accounted for by the theory of supererogation. This seems to me to be inevitable and to contain no methodological flaw (compare this to Rawls's doctrine of 'reflective equilibrium').

The philosophical problem of supererogation is twofold: theoretical and moral (i.e. meta-ethical and normative respectively). Basically it bears upon the relationship between supererogation and duty, and thus upon the limits of duty. Theoretically, the concept of supererogation gives rise to what may appear to be a paradox: on the one hand, acts of supererogation are, by definition, distinguished from acts of duty; on the other hand, they have meaning only in the framework of a moral theory based on the concept of duty. Now a completely non-deontological theory – that is to say, a theory based on a concept other than duty (virtue, sympathy, etc.) – cannot accommodate supererogation, because if there is no duty, then a fortiori there cannot be action which transcends duty. On the other hand, a purely deontological theory (like Kant's) does not leave room for supererogation either, for supererogation is a class of non-obligatory acts. Supererogation, being different yet related to duty, can be accounted for neither by a theory which attaches no importance to deontic concepts, nor by a theory which takes duty as exhausting the whole realm of moral behaviour.

It looks, therefore, as if the suggested theory of supererogation should fuse elements of both a deontological and a non-deontological type of ethics. We shall see that supererogation is intimately connected with virtuous traits of character, benevolent and

3

altruistic motivation, and aspiration to moral ideals. Nevertheless, the concept of supererogation can be understood only in relation to duty, and this makes the more deontologically oriented theories more appealing and promising to our discussion.

Analysing supererogation in deontological terms opens the door to another puzzle: how can supererogatory acts be so valuable and important, and yet not obligatory? How can a morally good action be non-obligatory in a basically deontological theory? This is sometimes referred to as the 'good–ought tie-up', which will be discussed in the following chapters. The usual kind of solution to this problem is reductionism – an attempt to analyse supererogation in deontic terms (e.g. as an imperfect duty, a super-obligation, a less stringent duty, a duty in an ideal world, or a permission to abstain from doing what is required by practical reason).

While purely deontological theories can be called 'anti-supererogationist', reductionism is an attempt to modify and extend deontological theory to accommodate supererogation as a limiting (or often marginal) case. This half-way solution I shall call 'qualified supererogationism'. The purpose of this work is to set up a theory which will be 'unqualified', that is to say not based on any reduction of the supererogatory to the obligatory.

The moral or normative problem of supererogation mainly concerns the demarcation of duty and 'beyond duty'. Even those who accept an ethical theory allowing for supererogation as a distinct category of moral action find the problem of demarcation highly controversial. Where does the limit of our duty to help others lie? Do we owe economic assistance to people in India as a duty? Does (or should) Oxfam appeal to our sense of duty, or rather to our generosity and moral ideals? These are substantive questions often debated in non-philosophical circles. Their solution depends on the way in which we understand the meaning of 'duty', but not only on that. People who share the same meta-ethical understanding of the concept of duty may differ in their moral judgments concerning its limits. Reflecting on many of the day-to-day controversies about moral issues would show that much rests on the problem of demarcation of supererogation and duty.

The dispute between Catholics and Lutherans regarding supererogation is at least partly a normative one. It concerns the scope and limits of religious duty, and the amount of 'good works' necessary for the salvation of the soul. Even if saintly acts are theor-

4

etically possible, the actual possibility of human beings doing such acts remains an open question, and with it the justification of expecting or encouraging people to act supererogatorily. But the theological debate within Christianity serves as a model both for the theoretical and for the moral problem of supererogation.

So the theory of supererogation turns out to be logically related to a theory of duty. The very meaning of supererogation is dependent on what is understood by duty. If supererogatory acts are those acts which go beyond the call of duty, it makes a vast difference whether we mean by 'duty' any moral requirement that is 'binding', or just a requirement derived from one's role, job, or function; whether 'duty' designates also what we normally call 'obligation', or is distinguished from it; whether duty is necessarily a universalizable requirement, or may also designate personal commitments. An analysis of these various alternatives will show that not every duty (and not in all of its meanings) can be 'excelled' in a supererogatory way. Reductionism will however be rejected under all the possible interpretations of duty.

The logical relation between supererogation and duty will be characterized in this work by two features: *correlativity* and *continuity*. Correlativity means that acts of supererogation derive their special value from their being 'more than duty requires'; i.e. they have meaning only relatively to obligatory action. This is why a theory of supererogation must be of a quasi-deontological type. The other feature – that of continuity – is to be understood also in terms of the logical interdependence of the concepts of supererogation and duty. Not every non-obligatory good act is supererogatory. It has to be *morally* good, its value being of the same *type* that makes obligatory action good and valuable. Obviously, the definition of 'morally good' is highly controversial, and the term is analysed in various ways (e.g. utility, happiness, virtue, etc.). Yet whichever definition is adopted, supererogation should be characterized as realizing *more* of the same type of value attached to obligatory action. That is to say: there is a common and continuous scale of values shared by supererogation and duty. How supererogatory acts that consist of over-subscription (like paying more than is owed) display this feature of continuity can be easily seen; other cases of supererogation (like mercy or volunteering) contain this feature too, but not in such a clear manner as in the former case. This logical condition of continuity is necessary if a Nietzschean morality, for instance, is to be excluded from what is covered by the definition of supererogation. The pursuit of non-obligatory (and non-moral) personal ideals or aesthetic value is not supererogatory, even if it is good and praiseworthy.

So far we have been stressing the logical dependence of supererogation on the concept of duty. It should however be noted that the dependence relation works both ways. A theory of supererogation shows that it is necessary for any theory of duty to point out the limits of duty, and the possibility of doing more than is required by it. Supererogation is a complementary part to any theory of duty. This is due to moral reasons of two kinds: those limiting the grounds for obliging people to work for the good of others, and those pointing to the value of the very existence of action which is voluntary and free from the constraints of moral duty.

The interrelation between supererogation and duty is perhaps the most fundamental one for our investigation. There are, however, further concepts to which supererogation also relates in relevant ways. Some philosophers try to analyse supererogation in terms of 'good' and 'bad', defining a supererogatory act as that which is good to do but not bad not to do. This definition is of course very crude and open to much criticism. The first half of the definition seems to be trivially true, but, for reasons stated in the preceding paragraphs, includes too much. The second half is unsatisfactory, because 'bad' can be interpreted either in an impersonal way (e.g. the overall loss in the world), or in a personal way (not bad *for x* not to do). In the former the definition seems to be false; in the latter it involves the problem of agency and responsibility which lies beyond the concepts of good and bad. Still, it is true that acts of supererogation are necessarily good and carry a moral value usually in terms of other people's happiness or welfare (although not in the case of some of the Evangelical Counsels, which are the Christian examples of supererogation). And there is also a sense in which failing to act supererogatorily is not considered to be 'bad'.

Another definition bearing the same structure as the previous one suggests that supererogatory acts are those which it is right to do but not wrong not to do. Whatever its merits, this definition shifts the focus to the question of rules and an act's conformity to rules. For those who interpret 'right' and 'wrong' in terms of conformity to rules, an act is supererogatory if it conforms to certain rules, but its omission does not violate any rule. At a first glance this seems an improvement on the above-mentioned definition in terms of goodness and badness. Yet it is frequently disputed whether supererogation is rule-determined at all. Some philosophers argue for a rule-free morality, and even if their arguments are not acceptable for the whole of morality, it may be the case that they characterize the supererogatory part. The latter view is adopted in this work. The view claiming that supererogatory acts conform to non-institutional or less binding rules will be criticized as being a version of reductionism. Not confined by any rules, supererogation is an open-ended category, based on personal decision which can be described as discretionary. Generosity in personal relations, or pardon in more institutionalized circumstances exhibit this rule-free aspect of supererogation.

Supererogation is normally associated with the concept of virtue or virtuous action. But one should take care not to take virtue as the defining property of supererogation. Although saintly and heroic acts are truly virtuous, not every type of supererogatory behaviour manifests virtue, and not every virtuous act is supererogatory. Furthermore, some acts which are obligatory reflect a virtuous trait of character no less than a supererogatory act. The relation between supererogation and virtue raises the problem of the *agent* of the act in question. Is there any necessary correlation between acting supererogatorily and having a special personality trait? Those who argue for such a correlation between acting supererogatorily and being virtuous try to define a supererogatory act as that act whose performance should be praised, although its omission should not be blamed. Others go further and describe it as an act which should be rewarded, although its omission should not be punished. The view implied by this claim is that only acts which do more than is required as duty deserve praise or reward, all other morally relevant acts being either 'merely right' or punishable. I find this theory too schematic, mainly because the grounds for praising or blaming people for what they do or fail to do include many other factors besides the moral binding force and the value of the act. Degree of risk and sacrifice, the agent's past and his character, conditions under which the act was performed, are all very important in justifying praise, blame and excuse.

Finally, supererogation is often analysed in terms of reasons for action (and in relation to 'ought'). It is hard to say whether 'ought'-statements apply to supererogatory acts, i.e. whether a

7

supererogatory act is something a person *ought* morally to do although it is not his duty. Of course, much rests on the meaning of these terms. A wide interpretation of 'duty' renders this definition inconsistent. But there are other interpretations too, which allow for locutions such as 'not being a relation of John and not being responsible for his plight, you did not have any duty to help him; nevertheless, you ought to have helped him'. This, however, is hardly a case of supererogation.

A more sophisticated analysis of supererogation in terms of 'ought' and reasons for action suggests that one ought to do a supererogatory act, yet one is also permitted not to do it. This theory tries to avoid the apparent inconsistency by treating the permission as a second-order reason for action, which entitles us to ignore (first-order) reasons for doing the act in question. This analysis of supererogation will be contested on both logical and ethical grounds.

Supererogation may thus be analysed in various terms, in relation to the different basic concepts of ethical theory and moral discourse: duty and obligation (in terms of requirement); good and bad (in terms of value); right and wrong (conformity to rules); virtue and vice (traits of character); praise and blame or reward and punishment (the reaction of others); and 'ought' (reasons for action). These are all relevant aspects of supererogation, but none of these pairs of concepts is sufficient to define it. Each one of these pairs has been used by some ethical theory as a basis for explaining supererogation. In the following chapters these theories will be discussed and criticised.

The above-mentioned pairs of contrary terms can be utilized in definitions of supererogation because these terms stand in asymmetrical relations to each other in the context of acting and forbearing. A supererogatory act is an act which it is good (right, praiseworthy, virtuous) to do, but not bad (wrong, blameful, evil) not to do. This is the reason why traditional deontic logic will not do for supererogation, for 'obligatory' and 'forbidden' stand in symmetrical relations (if an act is forbidden it is obligatory not to do it, and vice versa). Non-performance of a supererogatory act cannot be judged or appraised by means of terms contrary to those used in judging or appraising its performance. Only in the case of non-performance of obligatory acts can such contrary terms be legitimately used.

In this work I shall argue for a view that will be called *unqualified supererogationism*. This view not only acknowledges the possibility and existence of supererogation, but treats it as absolutely irreducible to duty. Acts of supererogation are characterized as purely voluntary, optional, and in a sense arbitrary, that is, not determined by universal standards or rules. Underlying such a contention is the view that holds human beings to be autonomous individuals having a basic right to pursue their own ideals and projects, sometimes regardless of the public or general good. People are not just tools for the promotion of good or for maximizing value and happiness in the world. Their duty towards others is limited, and moral considerations of what is obligatory do not come into every moral deliberation.

This is the negative aspect of unqualified supererogationism, for it merely provides the grounds for the possibility of supererogation. But there is a positive side too. Only an analysis which presents supererogation as an irreducible moral category does justice to its special worth and value. This special worth is derived from the act's being over and above what is required. The value of supererogatory acts consists not just in the increase of the net amount of goodness (welfare, happiness, utility) in the world, but also in their being totally optional and voluntary. Although heroic sacrifices and great acts of generosity are invaluable because of their consequences (in terms of utility and goodness) there are supererogatory acts which do not radically tilt the balance of good and yet deserve special praise. (Forgiveness and volunteering are good examples of this.) And even the heroic and beneficent acts are praiseworthy partly because they are not obligatory.

This intrinsic value attached independently of its utility to the act's being non-obligatory may help us to understand why some of our social organizations and institutions are built so as both to enable and to encourage supererogatory behaviour. It is felt by many people that a system of blood donation based on voluntary giving is morally superior to a system based on commercial exchange and economic utility (or, alternatively, it is superior to a system which legally requires the donation of blood). The same point is made by the habit of asking for volunteers where no clear procedure of selecting a person to perform a dangerous job can be applied. This habit is usually preferred to arbitrary choice, e.g. by a military commander.

Generally, supererogation provides moral agents with the opportunity of exercising and expressing virtuous traits of character, of acting altruistically, and of fulfilling their individual ideals, opportunities which are denied to them in the sphere of the morality of duty and obligation. And this itself is one of the justifications for the distinction between supererogation and duty.

So although relatively rare, supererogatory action is not of marginal importance, either morally or theoretically. It is therefore surprising how little attention has been paid to it in past and current ethical doctrines. Supererogation raises a challenge to any moral theory, especially a deontological one, for it bears on some of the central points and issues of morality: the limits of duty, the relation between goodness and obligation, the logic of obligatory action (deontic logic), the flaws of utilitarianism, and the personal dimensions of moral behaviour. Indeed, the way a theory treats the problem of supererogation and whether it can be adjusted to contain it serve as criteria for its adequacy.

In the first part of this work we address ourselves to a critical discussion of some of the major ethical theories (or types of theories) of the past: Christianity, Aristotelianism, Kantianism, Utilitarianism and Contract Theory. The discussion, however, is not intended to be a historical one. It is not a systematic survey of the evolution of the concept, nor is it exhaustive. Most philosophers mentioned in this part did not use the term *supererogation*, some of them did not even face the problem of supererogation directly. Much of the discussion should thus be seen as a 'reconstruction' rather than a history.

One of the objectives of the first part is to investigate what type of theory can best accommodate the phenomenon of supererogatory acts. Yet the discussion does not presuppose the truth of any specific ethical theory. The treatment of supererogation is just one criterion of the acceptability of a theory, and as other criteria cannot be discussed here, this question of truth will not be prejudged. Still, the problem of supererogation permits classical and current theories of morality to be explored from an unusual angle, and such an exploration may underline both some merits and some flaws and inconsistencies in those theories.

The second part of the work is analytical and constructive. It contains an outline of a theory of supererogation. Its aim is to define the concept of supererogation, to study its relation to other moral concepts, and to justify its special status. The chapters of this part contain a detailed discussion of contemporary theories devoted specifically to supererogation. Most of the philosophical literature dealing with the problem of supererogation dates from the last two decades, originally as a reaction to J. O. Urmson's pioneering article 'Saints and Heroes' (Urmson, 1958). Most of the work done during these years is piecemeal, and no systematic or extensive study of the subject has yet been undertaken.

PART I

The view of some major ethical theories

1

Theological origins in Christianity

1.1 THE RELEVANCE OF THE CHRISTIAN DOCTRINE

The subject of the *opera supererogationis* aroused one of the most heated theological disputes in the sixteenth century. Being a necessary theoretical justification of the institution of Indulgences, 'works of supererogation' were naturally a target of primary importance for the fierce attacks made by the Reformers on the Roman Catholic Church. Moreover, this debate touched upon the fundamental issues which divided the two parties: justification by works, the relation between human effort to achieve salvation and God's grace, freedom of the will, the source of merit, and the possibility of fulfilling God's commandments.

Although this study is concerned with the concept of supererogation in ethical theory and with the nature of supererogatory behaviour in secular morality, the theological background may serve as a suitable starting point for two reasons. Firstly, historically speaking, Christian theology is the origin both of the concept and of the formulation of the problem of supererogation. Nowhere can a clear discussion of the relation between duty and 'above duty' be found before Christianity, and up to our own time Thomas Aquinas (together with his Protestant critics) remains one of the most systematic writers on that problem. Secondly, there are theoretical reasons for tracing the theological origins of the concept. Christian (Catholic) morality may be characterized by four features: (a) it is based on duty (and not solely on virtue), (b) its source and authority is heteronomous, (c) its axiological framework is teleological, and (d) it assumes freedom of choice. In a more theological nomenclature, men's behaviour according to (Catholic) Christianity is governed by commandments (a), which are issued by divine external authority (b), and whose fulfilment is a means of achieving a specified end – the salvation of the soul (c), the agent having the freedom to choose his ends and means (d).

15

Now, a morality characterized by these features naturally allows for supererogation. For, being founded both on the concepts of duty and virtue, it meets the conditions of correlativity and continuity to which we briefly referred in the Introduction. Heteronomy means that the authority of the precepts by which we are bound is external to us. This relation of obedience to the requirements of a superior authority allows for acts which surpass these requirements more naturally than if we ourselves were their source and authority, because the gap between what I *have* to do and what I decide to do beyond my duty is harder to explain if I myself am the authority on what ought to be done.[1] Finally, a teleological theory leaves room for supererogatory acts in the sense that the same end can be achieved by various means – some of which are strictly necessary, others, just optional (such as those that guarantee the achievement of the end more speedily). This variety of means to a given end implies freedom of choice.

Obviously, there are other types of morality which are not characterized by these four features and yet have a supererogatory dimension. But the type of ethical theory expounded by medieval Christian theology is particularly illustrative for our purposes. The confrontation between the Catholic tradition and the Reformation includes most of the problems to which we will address ourselves in the analysis of supererogation. As there are interesting analogies between Christian and secular moralities with regard to supererogation a short exposition of the concept of supererogation in the religious context may be helpful. Indeed, the very idea of acting over and above one's duty quite often has religious overtones, especially when we talk about such behaviour as 'saintly'.

1.2 THE NEW TESTAMENT AND THE CHURCH FATHERS

Both Catholics and Protestants tried to base their case on the Scriptures. The New Testament, as we shall see, lends support to the interpretations of both parties. Although supererogation is not discussed as such in the New Testament the term *supererogation* dates back to the Latin version of the Bible, in which it occurs only once – in the parable of the Good Samaritan. After paying the innkeeper

---

[1] Nevertheless, supererogation is logically compatible with autonomy; it is only harder to explain for psychological reasons, as we shall see in the discussion of moral modesty (see below, 6.5).

'two pence' for the care and expenses of the robbed and wounded man, the Samaritan adds: 'and whatsoever thou shalt spend over and above (*quodcumque supererogaveris*), I, at my return, will repay thee' (Luke x, 35). This expression can certainly be understood as having no special meaning beyond what it literally expresses, namely a promise to compensate the innkeeper for extra expenses, not covered by the 'two pence'. But supererogationists can still point to the fact that even if what the Samaritan did up to that stage (saving the victim's life, taking care of him, etc.) was his duty, his promise to pay for further expenses was clearly beyond his duty; and as such this deed was especially meritorious and worthy of exemplifying what Jesus meant by 'love thy neighbour as thyself' (which is the moral of the whole parable).

Yet, since the story of the Good Samaritan does not clearly imply a distinction between duty and the non-obligatory virtuous act, it is not the *locus classicus* referred to by later supererogationists. The idea of supererogation is more explicitly contained in other passages, in which two types of norms are contrasted with each other – those which are commanded, and those which are just recommended. In the story of the rich man Jesus is asked 'what good shall I do that I may have life everlasting?', to which he replies: 'if thou wilt enter into life, keep the commandments', but adds: 'if thou wilt be perfect, go sell what thou hast and give to the poor and thou shalt have treasure in Heaven. And come follow me' (Matthew xix, 16–24). Another widely used source for later doctrines of supererogation is the recommendation of virginity and chastity. In Paul's words: 'Now, concerning virgins, I have no commandment of the Lord: but I give counsel, as having obtained mercy of the Lord, to be faithful. I think therefore that this is good for the present necessity: that it is good for a man so to be ... But if thou take a wife, thou hast not sinned' (I Corinthians vii, 25–8).[2]   But these are by no means the only sources from which supererogationists could draw their evidence. Jesus urges his Disciples to love their enemies (Matthew v, 44), to be merciful and forgiving (Luke vi, 36–7), and to be charitable in all their deeds. He blesses the rich man Zacheus for his habit of restoring fourfold to any man who has been wronged by him (Luke xix, 8), and generally preaches the morality of love and aspiration to perfection. Those norms can all be interpreted as supererogatory, as recommending acts and attitudes

[2] And see also Matthew xix, 12: 'He that can take, let him take it.'

which go well beyond the strict word of the law. In fact, they are part of the New Law – the Law of Liberty, which is constantly contrasted to the Old Law – the Law of Bondage, of the Jewish religion and the Old Testament.

The systematic theology of supererogation cannot, however, be found in the New Testament. Alluding perhaps to the passage quoted above from I Corinthians, the Church Fathers drew a distinction between the recommended and the strictly obligatory types of norms. The former became known as the 'counsels' (*consilia*), while the latter were termed 'precepts' (*praecepta*). Originally, the list of counsels (or Evangelical Counsels) included just three recommendations: perpetual poverty, perfect chastity and perfect obedience;[3] the precepts were the Ten Commandments, or rather the five mentioned by Jesus in Matthew xix, 18–19 (which except for that of honouring one's parents are typically negative, i.e. prescribe forbearances). Historically, the evolution of the doctrine of the Evangelical Counsels was stimulated by the need to provide a theoretical justification of the monastic ideals, whose importance became so marked in the third and fourth centuries. The monk's life was distinguished from the ordinary Christian way of life by his total withdrawal from the worldly pleasures of the flesh, property, and pride.[4] And although some measure of satisfaction of these human needs was permitted by Christianity, it was necessary to indicate the merit of such an absolute renunciation.

To mention just a few examples from the Patristic literature, the Shepherd of Hermas says: 'And if thou do any good thing beyond God's commandment, thou shalt win for thyself more exceeding glory, and shalt be more honourable with God than thou wouldest have been' (Taylor, 1906, Fifth Similitude, ch. 3, 3). Tertullian goes a step further claiming that strictly speaking only those non-obligatory acts are meritorious, because they alone are performed out of real freedom (the precepts are obeyed mainly out of fear and as a matter of necessity). God has ordained a special field of liberty (*licentia*) in order to give us an opportunity to act supererogatorily,

---

[3] Obedience is not explicitly formulated as a counsel in the New Testament, but later theologians understood the norm 'follow me' as implying this counsel. Cf. John x, 27 and Matthew xix, 21. The counsel of obedience recommends humility as a means to total preoccupation with God and the denial of selfish pride.

[4] 'For all that is in the world is the concupiscence of the flesh and the concupiscence of the eyes and the pride of life . . .' (I St. John The Apostle, ii, 16). This is the only place in the New Testament where the three cardinal counsels are listed together.

and this 'licence' is the only way to test whose acts are really meritorious by 'a trial of discipline' (Tertullian, *On Exhortation to Chastity*, ch. 8). Tertullian quotes I Corinthians x, 23 ('All things are lawful for me: but all things do not edify') to support his distinction. This notion of freedom, which turned out to be highly controversial in the Reformation, is surely central to any theory of supererrogation. Tertullian's examples are not confined to the three original counsels. He mentions voluntary penance, patience, fasting, and martyrdom – the greatest sacrifice of all. Yet at this stage there is no mention of the possibility of transferring the over-abundant merit of the Saints to other people.

In St. Ambrose and St. Augustine an explicit distinction between precepts and counsels is to be found for the first time. In the case of Ambrose it is in the context of the idea of chastity (Ambrose, *Concerning Widows*, ch. 12); in Augustine the distinction is associated with the story of the rich man (Augustine, *Letters*, 157; *Holy Virginity*, ch. 14). However, their discussions are still confined to the particular Evangelical Counsels, and the more systematic account of supererogation had to await the Schoolmen.

The most important motivation for developing a doctrine of supererogation is connected with the institution of Indulgences. The idea of indulgences is that remission of penance and temporal penalties attached to sin is conferred upon those who have acted in a meritorious way, mainly by contributing money to the Church. The system of Indulgences was used at first for the purpose of 'compensating' those who took part in the Crusades. But it did not take much time for the system to become 'commercialized', that is used for the financial benefit of the Church. Now these indulgences were believed to be drawn from what came to be known in the fourteenth century as the Spiritual Treasury of The Church committed to the Pope (and some of his Bishops). This 'treasury' was said to contain the superabundant merit of Jesus and the Saints, whose good works excelled what was necessary for their own salvation. This excess of merit was bequeathed to the Church in order to help sinners to achieve everlasting life. The Scholastic theologians of the Thirteenth century – notably Albertus Magnus, Alexander of Hales, and most systematically Thomas Aquinas – provided the philosophical justification for that system.

19

In the *Summa Theologica* Aquinas gives a general account of supererogation, which is theoretically based on the distinction between precepts and counsels: 'a commandment implies obligation, whereas a counsel is left to the option of the one to whom it is given' (Aquinas, *Summa Theologica,* I, II, Q. 108, Art. 4). The commandment is binding; the counsel, only recommended. The commandment expresses a necessity; the counsel is given as a matter of free choice of the agent (compare Tertullian's *licentia*). But in what sense are the commandments 'necessary'? This is explained by the teleological nature of Christian morality as seen through the Aristotelian eyes of Aquinas: 'the commandments ... [are] about matters that are necessary to gain the end of eternal bliss ... the counsels are about matters that render the gaining of this end more assured and expeditious'. This distinction, which is put in teleological terms, presupposes another distinction, that between the Old Law and the New Law. It is only the New Law, the Law of Liberty, which presents the agent with a specific end – that of salvation. The Old Law does not specify such an end. Hence, it is natural that the New Law should allow for various means of achieving that end, whereas in the Old Law strict adherence to the commandments is the only possible way of leading a religious life. This is why the Old Law is called 'the Law of Bondage'. The New Law, however, has two aspects: as a *law* it prescribes the minimum required for gaining an everlasting life; but as a law of *liberty* it adds advice and recommendations for quick and 'guaranteed' ways of securing this end.

This particular explanation of the function of the counsels, however, is not the complete doctrine. It stresses the role of supererogatory action as a better means to a particular end, i.e. as a form of expediency. But there is surely more to the ideals recommended by the counsels. Those who pursue them try to achieve a *better end* than those who are satisfied with fulfilling God's commandments. In Aquinas's own words, this higher end is the 'perfection of human life', which is man's total preoccupation with God (Aquinas, *Summa Contra Gentiles*, bk. III, pt. II, ch. 130). This explains why works of supererogation are often referred to as *opera meliora* (better acts), for they are good not only in terms of expediency, but also in themselves – as aiming at a better ideal than acts commanded by God. Accordingly, 'man is *counselled* to forgo the lesser goods for the sake of the greater' (ibid.).

This latter interpretation of the counsels in the *Summa Contra Gentiles* is closer to what we understand by supererogation in secular morality. Nevertheless, it is perfectly compatible with the more self-regarding account of the *Summa Theologica*. In both cases the indulgence in the worldly pleasures of property, flesh, and selfish pride is said to be the main obstacle to salvation and perfection respectively. The aim of the counsels is to remove this obstacle as far as possible, so that (in the latter case) man's attention to God will be undivided, and so that (in the former case) he will not be tempted to 'make use of things corporal and earthly [not] according to the order of reason'.[5] But the teleological nature is preserved in the explanation of the counsels in terms of perfection, for Aquinas emphasizes that chastity, poverty, and obedience are not 'themselves perfections', but only 'dispositions to perfection', i.e. ways to ensure unobstructed love of God (ibid.). These 'dispositions' are also said to be *signs* of perfection; the fact that a man succeeds in renouncing all worldly goods is evidence of his love of God. In other words, the precepts are intended to remove things which are *contrary* to charity, while the counsels are meant to remove things that *hinder* acts of charity. The counsels are 'instrumentally' necessary to perfection (Aquinas, *Summa Theologica*, II, II, Q. 184, Art. 3). And they are supererogatory, because although necessary to perfection, they are superfluous for salvation.

It is important to note that the interpretation of the counsels as recommending '*better* works' gives the counsels an 'open texture'. Unlike the lesser goods which are the subject of the precepts, the 'greater goods are not definitely fixed in the individual'. The second objection in the Article discussed above (Aquinas, *Summa Theologica* I, II, Q. 108, Art. 4) takes this fact as implying the impossibility of giving 'definite counsels', to which Aquinas replies cryptically by saying that the things that are simply and absolutely the greater goods are fixed.

The commandments are directed to everyone. Who are the subjects of the counsels? In reply to the first objection in Article 4, Aquinas admits that although the counsels are 'in themselves ex-

---

[5] This temptation is hard to overcome, as the story of the rich man in Matthew teaches. If it is easier for a camel to pass through the eye of a needle than for a rich man to be saved, it might be advisable for the rich to give up their property altogether.

pedient to all', many human beings are not 'inclined to such things'. Thus, the actual range of application of the counsels is limited to the few, and conditioned by the agent's desire for perfection and by his capacity to observe them.

Aquinas also distinguishes between absolute observance of the counsels and observance in a 'restricted sense' (ibid.). This distinction is theoretically significant, for it allows for individual acts of supererogation which do not demand total renunciation of worldly pleasures. The monk, for example, who chooses chastity, poverty, and obedience as a *way of life*, that is as an ideal which should be pursued constantly and for an indefinite time, is indeed a 'saint'. But one can also follow the Evangelical Counsels in isolated cases like giving alms, refraining from sexual intercourse for a limited period in order to devote oneself to prayer, or forgiving one's enemies. For Aquinas these are all supererogatory acts, since it is not one's duty to refrain from lawful carnal pleasures, nor is one bound to give alms or to refrain from seeking justice. But although Aquinas does not say so explicitly, it is clear that absolute observance of the Evangelical Counsels is a necessary condition for being venerated as a Saint.[6]

The distinction between counsels and precepts is suggested by Aquinas in the wider context of the discussion of the New Law. And it is philosophically important to see it in that context, for the fact that Jesus gave some counsels in addition to the precepts is believed to be exactly the advantage of the New Law over the Old one, which leaves no room for supererogatory ideals. The New Law can be 'the law of perfection', charity, and love only because it allows for a variety of ways of attaining salvation. This variety admits degrees of perfection and presupposes that not all people can respond equally to the 'recommendations' of the law. A law which does not have this open texture is (like the Old Law) just 'a pedagogue of children', purely authoritarian (Aquinas, *Summa Theologica* I, II, Q. 107, Art. 1).

So far we have been looking at the distinction between precepts and counsels as defined and analysed by Aquinas. But how is the distinction applied in concrete cases? One objection, considered by

---

[6] The Roman Catholic Church has well-defined and strict procedures for the Canonization of Saints. It is only those who display virtue in a 'heroic' way who deserve to be venerated as Saints; so even absolute observance of the counsels may not be sufficient for that purpose – *a fortiori* observance in the restricted sense.

Aquinas himself, is that the counsels 'are unfittingly given in the New Law: both because they are not all mentioned; and because they are not distinguished from the commandments' (Aquinas, *Summa Theologica* I, II, Q. 108, Art. 4, Obj. 4). In the New Testament some matters pertaining to the life of perfection are considered as precepts, e.g. 'love your enemies'. Aquinas' reply to that objection is unconvincing, yet it is illuminating for our purposes. He says that the precept 'love your enemies' is concerned with the 'preparation of the mind' (that man should be prepared to do good to his enemies 'when there is a need'), while actual good behaviour towards an enemy ('when there is no special need') is given merely as a counsel. Aquinas tries to save his interpretation of the Bible and his theory of counsels by distinguishing between man's general dispositions and his concrete actions. But it seems that the converse of Aquinas' thesis is true: the general disposition to love one's enemy can only be recommended, while particular benevolent acts towards an enemy can be demanded – at least under some conditions. And what are these conditions? Aquinas refers to this question only in terms of 'when there is (or is not) a need'. But this is exactly the objector's problem – when *is* there a need?

This brings us to the difficult problem of demarcation of the supererogatory and the obligatory. For example, is almsgiving a matter of precept or a matter of counsel? Aquinas answers that question by saying that *generally* almsgiving is a precept, being 'a necessary condition to the love of our neighbour'. Yet, he adds, it is a precept only if certain conditions relating to the relative wealth and need of the benefactor and the recipient obtain. The giver should give only 'of his surplus' (that which is beyond his own needs), and the recipient has a right over the gift only if he is in need (indeed in such a need that can only be relieved by the giver). Otherwise, acts of almsgiving are supererogatory (Aquinas, *Summa Theologica*, II, II, Q. 32, Art. 5 and Art. 6).

It is not clear whether beneficence is considered by Aquinas as supererogatory. As in the previous case of almsgiving, he restricts the duty to perform beneficent acts to certain 'circumstances', implying that under other circumstances these acts are supererogatory (ibid., Q. 31, Art. 2). But this can also be understood as implying a conception of beneficence as an imperfect duty, that is a general duty which ought to be realized but not in every particular opportunity. As will be shown (cf. below, 6.2) these two interpretations are incompatible, as supererogation cannot be reduced to imperfect duties.

As for mercy, Aquinas does not mention it as an object of the Evangelical Counsels, yet he seems to treat it as supererogatory. According to Aquinas there is no contradiction between mercy and justice, for mercy is 'something more than justice' (Aquinas, *Summa Theologica*, I, Q. 21, Art. 3). The Scriptural basis of this view is found in a passage from James ii, 13: 'mercy exalteth itself above judgment'. Acts of mercy are regarded as analogous to acts of liberality or bestowing gifts: the case of 'one who pardons an offence committed against him' is similar to the case of 'a man who pays another two hundred pieces of money, though owing him only one hundred'. It seems that for Aquinas mercy and pardon are not just supererogatory, but supererogatory in the same way as bestowing gifts is 'over and above' one's duty, that is – in the sense of over-subscription. This claim will be contested in 7.7.

Aquinas' view of gratitude should also be mentioned, as it is connected with the subject of supererogation. Gratitude is a precept, a duty; ingratitude is *always* a sin. Furthermore, gratitude is an obligation of a special kind: it demands repayment over and above what was given. The logic behind this special requirement is that as the benefactor 'conferred the favor gratis without being bound to do so ... the beneficiary is under a moral obligation to bestow something gratis in return'; and this condition is not met 'unless he exceeds the quantity of the favor received' (Aquinas, *Summa Theologica*, II, II, Q. 106, Art. 6). As the act of gratitude cannot itself be 'gratis' (as the original supererogatory act was), the only *free* element left is the amount of favour returned – i.e. the quantity in excess of that which was given originally. So, in a way, gratitude is a duty to act supererogatorily, to repay more than is due according to the principles of justice.[7]

Aquinas' distinction between the obligatory and the supererogatory raises the problem of the relationship between two other concepts: law and virtue. Works of supererogation are typically virtuous, but are they prescribed by law? The natural answer is that they are not, as these acts are the object of counsels rather than pre-

---

[7] And the case of gratitude should be well distinguished from that of restitution, which 're-establishes equality where an unjust taking has caused inequality'. Restoring *more* is not a duty at all in that case, but rather supererogatory (Aquinas, *Summa Theologica*, II, II, Q. 62, Art. 3).

cepts. But this statement leads to the conclusion that not all acts of virtue are prescribed by law. This conclusion seems valid for the *religious* law of the Bible (The Divine Law), but is it also valid for the *moral* (natural) law?

Aquinas' answer runs along the following lines: 'To the natural law belongs everything to which a man is inclined according to his nature'; rationality is the 'proper form' of man; since every being is inclined to operate according to his form, man has a natural inclination to act according to reason; and this type of action is the definition of virtue. The conclusion is that all virtuous actions are prescribed by the natural law (Aquinas, *Summa Theologica*, I, II, Q. 94, Art. 3).

With such a conclusion, how can supererogation be justified? Aquinas replies that when considered as virtuous, all virtuous actions are prescribed by natural law, but when considered 'in themselves' (i.e. as actions of a certain species), virtuous actions are not always prescribed, because our nature does not incline to them 'at first', and their value is acknowledged only after 'an inquiry of reason'. That is to say: from the point of view of virtue and perfection (the point of view of the Eternal Law) it would be natural for us to perform these virtuous actions, but as human beings are not perfect (they are 'ill-disposed' and 'not fully rational') there are virtuous actions which cannot be commanded by the natural law (or, for that matter, by the religious law).

The same question is raised with regard to the Human ('positive') Law: does it prescribe all virtuous actions? The answer is that though every act of virtue can be prescribed by the law (as the law is directed to the common good), the human law does not actually prescribe every act of every virtue, but only some acts of each virtue – those pertaining to the common (social) good of justice and peace, or those which are directly 'ordainable to the common good' (ibid., Q. 96, Art. 3).

Elsewhere Aquinas is more explicit: the human law is concerned only with *external* acts which have effects on society (or on other human-beings). Therefore, it makes precepts only about 'acts of justice'. Acts of other virtues are commanded by the human law only if they are directly related to justice. On the other hand, other virtuous acts are commanded by the Divine Law, because the latter is concerned with man's relation with God. The scope of precepts in the Divine Law is wider and includes not only other virtues than justice, but also the *internal* actions (intentions, passions, etc.). Yet only the actions whose absence undermines the very 'order of virtue' are commanded by the Divine Law as precepts, while actions of perfect virtue are given as counsels and admonitions (ibid., Q. 100, Art. 2; see also below, 8.2, 8.3).

Aquinas draws parallel conclusions for *vices*. The human law does not forbid all vices, but only 'the more grievous' ones, the reason for this being man's imperfect nature. Human law forbids only those actions which endanger the maintenance of social life as such (ibid., Q. 96, Art. 2). But it should be noted that though the human law does not forbid all vices, the religious law does, as it is concerned not only with a minimum of tolerable life in society, but also with the salvation of man. So the symmetry of virtue and vice in relation to obligation and supererogation is broken in the case of the Divine Law. While the human law does not deal with both supererogatory acts and bad but permissible acts, the Divine Law allows for non-obligatory good acts (supererogation) but prohibits all evil acts. There are no negative counsels – i.e. recommendations to refrain from doing evil; these are all subject to prohibitions (6.3).

Finally, Aquinas is also aware of the institutional–practical implications of a theory which allows for supererogation. In fact, it is partly in order to justify these implications that the theory is spelt out in such detail. Aquinas accepts the widespread custom of Indulgences and tries (although somewhat reluctantly) to justify it in theological terms: 'The reason why they [the Indulgences] so avail is the oneness of the mystical body in which many have performed works of satisfaction exceeding the requirements of their debts . . . So great is the quantity of such merits that it exceeds the entire debt of punishment due to those who are living at this moment (Aquinas, *Summa Theologica*, Supplement, Q. 25, Art. 1). Furthermore, 'one man can satisfy for another', and this is how the 'superabundance of satisfaction' of the Saints can be used for the benefit of others. These merits are the property of the Church (for whose sake the Saints acted), and therefore can be transferred and then distributed by those who rule the Church.

1.4 THE REFORMATION

Both this theory and the institution it was meant to justify aroused the most virulent attacks by the Protestants in the sixteenth century.

The theory was treated as absurd and even blasphemous for reasons which will be discussed presently. The institution of Indulgences was taken as a symbol of the corruption of the Roman Catholic Church (and indeed, even those who supported the idea of Indulgences had to admit that it became an easy way of filling the Church's coffers, and was widely abused by the Bishops). The cult of Saints and the ideal of monastic life, which are connected with the notion of supererogation, were also criticized by the Reformation. Yet our purpose here is restricted to a discussion of the anti-supererogationist attitude of Protestantism which, among other things, clearly had an effect on Kant's view of the problem.

Luther's critique of supererogation must be understood in the wider context of his deontological approach and his denial of the freedom of the will. Human 'works' are never sufficient for attaining salvation. Without God's grace no amount of good works has any meaning, and it is only through God's will that we can do the good acts at all. Man is justified by faith alone. Our duty (towards God) is infinite and can be never wholly fulfilled. A very strict morality of duty was established, which was substituted for the Catholic one that allowed for degrees of perfection, for the possibility of overstepping the demands of duty, and for the existence of freedom of the individual regarding the nature of his religious life. This rigorous anti-supererogationist morality is best expressed by Luther's own words in his 'Explanation of The Ninety Five Theses' (Thesis 58): 'no saint has adequately fulfilled God's commandments in this life. Consequently the saints have done absolutely nothing which is superabundant. Therefore they have left nothing to be allocated through indulgences' (Luther, *Works*, Vol. 31, p. 213 and section 58 passim). Even acts of martyrdom and self-sacrifice are not over and above one's duty; they too are required. Even saints have to pray, confess, and be forgiven for their sins. Their acts are examples to be imitated, rather than creating a surplus to be used for the remission of punishment. Even Jesus's works, which clearly are 'superabundant', do not form a treasury of merit which can be distributed as 'indulgences' (not even by the Pope, as he has no divine powers of forgiveness).

Calvin's remarks are also unambiguous with regard to supererogation: 'man ... has no works in which he can glory before God, and ... hence, deprived of all aid from works, he is justified by faith alone' (Calvin, *Institutes of the Christian Religion*, bk. III, ch.

xvii, 8). The Catholic doctrine of justification by man's own actions is wrong and 'There is nothing more solid in their dogma of compensation by means of works of supererogation... all the righteousness of men collected into one heap would be inadequate to compensate for a single sin' (ibid., bk. iii, ch. xiv, 13). Like Luther, Calvin is both a strict deontologist and a critic of the free-will thesis: 'let us not boast of voluntary liberality in matters of necessary obligation' (ibid., 14). The doctrine of supererogation is called 'a patchwork of sacrilege and blasphemy', as there can be no surplus of merit even through acts of martyrdom (ibid., bk. iii, ch. v, 3).

Finally, the Anglican Church also denounced the Roman Catholic doctrine of supererogation on similar grounds. The text of Article Fourteen of The Thirty Nine Articles runs as follows:

> Voluntary works besides, over and above God's commandments, which they call works of supererogation, cannot be taught without arrogancy and impiety. For by them men do declare that they do not render unto God as much as they are bound to do, but that they do more for His sake than of bounden duty is required: whereas Christ saith plainly, When ye have done all that are commanded to you, say, we be unprofitable servants (Gibson, 1898, p. 424).

This last sentence, quoted from Luke xvii, 10, was held by all the critics of the Catholic doctrine to be the Scriptural proof of their anti-supererogationist view.[8] Whatever man does, he remains an unprofitable servant of God, totally dependent on His gratuitous grace and mercy which he does not deserve. Thus, in the words of Thomas Becon, Opera Supererogationis should be more appropriately named 'opera superarrogantiae', or according to John Bradford works of supererogation are merely 'works of superabomination', because they presuppose options which do not exist. God alone, through Christ's works, can redeem us.

There is an attempt in Protestant theology to maintain the distinction between precepts and counsels by seeing counsels as a special kind of precept. The counsel now becomes a sort of subjective duty, a precept *for some people*. Thus, some modern theologians (e.g.

---

[8] The Catholic tradition interpreted this verse as referring only to those who did not excel their duty. Those who *did*, like the Saints, are not 'unprofitable servants' (Cf. Ambrose, *Concerning Widows*, ch. 12).

Schüller, 1966, pp. 61–75) interpret the 'counsels' of the New Testament as precepts for those who are granted *charisma* or have some special vocation. The problematic passage in I Corinthians vii is read by Protestants as commanding chastity for anyone who is in that special 'state' which enables him to remain chaste (Glaser, 1970, p. 285). The Evangelical Counsels are not recommendations to the individual, which he is free to follow or to reject. Freedom is possible only within the framework of Divine Law, and the Catholics mistakenly thought that freedom presupposes some area of action which does not fall under God's commandments only because they took the State law as a model for Divine Law (Schüller, 1966, p. 67). Thus, in the Protestant view there are people who can fulfil their duty only by following counsels like those of virginity or poverty. Those counsels apply to the people who can lead a chaste life *only* by remaining virgin. For those people the counsel of virginity becomes a strict obligation. And they deserve no special praise for doing more than others.

But of course the Catholic may ask how we are to treat the virginity of people for whom it is not a necessary means of fulfilling the duty of chastity. More generally, it is quite absurd to claim that *any* virtuous act – no matter how much sacrifice is involved – is a duty, i.e. a necessary means (for an individual agent) to the end of obeying God's commandments. Our theory of supererogation in secular morality will also contest the Protestant conception of freedom, and will follow the Roman Catholic thinking (8.3).

Although it was never discussed under this heading, the gratuitous act of God's granting grace and mercy to his 'unprofitable servants' can itself be viewed as a supererogatory act. In Catholic theology *some* principles of the proportion between man's deeds and God's rewards (or punishment) are believed to govern God's relation to man. In Protestantism, however, no such principles obtain, and any reward bestowed by God is undeserved and is due to the gratuitous operation of grace. Thus, since man is necessarily sinful and unworthy of salvation, God's mercy is always beyond what is man's *due*. In that respect, God can be said to act 'supererogatorily'. This of course is a rather special case of supererogation, because usually God is not believed to have any duties at all, *ipso facto* does not act beyond his duties. The logical and theological problem of supererogatory action of a perfect being will be raised again in the discussion of the nature of mercy (7.7).

When we come to draw the philosophical conclusions from the theological discussion of supererogation we must obviously bear in mind the fundamental difference between secular morality and religious morality. In the former case, both duty and virtue are judged according to purely human standards, primarily the effects of the agent's acts on other people and society as a whole. In the latter case, duty and virtue are interpreted as mainly characterizing the relation between man and God. This difference is reflected in the respective views of supererogation of the two types of ethical theory. For the Christian supererogationist doing more than is required is intended 'to please God', to achieve perfection, to guarantee a speedy salvation. In secular morality, supererogatory acts are basically those which are highly beneficial to others. While the emphasis in the religious case is on the *self*-regarding value of supererogation, the concept in the non-religious context is related to *other*-regarding benefits. It is therefore natural that Christian morality puts forward the ideal of supererogation in terms of 'counsels', since we usually advise people as to the means of achieving an end to which they are naturally inclined. On the other hand, in secular morality people are *encouraged* to act supererogatorily rather than *advised* to do so, for it is the *end* which we try to convince them to adopt rather than the *means* to an end which they already pursue.

We should not ignore however the other-regarding aspects of supererogatory behaviour in Catholic theology. Although virginity and obedience do not directly benefit other human beings, poverty and mercy certainly do have other-regarding effects. Furthermore, the doctrine of a Spiritual Treasury makes the self-regarding virtues useful to other people. Although the meritorious acts of the saints are not originally meant to benefit other people (but rather the Church), they eventually become beneficial to those who are granted indulgences.

The important difference between religious and secular ethical theory does not mean that the *meaning* of supererogation is radically different in the two cases. The logical features of the concept of supererogation are displayed by the two theories in similar ways. It is only the type of relations to which the concept is applied which is different. Otherwise, the analogies between the object of the

30

Evangelical Counsels and what we call supererogatory acts are quite close. In both cases the act in question is only expected of a few people, that is, not universally demanded. It is only necessary for the achievement of an ideal which is 'higher' than the end of those acts which are obligatory. Yet this ideal is higher on the same *scale* as the one on which the end of the obligatory action is situated (that is to say *more* perfect, like virginity in relation to monogamous marriage on the scale of chastity, or absolute poverty in relation to obligatory almsgiving on the scale of charity, etc.). This shows that the Christian concept of supererogation meets our condition of continuity. In both types of morality the supererogatory act is that which is only 'recommended' – i.e. it is not binding, and consequently failure to perform it is not reprehensible and does not entail punishment, although doing it deserves praise and special rewards. Supererogatory behaviour is a matter of free choice, and as it has this element of pure option, a theory of freedom of the will is necessarily presupposed. Tertullian's idea of a special sphere of liberty ordained to man in order to test his virtue is especially relevant to the supererogationist view. The freedom of choice underlying supererogation is not just freedom from (physical) constraint, but also from moral obligation. In that sense the freedom exemplified by supererogatory behaviour is more far-reaching than that assumed by other types of moral action. Both in Christian and non-religious morality supererogation partly determines the standards of perfection; that is, exceeding duty is in itself a criterion of perfection, and this perfection – unlike duty, which is well-defined by the 'minimum required' – allows for an indefinite number of degrees and has no specified limits.

This last feature is of course contested by anti-supererogationists who have either a different notion of perfection, or do not believe that perfection is an attainable ideal for human beings. Moral perfection – if at all realizable – can, according to anti-supererogationists, be achieved only by strict obedience to duty. The supererogationists believe that it can be achieved only by going beyond duty, and that the very act of exceeding duty is virtuous and praiseworthy. In that respect Protestant theology resembles Kant's view of supererogation, while the Roman Catholic approach can be grouped together with ethical theories which allow for supererogation, and with Aristotelian ethics which allows for degrees of perfection (although perhaps not for supererogation in our sense as we shall see in the next chapter).

Still the Catholic concept of supererogation, especially in regard to its practical implications, remains unconvincing. The idea of supererogation creating a spiritual bank of merit which can be distributed by the Pope is unacceptable to those who do not share some of the metaphysical assumptions implied by the Christian doctrine. Moral merit is usually thought not to be transferable from one person to another via a 'reservoir'. It cannot be stored and distributed in a mechanical way in moral transactions. Yet if the Catholic doctrine is viewed in the light of its specific teleological character, then the theory gains some plausibility. Human beings are required to do certain things in order to achieve a specific end. If they fail to do them, they are punished, yet if they do more than is required, a certain surplus is created. As this surplus is extremely valuable, it is hard to conceive that it is just superfluous. It must entail some reward, either to the agent himself or to others. This is the logic of the argument supporting indulgences, but also of the very idea of Jesus's atonement for everybody's sins (an idea which is accepted by the anti-supererogationist Protestants as well).

A secular theory of supererogation, being devoid of this metaphysical assumption of the possibility of the divine transfer of merit, can have no practical implications analogous to indulgences. Since the end of our moral *duties* is not self-regarding (like salvation), the surplus of merit created by supererogatory acts does not pose a problem. This surplus does not lie idle, nor is it superfluous, for by definition it is concerned with other people's good and well-being, and does not have to be mysteriously transferred. There is only one way in which supererogation can counterbalance moral transgression, and that is as mitigating circumstances taken into consideration when we judge the agent for his misdeeds. But in that case no transference of merit takes place. It is just that the supererogatory action reflects on the agent's character in a way that makes us tend to judge his misdeed as a matter of incidental weakness. In no way does the supererogatory behaviour compensate for the agent's violation of the moral law, nor, *a fortiori*, for the moral wrong-doings of other people.

The theological discussion of the relation between law and virtue raises some interesting points which are relevant to a non-religious theory of supererogation. It is indeed a disturbing question why *all* virtuous acts are not demanded by 'law', i.e. by moral duty. The possibility of supererogation hinges on the answer to this question (as we shall see in 8.1). Now, for Aquinas the reason for not enforcing every virtuous act by means of the Human Law (which is analogous to what we call 'the legal system') is that the purpose of this law is restricted to the regulation of the 'external' acts of human beings who are to live in justice and peace. And not every virtuous act is necessarily a matter of justice. As for the natural law (what we would call 'the moral law'), the reason for not prescribing every virtuous act is different: it relates not to the purpose of the law (which in that case is much wider than that of the Human Law, covering all virtues, not only that of justice) but to the imperfection of human beings who are the subjects of this law. So although morality prohibits us and obliges us to do certain things which are not prohibited or prescribed by the law of the state, even in the moral law there are virtuous acts which are left to the free choice of the agent. And as for the third type of law, the Divine Law of God, why should it not demand of human beings to act virtuously also in those cases 'to which they are not naturally inclined at first'? Here again there is a third type of reason supporting the non-enforcement of every virtuous act. This is the idea of freedom to seek perfection which underlies the New Law, the law of liberty, as against the over-legalistic and authoritarian law of the Old Testament. This argument is not explicitly stated by Aquinas, although it is implied in his attitude towards the New Law. In Q. 108, which describes the distinction between counsels and precepts, Aquinas fails to provide a justification of the value of those counsels *as* counsels. (If Jesus's counsels are 'supremely useful and becoming', why should they not be given as precepts?)

So we find in Aquinas three different arguments for leaving some virtuous acts to free choice, rather than applying the 'law' to them. But, as we will see later, for good acts to be not legally obligatory is a necessary but not a sufficient condition for being classed as supererogatory. Therefore, it is only the latter two which serve to support the possibility of supererogation. Although these two arguments are not incompatible, they make it hard for us to decide whether Aquinas presents a qualified or an unqualified version of supererogationism. The argument of imperfection of human beings seems to support the former interpretation, while the argument of the intrinsic value of *licentia* seems to justify an interpretation of the latter type. I would not like to pursue that exegetical problem further. It should only be noted that Aquinas's discussion of the three reasons for not prescribing every virtuous act by means of 'law', is part of his treatment of the general relation between law and virtue rather than of his view of supererogation. The latter subject is specifically mentioned in the context of the nature of the New Law, that is in relation to the religious, Divine Law (the other two types of law do not contain counsels). And this fact renders the interpretation of Aquinas's view as unqualified supererogationism more plausible. Contrary to Aquinas, my aim is to present an unqualified version of supererogationism which will be part of the 'natural law' in the sense of a non-religious morality.

2

The morality of virtue:
the Greco–Roman view

2.1 SUPEREROGATIONISM IN A SECONDARY SENSE

The dispute between theories which do and do not recognize supererogation as a distinct ethical category can be of two types. It may either imply a disagreement concerning the status of supererogatory acts within a general theory that is shared by the disputing parties, or involve two radically different theories which have no common ground for discussing the concept at all. The former type of dispute I shall call 'internal', the latter 'external'. The internal type alone can strictly speaking be called a 'dispute', since in the case of an external disagreement the two theories do not have any point of contact, or – in more precise terms – they cannot argue about a concept which in the one theory has no specific meaning. This type of controversy involves what is sometimes referred to as 'incommensurability' of philosophical (or ethical) theories, an attribute which makes rational–critical argument between two theories problematic or even futile.

The theological dispute between the Catholics and the Protestants, discussed in the last chapter, is a typically internal disagreement between supererogationists and *anti*-supererogationists. Both sides have an ethical theory which is based on a concept of duty and on metaphysical assumptions relating to the divine source of duty, man's relation with God, the immortality of the soul, etc. Furthermore, Catholics and Protestants have many religious and moral values in common. Their dispute over the concept of supererogation concerns the specific problem of the scope of duty, or of man's ability to do more than is required of him. Although Protestant anti-supererogationists can grasp the Catholic idea of supererogation, their aim is to deny its applicability. This is, therefore, an internal dispute.

But when we discuss classical theories of morality, like Aristotle's, we are immediately confronted with the problem of the incommensurability of the conceptual framework of Aristotle's theory with that of supererogation. It is not only impossible to find in Aristotle any specific reference to that special class of actions, but it is also hard to reconstruct an Aristotelian interpretation of the very idea of supererogation. This is a typical example of an external disagreement. Such a theory, then, can hardly be called anti-supererogationist, for although it does not recognize the theoretical or moral importance of supererogation, it does not *deny* it either (as Protestants, Kantians and some utilitarians do). It is a type of theory which does not give rise to the *problem* of supererogation.

For those who treat every dispute between incommensurable theories as inevitably futile, the external disagreement between the Aristotelian view and supererogationism cannot be discussed or resolved rationally. Yet I find the external alternative to a theory of supererogation relevant to our study, and illuminating, not only historically but also theoretically. This may be due to the fact that the distinction between internal and external is a *relative* one, which means that although the idea of supererogation, as we understand it, is in itself alien to classical morality and ethics, there are strong similarities between some of the classical 'virtues' and what we would call supererogation. In other words, classical ethics contains supererogatory elements in it, moral values and theoretical distinctions which could be classified as supererogatory by the supererogationist. This, I believe, suffices to justify a short examination of Greek and Roman ethics before embarking on the more detailed discussion of the anti-supererogationist views of Kant and some utilitarians.

Generally speaking classical ethics is incongruous with theories which raise the problem of supererogation, since it is axiological rather than deontological. It takes as its basic conceptual framework the notions of goodness, virtue, and perfection rather than those of duty, right, and justice. It aims at a definition of the good man and the good for man, rather than at a formulation of a system of interpersonal principles of just and obligatory action. Such an axiologically oriented ethics is more concerned with actions which manifest good character and noble personality than with actions which can be justifiably required as duties of persons who are not initially (or naturally) inclined to perform them. In that respect classical morality is

36

more self-regarding, taking the point of view of what is good for the agent. Deontological ethics is more other-regarding, being concerned with the agent's duties towards his fellow beings and society as a whole. An axiological ethics can thus hardly accommodate supererogation, as it has no tools to distinguish between the obligatory and the supererogatory.

Furthermore, classical morality is fundamentally the morality of virtue. Even justice – which in our eyes is concerned with fair distribution and impersonal principles of what is morally required – is, for the Greeks, primarily a virtue of the 'moral man', a trait of character. It is not only a property of political institutions and social organizations but also of the individual, i.e. a harmony between the different elements of the soul (according to Plato). In that sense, the just man is the righteous, or virtuous man, and not just someone who is fair in his dealings with others. Now, a virtue is defined by Aristotle as the *mean* between two extremes, and as such it cannot be excelled without loss of value. Virtue is a fixed ideal which can, in principle, be achieved, but not surpassed. One cannot go beyond justice (at least in one sense) without upsetting the proper balance between the different elements of the soul (or of the social order in question). And the same applies, as we shall presently see, to other virtues which seem to have a supererogatory element in them.

As the Greek concept of justice differs significantly from our concept of justice, so should *arete* be distinguished from (Christian) *virtue*. Greek 'virtue' is a well-defined ideal which determines the *right* way, amount and circumstances of good actions. Being itself 'excellence', *arete* cannot be excelled. Christian virtue on the other hand is of an open-ended nature. It is not governed by rules which put limits on the actions which exemplify it. Thus, charity has no limits and seems to be guided by a principle of 'the more, the better'. This difference between *arete* and Christian virtue is of course also reflected in the content of the values held by the respective ethical systems. While Greek morality commends *moderation*, Christian morality tends to praise the *extreme*. In the one case we find the values of friendliness, temperance, calculated courage, limited beneficence and, of course, justice. In the other case we find counsels of poverty, chastity, humility, and self-denial, that is recommendations to act beyond the requirements of justice. Greek self-assertion is replaced by Christian abnegation.

Given these structural differences between the two externally

37

divergent theories, can supererogation be given any meaning in an Aristotelian ethics? In the strict sense of the word, supererogation has no place in classical ethics, since the two conditions of correlativity and continuity with duty do not seem to be met. Nevertheless, classical ethics can be described as supererogatory (in a secondary sense) exactly because it is not based on duty. The fact that the morality of the good man consists mainly in actions which are not governed by reciprocal, universalizable prescriptions and by demands backed by sanctions makes these actions optional, free, and dependent on some measure of individual discretion. And these are characteristically supererogatory features.

2.2 POPULAR MORALITY

As an illustration of these supererogatory elements in the classical moral view let us first look at popular morality. Social interaction in the ancient world was much more based on what sociologists and anthropologists call 'the gift relationship' than it is in today's Judaeo-Christian civilization.[1] This system of non-economic giving and taking served as a method of unilateral and multilateral social transfer. It was not legally institutionalized or governed by principles determining definite rights and duties. Being an uncommercialized system of exchange, it gradually died out with the ascending use of money and the legislation in the sphere of commercial transaction. It should, however, be borne in mind that in the act of giving, a return was expected, and it was indeed an 'obligation' to express gratitude by returning a gift or favour – and, if possible, a larger and worthier one.[2]

This practice of giving in expectation of a return has the dual character of establishing friendship and asserting one's worth (Hands, 1968, p. 28). These two aims can hardly be achieved merely by conforming to legal or even moral norms prescribed by a deontically oriented system of justice. In that respect the idea of voluntary giving is of a supererogatory nature. For by doing someone a favour or giving a gift the benefactor does something to which the benefi-

---

[1] See, for example, Mauss, 1954, which primarily studies primitive societies; and Titmuss, 1973, which studies the gift relationship in the context of blood-donation. For further discussion of this topic, see below 7.3.

[2] Compare to Thomas Aquinas's suggestion that a supererogatory gift deserves a slightly larger gift in return (see above, 1.3).

ciary has no right. He may deserve it, but still not have any *claim* to it. By such an act of beneficence the benefactor expresses his personal concern for the beneficiary, for otherwise why should he have bestowed the benefit on him. And he also earns honour, for he had no *duty* to act as he has done. This personal dimension of moral behaviour that is not guided by duty is, as we shall see in chapter 8, one of the intrinsic values of supererogation. And although we would usually wish to restrict supererogation to those acts which go beyond a *specific duty*, the fact that classical morality had a much less elaborate notion of duties and rights does not mean that the voluntary system of giving cannot be treated as supererogatory, at least in a secondary sense.

If we examine the duty of gratitude we can similarly trace a supererogatory element in the gift relationship. For although it is true that in Greek morality beneficiaries had a 'duty' to show gratitude, it was not a duty in the sense of returning borrowed money or fulfilling a promise. It was not only the material benefit which had to be acknowledged, but also the generosity, benevolence and nobility of the benefactor, i.e. the supererogatory nature of the gift. So although one gave in expectation of a return of a comparable gift, one also expected gratitude – a recognition of the benevolent character of the original act of giving. The gift combined economic ends with supererogatory ideals.

Similar supererogatory elements can be found in the system of financing public projects in Greece. Hands notes that in the *polis* there was no system of taxation in the modern sense (Hands, 1968, p. 40). Rich people were expected to contribute to public funds whenever there was a need. No definite amounts were specified, and the system was meant to be voluntary. The donor could not, in that case, expect any kind of return besides honour and good reputation. Again, this system cannot strictly speaking be called supererogatory, for it does not consist of payments over and above one's share in the taxes prescribed by law. Further, it is not supererogatory because omission entailed some form of sanction, mainly public shame. Nevertheless, it is supererogatory in the sense that the amount paid was left to the discretion of the individual donor, and was considered as reflecting on his moral character and generosity. By contributing generously to a public enterprise the rich citizen had an opportunity of exercising moral and political virtue in a way which cannot be displayed in a system based on income-tax laws. And such a system of financing public expenditure is supererogatory also in the sense that giving was always made to *appear* as a generous and honourable act.

Some sort of distinction between duty and supererogation can be found in classical popular morality. According to Hands small acts of charity (giving a penny to a beggar, or water to the thirsty) were not considered 'honourable' because they were absolutely required (Hands, 1968, pp. 46–7). Their small cost to the donor, plus the relatively great benefit to the recipient, made them obligatory and morally insignificant as well. No return could be expected, even of an immaterial kind (honour). Only the greater acts of beneficence were morally praised and entailed a duty of gratitude and moral desert. Only the truly generous acts could create friendship and earn the benefactor honour. This of course explains why – unlike Christian (and Jewish)[3] morality, which praises anonymous giving – the Greeks and Romans found nothing wrong with confining one's 'supererogatory' behaviour to public circumstances, in which the action could also be *seen* to be done. For neither honour nor friendship can be earned by anonymous giving.

To conclude this section, we may point to the fact that beneficence in classical morality served both as a form of economic transaction and as an altruistic gesture. To our modern eyes these two functions may appear incompatible, but for the Greeks and the Romans they were not. For although gifts and the contribution of money had an economic function and were based on reciprocity and the expectation of a return, they were also means of expressing a virtuous character, of creating friendly relations and of earning honour. And the term *philanthropia* should be understood in this wider sense. Although strongly self-regarding, classical morality had a supererogatory dimension. Large parts of the social and political life were meant to be based on supererogatory behaviour.

2.3 BENEFICENCE AND ALTRUISM IN ARISTOTLE AND SENECA

The writings of moral philosophers like Aristotle and Seneca contain similar elements of a supererogatory nature. Seneca's defi-

---

[3] In Maimonides's Scale of Charity, charitable acts which involve the anonymity of both benefactor and beneficiary are considered to be superior to other, more personal forms of giving.

nition of *beneficium* seems indeed supererogatory: 'It is the act of a well-wisher who bestows joy and derives joy from the bestowal of it, and is inclined to do what he does from the prompting of his own will' (Seneca, On mercy, *Moral Essays*, vol. 1, p. 23). Beneficent acts are performed spontaneously, as a matter of natural inclination, rather than out of a sense of duty or as the discharge of an obligation. This makes them praiseworthy and honourable. Seneca emphasizes the intention accompanying the act which is more important (morally speaking) than the material benefit bestowed. The supererogatory nature of beneficence lies, then, in the 'spirit of the action', in 'the intention of the giver or doer', not in 'what is done or given'. It is, therefore, relevant to know *how* the action was done, and praise is attached only to beneficent acts that were done without hesitation, with ease, without being asked for, etc. Unlike our 'deontic' concept of supererogation, which is primarily associated with the value of the act itself (being *more* than is required), the Greeks and Romans credited those who were motivated by a virtuous disposition with special moral praise.

Seneca clearly distinguishes between the relationship of giving and returning and that of commercial transaction. Both are reciprocal and impose obligations on the receiving party. But while a debt (in the latter type of relationship) places an obligation on the debtor to pay back, to settle his debt, the beneficiary (in the former type of relationship) is required to be grateful. While the obligation of the debtor applies merely to the payment itself, the beneficiary of a supererogatory act must acknowledge the benevolent attitude of his benefactor. And although the benefactor may expect a 'return', he has no right to demand it, for a gift in return is necessarily a voluntary act analogous to the voluntariness of the beneficent act itself (Seneca, *Ad Lucilium: Epistulae Morales*, vol. 2, p. 225). Seneca is clearly aware of the free nature both of beneficence and of gratitude when he precludes any type of legal intervention in the relations between benefactor and beneficiary:

First of all, the best part of a benefit is lost if it can become actionable, as is possible in the case of a fixed loan or of something rented or leased. For the most beautiful part of a benefit is that we gave it even when we were likely to lose it, that we left it wholly to the discretion of the one who received it. . . . In the second place, although to repay gratitude is a most praiseworthy act, it ceases to be praiseworthy if it is made obligatory. . . . There is no glory in being grateful unless it would have been safe to be ungrateful (Seneca, De beneficiis, *Moral Essays*, vol. 3, pp. 137, 139).

41

These comments show Seneca's awareness of the intrinsic value of actions which are not governed by principles of strict obligation. So although there is a sense in which beneficence and *a fortiori* gratitude are morally required of persons (and in that sense cannot be considered supererogatory), the logic of these concepts implies voluntariness, immunity from legal action, and individual discretion. In that sense, gratitude and *a fortiori* beneficence are both supererogatory.

Yet even if interpreted as supererogatory, beneficence should have limits. According to Seneca, gifts should never be too large (relative both to the donor and to the recipient). One should never make a gift which one should be ashamed to ask for; and one should give only to persons who are in need, and usually not to the extent of bringing need upon oneself (Seneca, De beneficiis, *Moral Essays*, vol. 3, pp. 77, 79). Moderation restricts the scope of supererogation, and altruism is confined to circumstances in which the well-being and self-respect of both giver and recipient are not impaired.

Although being the most systematic of all ethical theorists of the classical period, Aristotle is unclear in matters concerning our problem. In a typically axiological theory like Aristotle's ethics, supererogation (in the strict sense of the word) has no place, for it suggests no theory of moral duty and obligation. Supererogation, however, can also be defined in relation to the concept of justice, that is as a category of virtuous action which goes beyond what is simply 'just'. And as justice plays a major role in Aristotle's ethics, one may ask whether he also recognizes such a moral category.

Aristotle is rather ambiguous on that, leaving ample room for interpretation and reconstruction. The problem lies basically in his definition of justice which, in one of its senses, is quite different from what we commonly understand by it. Contrary to our distinction between justice and virtue (which seems to be presupposed by a theory of supererogation), Aristotle tells us that they are in fact the same. For, 'justice, alone of the virtues, is thought to be "another's good"', and this makes it not only superior to all virtues but identical with 'virtue entire' (*Ethica Nicomachea*, 1130a). This concept of justice does not refer to an impersonal system of duties and rights, claims and counter-claims, which can be supererogatorily surpassed, but rather to the personal relationship between the virtuous individual and those who deserve to benefit from his virtue. This personal nature of justice is indeed a most fundamental one for Aristotle, and this is reflected in the intimate connection of justice and friendship. One cannot be unjust towards other people and yet be their friend, and making friends is sufficient to avoid unjust behaviour (*Ethica Eudemia*, 1234b). Furthermore, Aristotle claims that 'justice and injustice are specially exhibited towards friends', which may strike us as odd, since we usually take justice to refer mainly to our relations with people with whom we have no personal relations. For Aristotle, however, friendship (like justice) means something wider: 'it is thought to be the special business of the political art to produce friendship' (*Ethica Eudemia*, 1234b, and cf. *Ethica Nicomachea*, 1155a).[4]

Nevertheless, Aristotle talks of justice in a narrower sense too, i.e. not that which is identical with virtue, but that which is 'a *part* of virtue' (*Ethica Nicomachea*, 1130a). This is called 'particular justice', and has either a distributive function or a rectifying one. This concept of justice is similar to the way we understand the term. Now, while 'general' justice cannot be surpassed (for it 'bids us practise every virtue and forbids us to practise any vice', *Ethica Nicomachea*, 1130b), particular justice certainly can be surpassed; in distribution, one can take a smaller share than one's due; in rectification of an injustice, one can make a larger compensation than the one required in terms of what Aristotle calls 'equalization'. These clearly are cases of supererogation, which, although not explicitly mentioned as such by Aristotle, are compatible with his theory; they are admirable because justice is concerned with 'another's good'.

This interpretation is further supported by other remarks made by Aristotle with regard to the nature of justice. A distinction is drawn between 'private justice' and 'justice towards others' (*Ethica Eudemia*, 1235a). While the former is 'practised to friends' and 'depends on ourselves alone', 'justice towards all others is determined by the laws, and does not depend on us'. It seems that justice towards others is analogous to the legal concept governing the

---

[4] This attempt to blur the distinction between justice and friendship is reminiscent of Paul Tillich's assimilation of justice and love in his theological (anti-supererogationist) argument: 'love does not do more than justice demands . . . [it] is the ultimate principle of justice . . . and creative justice is the form of reuniting love' (Tillich, 1954, p. 71).

sphere of claims and counter-claims, rights and duties. It is objective and universal, and is expressed in impersonal laws. The private kind of justice is however personal, both in its being applied towards *friends* and in its being decided freely by the *individual* agent. This could be called metaphorically 'supererogatory justice', for it allows – indeed recommends – surpassing the requirements of justice in the legal sense.

Aristotle clearly rates private justice higher than impersonal justice, which is applied in an anomymous manner. Its supererogatory nature is manifested in the fact that while the just man (in the legal sense) needs friends, true friends have no need to resort to this kind of justice.[5] Furthermore, when in the same passage Aristotle says that it is the aim of law-givers to care more for friendship than for justice, he seems to be implying that a system of principles of distributive and rectifying justice is no more than a necessary evil, and that ideally, if everyone behaved supererogatorily, in the light of 'the truest form of justice', there would be no need for distributive and rectifying principles. But again we should be cautious not to press the analogy between private justice and our notion of supererogation too far, for in Aristotle's theory 'the truest form of justice' is *based* on friendship, on the natural and personal relationship between persons, while our concept of supererogation applies to actions towards strangers as well, and friendship is – at most – *a consequence* of supererogatory behaviour. Still, human interaction based on supererogation is indeed superior to that based on legal justice in the sense that a habit of, for example, paying more than is due makes distributive and rectifying principles of justice superfluous.

The distinction between these two types of justice is supplemented by a parallel distinction between two types of friendship – the 'civic' and the 'moral' (*Ethica Eudemia*, 1242b ff.). The former is contractual in its essence, that is based on an agreement (as in a commercial transaction), and has utility as its aim. The latter is based on virtue and is nobler than civic friendship, for it is more concerned with the purpose, which is making friends 'through virtue', than with achieving the end for which civic friendship is established. The moral type of friendship yields supererogatory behaviour. By defi-

---

[5] 'And the truest form of justice is thought to be a friendly quality' (*Ethica Nicomachea*, 1155a). This form of justice is probably identical with 'private justice' of the *Ethica Eudemia*.

nition it cannot give rise to any recriminations or legal intervention, as it transcends the world of just claims and fixed amounts of payments. It is supererogatory also in relation to the friendship of utility which is based on moral trust rather than on legal contract. For although this kind of friendship gives the impression of being moral in its essence, it is still contractual and has usefulness as its aim. In other words, except for the element of trust which makes it moral rather than civic, this kind of friendship is based on the contractual kind of justice rather than on virtue, and hence often leads to mutual recriminations. So the civic friendship is governed by justice in the narrow sense, whereas moral friendship is guided by 'true justice', that which is identical with virtue. But again, we should take care not to overstate the significance of these distinctions for our moral theories, because on the one hand we usually refrain from treating friendship as a *moral* type of relationship, and on the other hand we do not consider the contractual (civic) relationship as a form of friendship.

Aristotle's discussion of beneficence, liberality, and magnificence reveals some supererogatory features which resemble those found in Seneca. Beneficence is an other-regarding virtue, meaning that the beneficent act should be intended to benefit another person, and should not just be accidentally useful. Unlike the legal relation of creditor–debtor, the relation between the benefactor and the beneficiary involves a personal, friendly attitude, which is expressed on the one hand by the special love of the benefactor for those who benefit from his action, and on the other hand by the feeling of gratitude on the part of the recipient. This feeling of gratitude is an acknowledgment of the supererogatory, gratuitous nature of the beneficent act. The relation of benefactor–beneficiary is, however, asymmetrical: the benefactor is the active party, taking a free decision, while the person at the receiving-end is the passive party, and is clearly less free in the sense that he is under an obligation to be grateful (even if he is under no obligation to *repay*) (*Ethica Nicomachea*, 1167b–1168a).

Beneficence is supererogatory in its being more than 'particular justice' requires. The liberal man is one who gives to people to whom he *owes* nothing. This interpretation is confirmed by Aristotle's characterization of excessive giving (prodigality) as the mark of a 'foolish' man rather than of a 'wicked and ignoble man' (*Ethica Nicomachea*, 1121a). So although a foolish (and prodigal) person cannot be completely virtuous, he is not *unjust* by being what he is. Liberality is giving beyond what justice – in the narrow sense – requires, and being excessive in it cannot be blamed on grounds of injustice but merely on the independent grounds of lack of moderation. One can go beyond justice without being unjust. For, according to Aristotle, no one can be said to be 'voluntarily treated unjustly', i.e. taking less than one's share is not unjust as long as it is a voluntary act (*Ethica Nicomachea*, 1138a).

But if justice is taken in its wider meaning – as equivalent to 'virtue entire' – then beneficent acts are not supererogatory but simply just. One ought to give of one's own property to those who need and deserve it, provided one leaves enough for oneself. In that respect liberality is not more virtuous than justice. It is the manifestation of true justice, and it is expected of every good man who has the opportunity and means of giving. Related to that sense of justice, beneficence is not supererogatory, for it is restricted by principles of moderation ('the mean') which also limit the element of option implied in supererogatory conduct. These restrictions (giving the right amount to the right person at the right time) perhaps are analogous to the principles of distributive and rectifying justice (proportion, equalization). Giving is virtuous only if it comes from one's 'superfluities'. Otherwise, it is either foolish or even a vice, for it may be a sign of excessive self-indulgence, which is a common danger of supererogatory behaviour in general. This idea of beneficence can of course be contrasted with the Christian one which, as Thomas Aquinas remarks, is supererogatory and truly virtuous only if the agent gives part of what he *needs* (unlike the giving of one's surplus which is a definite duty).

Still, although beneficence is restricted to those who *deserve* to be benefited, it does not mean that they can claim it as their *due*. And although one should give only of one's *surplus*, it does not mean that one *has* to give everything one has in excess of one's needs (as a matter of distributive justice). That is to say, the restrictions placed on the exercise of beneficence do not mean that beneficent acts are not supererogatory. Similarly, the self-regarding gains of generosity (honour, pride, being praised as noble, etc.) are not inconsistent with supererogation (in the same way as divine reward or 'glory' do not diminish the value of Christian saintly acts).

Liberality is the virtue of giving and taking wealth, the mean between lavishness and meanness. But Aristotle adds that it is 'especially in respect with giving' that this virtue is exercised, 'for it is more characteristic of virtue to do good than to have good done to one, and more characteristic to do what is noble than not to do what is base' (*Ethica Nicomachea*, 1119b–1120a; and see below, 6.3). This again can serve to support a partially supererogatory interpretation of Aristotelian liberality: the asymmetry of doing good and refraining from doing evil in relation to moral praise (and nobility) is typical of acts which transcend justice. Gratitude is accordingly felt towards one who gives, not towards one who does not take; and the same holds for praise, as it is easier not to take than to give. On the other hand, in matters of justice (in the 'particular' sense), doing what one ought to is no more virtuous than refraining from wrong-doing.

Finally, the relation between *equity* and justice, briefly discussed by Aristotle (*Ethica Nicomachea*, 1137a–1138a), bears some similarity to the relation between supererogation and justice. Equity in a way is superior to justice, but in another way is no different from it. We praise the man who acts in an equitable manner *because* he does not stick to the strict rule of justice. Yet such a departure from the rule of justice does not involve injustice. Aristotle seems to solve this problem by resorting to another distinction between two kinds of justice: that which is embodied in universal law, as opposed to that which is manifested by the application of that law to a specific situation. Applying universal law to some particular cases, without any regard to their specific features, may lead to an injustice. Accordingly, equity is 'a correction of law where it is defective owing to its universality'. And the initial problem is solved since 'the equitable is just, but not the legally just but a correction of legal justice'. What Aristotle calls equitable is analogical to the supererogatory in our view, as it meets our condition of continuity: 'The equitable, though it is better than one kind of justice, yet is just, and it is not as being a different class of thing that it is better than the just.' There is, however, a crucial difference between equity and supererogation. For Aristotle reduces equity to absolute justice, and by that denies equity an independent supererogatory value. In other words: although one is within one's legal rights in acting according to justice (in the non-absolute sense) but not equitably, one is morally expected to be equitable, that is to 'correct' the defects of the universal principle of justice so as to be absolutely just. So the equitable–just distinction applies to the relation between our legal and moral duties rather than to the relation between supererogation and obligation. This, however, remains a matter of interpretation, because Aristotle makes no clear distinction between the legal and the moral in his theory, and when he talks of 'law' he definitely means something wider than the positive legal system. Whatever the correct reading of Aristotle is, equity can in principle be viewed as one type of supererogation. Yet it is a 'degenerate' one, because its corrective character makes it supererogatory only in the *qualified* sense: ideally it should have been part of justice, as Aristotle himself implies (cf. Aquinas, *Summa Theologica*, II, II, Q. 120).

We can conclude, then, that although the idea of supererogation in the strict sense of the word is alien to classical ethics (which can thus be treated as 'externally' different from supererogationism), a distinction between what is strictly required and what is virtuous and partly optional, is held both by moral philosophers and by 'ordinary men'. The Greco–Roman view of beneficence and gratitude, equity and perfect justice, friendship and noble behaviour contains important supererogatory elements. It should however be noted that unlike our notion of supererogation, which attaches special moral value to the very act of going beyond duty, classical morality does not view virtuous action as meritorious for that reason. In terms of the two conditions set out in the Introduction we can thus argue that although beneficent, equitable, and virtuous actions in general meet the condition of *continuity*, they cannot be treated as supererogatory in the strict sense of the word, because they do not fulfil the condition of *correlativity*.

3

The morality of duty:
Kant on supererogation

3.1 DEONTOLOGY VS. AXIOLOGY

A deontological theory, such as Kant's ethics, presents the theory of supererogation with a problem, which may be treated as the opposite of that posed by axiological ethics of the type discussed in the last chapter. For, while the very absence of a concept of duty in classical ethics makes it hard to give any meaning to the notion of acts which go beyond the call of duty, the all-embracing nature of duty in a deontological theory makes the idea of supererogation no more intelligible. In neither theory is supererogation accounted for as a separate moral category, but this is for diametrically opposed reasons: in the one case nothing which really is of a moral worth is obligatory; in the other case everything which is of a moral worth is obligatory.

This difference (in the reasons that make both axiological and deontological theories incompatible, at least prima facie, with supererogationism) explains why the issue in the case of classical morality is 'external', whereas in Kant's case it is 'internal'. In the former the condition of correlativity (of duty and supererogation) cannot be met for conceptual reasons, while in the latter the issue concerns the *scope* of duty, and the reasons for rejecting a realm beyond duty are more ethical and normative. It also explains why classical morality is not directly concerned with the problem of supererogation, while Kantian ethics sees it as a challenge which must be answered. The distinction between the externality and internality of the two disputes is also reflected in the fact that while in classical ethics the idea of supererogation has to be built into the theory by way of reconstruction, in Kant's case it can be understood in terms of the ethical theory proper.

The external differences between the morality of virtue and

supererogation make it impossible to refer to Aristotle as an anti-supererogationist. These obstacles do not apply to deontological theories, like those of the Protestants and Kant, which deny the possibility of supererogation on specific grounds. The reasons for refusing to recognize the existence and value of supererogatory acts vary in their particular content, but they support a common belief in the all-embracing scope of moral duty, which entails anti-supererogationism. Although Kant does not adopt the Lutheran argument against supererogation (i.e. the metaphysical impossibility of doing more than is commanded by God), it cannot be denied that in his rigorous morality of duty, and hence in the denial of supererogation, he is much influenced by his strict and typically Protestant moral upbringing.

All these contrasts between classical and Kantian ethics are, however, much too crude and do not represent the complexity of their respective attitudes towards supererogation. First, as has already been noted, the distinction between 'external' and 'internal' is relative, and as such, it is only partially useful. Secondly, 'axiological' and 'deontological' cannot be taken as purely and wholly characterizing Aristotelian and Kantian ethics respectively. Both popular morality and the ethical theory of the Greeks and Romans have been shown to contain distinctions between obligatory and non-obligatory (yet virtuous) actions. And similarly Kantian ethics, as we shall see in the present chapter, falls short of the rigidly deontological view often ascribed to it. Consequently, although Kant's disagreement with supererogationism is (relatively) internal, he cannot be labelled as an anti-supererogationist without qualification. Some of his writings hint at a more conciliatory approach towards moral actions which cannot be considered as duties, and reveal a tendency to recognize the value of certain supererogatory ideals. Still, Kant's view may also serve as a typical example of a deontological theory with its anti-supererogationist implications.

Before embarking on a detailed textual analysis a short note on the principal sources for the present investigation may be useful. Kant's ethical writings can be divided (and are divided in this way by Kant himself) into two groups: the 'preparatory' works and the 'systematic' works. The first group consists of the *Groundwork* (or *Fundamental Principles of The Metaphysic of Morals*) (1785) and the *Critique of Practical Reason* (1788); the second group includes the later *Metaphysic of Morals* (1797) and perhaps also the earlier work, *Lec-*

tures on Ethics. The terms 'Groundwork' and 'Critique' on the one hand, and 'Metaphysic' on the other hand suffice to explain this division, provided we understand them in their technical sense. The two works of the first group are usually taken to represent Kant's ethical views, but this is highly misleading, especially when one tries to get a complete picture of the details of his moral system. The preparatory works are more abstract, being concerned with the formal structure of practical reason and the moral law. The other, lesser-known works of the second group are more 'anthropological', as they deal with the systematic application of the supreme principle of morality. They are also less deontological than the preparatory writings, and express Kant's interest in the teleological aspects of morality – ethical ends, ideals, and virtues.

It is, therefore, natural that the *Metaphysic* and *Lectures* are not only more concerned with the problem of supererogatory acts, but that they also take a stand which is more favourable to them. In the application of the moral law Kant discusses the virtues of beneficence, gratitude, sympathy, and charity and the concepts of duties to oneself, praise, and merit. This discussion forces Kant to qualify his rigorous deontological principles (which in the preparatory works imply either a total disregard of supererogation or an anti-supererogationist view), and to adopt a more 'latitudinarian' theory, which inevitably raises the problem of supererogation. There is one important exception to the above-mentioned division: those passages in the *Critique* that deals with the psychological and educational aspects of the moral law. The last chapter of the Analytic (concerning the incentives of morality) and the last part of the book (the Methodology) contain some interesting remarks on the value and dangers of supererogatory action. Like the *Metaphysic* they are concerned with the application of the moral law and its influence on subjective human maxims. In that respect these chapters should not be classified as 'preparatory' (*Critique*, pp. 130, 249, and *Groundwork*, p. 57).

3.2 THE RIGOROUS THEORY: THE DENIAL OF SUPEREROGATION

An action that is neither commanded nor forbidden is merely *permissible*. . . . An action of this kind is called morally indifferent (*Metaphysic*, pp. 21–2).

Kant seems to be committed to what Urmson calls the threefold classification of actions from the point of view of moral worth, and if that is the case, then his theory is open to Urmson's criticism as 'inadequate' (Urmson, 1958, pp. 198–9). It is inadequate because it does not allow for supererogatory acts, that is acts that are permissible yet not morally indifferent. Furthermore, in the passage that follows the assertion quoted above Kant even questions the very existence of a category of morally indifferent actions, which raises the possibility of a bare twofold classification of actions (the obligatory and the forbidden). Although, I believe, Kant rejects such a rigid classification as characterizing the 'fantastically virtuous' man, the pedant 'who admits *nothing* morally *indifferent*' (*Metaphysic*, p. 71), this does not in itself weaken his denial of supererogation on the basis of a rigorous threefold division.

Given this deontic conceptual framework, how does Kant deal with actions which we would call supererogatory? On the one hand, supererogation is incompatible with a theory based on such parsimonious deontic logic because, by definition, no action can be morally better than that which is required as a duty. On the other hand, the theory of duty itself is formulated by Kant in a manner which suggests some distinctions of a supererogatory nature. Kant is torn between the rigorous theory of duty and the need to account for man's aspiration to perfection and virtuous ideals, between his Rationalism and Pietism. Kant never explicitly admits that there is an ethical problem involved in the status of acts which are beyond one's duty, nor does he mention the term 'supererogation'. Yet he can be shown to use (implicitly) two complementary strategies for solving the above-mentioned tension: reducing the supererogatory to the obligatory, and extending the meaning and scope of the concept of duty. The first strategy is typically anti-supererogationist; the second often just makes the reduction (the first strategy) more plausible, but may sometimes allow some room for supererogatory acts. These two strategies are not always clearly distinguished from each other, and should be understood merely as auxiliary tools of analysis and interpretation.

Kant's rigorous theory is basically anti-supererogationist, and accordingly he employs the first strategy to deal with the deviating case of supererogation. If we look at the features characterizing a moral act according to Kant we can list at least three important conditions:

(1) *Obligatoriness*: The moral act is never optional. There is a necessity in moral actions, which for human beings (having inclinations besides reason) means a duty, an imperative. The moral act is therefore always performed in obedience to a binding command or law.[1]

(2) *Universalizability*: An act is tested for its morality by the final and supreme test of the universalizability of the maxim according to which it is performed or chosen.

(3) *Duty as a motive*: An act is moral if and only if its motive is moral, which for Kant means that it is done for the sake of duty and out of reverence for the moral law. The morality of the act does not consist in its purpose or its results but solely in the formal principle of volition which governs the act.

Do these conditions exclude supererogatory acts from the realm of morality? Condition (1) is by definition incompatible with supererogation. It implies that failure to perform a moral act is reprehensible. But supererogation is the class of acts that are *optional* i.e. those, the omission of which is not considered wrong or punishable. Furthermore, the morality of supererogation claims that the special value of certain virtuous acts lies in their being optional, that is in the freedom (not in the Kantian sense) of the agent to choose not to do them. Volunteering is an example of a type of action which, due to condition (1), cannot and does not have moral value in Kant's eyes, although it is highly regarded by supererogationists.

Applying condition (2) to supererogation is more problematic. The two 'sub-tests' of the categorical imperative (based on the universalizability test) are: (a) can the relevant maxim be *conceived* as a universal law without contradiction; (b) can it be *willed* as such as a law without contradiction (*Groundwork*, pp. 55–6). The first sub-test (which is applied 'negatively' by Kant) does not concern supererogation, since a world in which everybody sticks strictly to his duties and does nothing beyond them is conceivable without contradiction. This is implied by Kant's own analysis of his fourth example (mutual help) illustrating the application of the categorical imperative. It may very well be a world which would lack some moral values and worth, but it can still be consistently imagined. A

---

[1] It is noteworthy that Kant mentions (*Groundwork*, p. 82) the Scholastic distinction between *consilia* and *praecepta*; but unlike Medieval philosophy, which uses this distinction as the basis of the concept of supererogation, Kant uses it to clarify the difference between the *prudential* and the *moral*. *Consilia*, thus, have no moral status; their value is merely empirical.

'positive' application of this sub-test to supererogatory action does not yield a contradiction either (we can easily imagine a world in which everyone acts on certain maxims of supererogation), and consequently we are led to the conclusion that such supererogatory maxims and actions are morally indifferent. Yet if there are supererogatory maxims which logically cannot be universalized (e.g. a maxim urging me always to do *more than others*), then it seems that supererogatory maxims are contrary to morality, rather than just indifferent to it.

As for the second sub-test it is more difficult to say whether it applies to supererogation, because it is not exactly clear what Kant means by a contradiction in the will. However, it seems clear that one can without contradiction will a world in which at least *some* supererogatory maxims have no normative force. One may be quite content to live in a world in which one neither receives charity from others nor is asked to give to charity. Generally, the universalizability test seems not to apply to supererogation because it tests particular actions in a negative way alone (an act is a moral duty if we cannot conceive or will without contradiction the universalization of the maxim of its negation). But supererogatory action is based on a positive definition of what is good and virtuous to do, rather than on a duty to avoid performing a forbidden act. The agent of a heroic act does not justify his action by the universalizability principle. On the contrary, he may regard his action as his *personal* duty or his individual ideal alone.

The third condition, that of the moral motive, cannot easily be applied to supererogation. Perhaps this is due to the fact that it invites even more criticism (than the two preceding conditions) as a condition of moral conduct in general, independently of supererogation. The problem is that even if we take Kant's side and admit that only morally motivated acts have moral value, how are we to apply this condition to supererogation? Kant says that acting for the sake of duty is the only moral motive. But can a supererogatory act be performed for the sake of duty in the sense of respect to a universally binding law? The agent may talk of a subjective duty (e.g. to realize certain personal ideals), or a feeling that he had to do the act, but this is exactly what Kant wants to avoid in his definition of 'moral'. Furthermore, the idea of non-obligatory good action requires that the result (or at least the intended result) of the act be of a certain nature, e.g. achieve *more* good than is demanded by duty.

But unlike condition (3), which is formal, this condition is material. Kant himself suspects that 'super-meritorious' acts are performed for the sake of pleasure, praise, or merit and are therefore incompatible with (3). He insists that 'actions . . . done with great sacrifice and merely for the sake of duty may be praised as noble and sublime deeds, yet only in so far as there are clues which suggest that they were done wholly out of respect for duty and not from aroused feelings' (*Critique*, p. 192, cf. p. 191). Although the restriction imposed by condition (3) on moral action in general is controversial, it is especially problematic with regard to supererogation. We can try to fulfil our duties 'for the sake of duty', but when we come to surpass the requirements of duty, can we still be described as acting for duty's sake? In most cases supererogatory acts *are* done from 'aroused feelings', like the love of a friend, of humanity or of God, and not (as Kant unfairly suspects) out of 'vain self-love' or 'to pride ourselves on our meritorious worth'. Supererogatory action is often the outcome of 'a spontaneous inclination' or 'an endeavor unbidden but gladly undertaken', which for Kant are motives characteristic of moral fanaticism. Most people would not agree with Kant's denunciation of volunteering as a conceited contempt of duty (*Critique*, p. 189). Kant's anti-supererogationism is expressed by his rejection of there being any moral value in actions 'to which we think we need no command'. Nevertheless, Kant is justified in his warning against moral self-indulgence which is often a by-product of supererogation, but seldom a by-product of action which is recognized both by society and by the agent as obligatory. It is true that psychologically reverence for the law makes us humble and restrains the 'empirical' feelings of moral conceit. But this does not justify the repudiation of the moral value of supererogation (or volunteering) in general.[2]

But if the three conditions for the morality of actions do not leave place for supererogation, what does Kant mean by 'noble and sublime deeds' or by 'super-meritorious acts'? I think that Kant's answer would be formulated in terms of overcoming obstacles and of self-restraint. 'Virtue is the strength of man's maxim in fulfilling his duty' (*Metaphysic*, p. 54, and cf. pp. 38, 42). The 'supererogatory' act is especially praiseworthy not because of its content, result,

---

[2] Kindness of heart and charitable feelings are inclinations which should be inculcated only if they are subordinated to principles. Otherwise they encourage 'unregulated conduct' which is morally worthless (*Lectures*, p. 193).

or relation to duty but due to the difficult circumstances in which it is performed. In a way this is a test for the morality of obligatory action in general, for according to Kant, the moral act is performed *despite* inclinations to do the contrary. So we can see that, faced with the problem of supererogation, Kant uses the strategy of reducing the deviating cases to suit his rigorous theory. Supererogatory acts are either moral in the same sense as all other moral acts, or do not carry any moral worth whatsoever. 'For all actions which are praise-worthy, if we only search [i.e. apply the two strategies] we shall find a law of duty which commands and does not leave us to choose what may be agreeable to our propensity' (*Critique*, p. 192). Simi-larly, 'One need only reflect a little to find an indebtedness which the vaunted hero has in some way incurred to the human race . . . which will prevent the thought of duty from being repressed by the self-complacent imagination of merit' (*Critique*, p. 252n).

In his later writings, confronted by problems involved in the application of the categorical imperative, Kant becomes aware of the difficulties in applying the strategy of reduction. This compels him to employ the second strategy, namely the extension of the concept of duty. That in turn allows him to make distinctions within the sphere of duty which either make the reduction of the supererogatory to the obligatory more plausible, or even make the supererogatory a possible ethical category.

3.3 THE LATITUDINARIAN THEORY: THE REDUCTION TO DUTY

Supererogation is sometimes described as a category of actions which, although morally good, cannot be exacted or demanded by others, that is to say actions over which the recipient has no right or claim. If that is taken as a defining characteristic of supererogation, then Kant in his broader theory can account for this disputed class of actions. In the *Metaphysic* (p. 39) he says that 'ethics contains duties which others cannot compel us (by natural means) to fulfill'. This is due to the fact that ethics is 'a doctrine of ends', and 'compulsion to have or to adopt ends is self-contradictory'.

Although the argument presented above sounds plausible, all that is admitted by Kant here is that duties which can (like *legal* duties) be exacted by others do not exhaust the whole realm of *moral duty*. Kant distinguishes between two types of moral duties: the external type, in which duty determines corresponding rights of others to exercise compulsion, and the internal one, where no such rights exist (*Metaphysic*, p. 41). The first type comprises the 'juridical duties'; the second the 'duties of virtue'. Being concerned with general ends rather than with specific actions, duties of virtue can be described as those which go beyond institutional or contractarian contexts (such as doing one's professional duty, or promise-keeping, truth-telling, etc.). While juridical duties are those which are either actually enforced or at least may be logically so enforced (setting aside practical or moral reasons for not doing so), duties of virtue exclude, by definition, any legal intervention. So although supererogatory acts can never be legally required, this does not mean that the Kantian distinction between the two types of duty makes room for supererogation. For the distinction between the supererogatory and the obligatory does not coincide with that between the morally required and the legally enforceable.

In the *Critique* (p. 256) Kant calls the first type of duties 'essential' and the second 'non-essential'. The former are based on other persons' *rights*, while the latter arise from other persons' *needs*. This formulation of the distinction between types of duties may again give the impression that Kant is trying to make room for supererogation. For it is true that we are often urged by someone's needs to perform an act which transcends our duty, whereas we are always expected to fulfil our duties independently of the needs of the person to whom the duty is owed as his right. Although the terms 'essential' and 'non-essential' may suggest different degrees of moral stringency, Kant does not in fact believe that duties of virtue are less important or less binding than juridical duties.

The failure of this distinction to accommodate supererogation is due to the fact that it is a distinction *within* the concept of moral duty. Supererogation is recognized only as a class of acts, which although obligatory, cannot be externally exacted. But there is no place for supererogation in the sense of moral acts which are not duties *at all*. Although some moral acts are such that we cannot be externally compelled to perform them, their internal binding force is no less stringent, they are no less universalizable, and their omission is no less wrong and reprehensible than of any other obligatory act. Kant adds that if 'someone does *more* in the way of duty than the law can compel him to do, his action is *meritorious*' (*Metaphysic*, p. 27).

Although it may again sound as if it implies supererogationism, this statement merely characterizes 'the meritorious' (in contrast to 'the due'), as that which can only be internally enforced, but not as the mark of supererogation. The meritorious action reflects on the virtue (strength of will) of the agent who does not require any external threat in order to be moral.

By that distinction between juridical duties and duties of virtue Kant widens the scope of the concept of duty (the second strategy), and consequently makes it possible to reduce supererogatory acts to acts of duty (the first strategy). This is a more refined way of expressing an anti-supererogationist view than that contained in the more rigorous formulations of the theory that were discussed in the previous section. It recognizes the moral value of the allegedly supererogatory acts, but does so only on the condition that in the final analysis they be treated as obligatory. Unlike the rigorous theory of duty, which either disregards or simply denies the moral status of supererogation, the more latitudinarian theory faces the deontic problem raised by these acts and tries to solve it by a combination of the two strategies.

Although no rights of 'exercising compulsion' correspond to duties of virtue, these duties entail a 'right in the sense of a *moral title*' (*Metaphysic*, p. 40). This general statement lies at the foundation of the Kantian reduction. We can take as an illustrative example the distinction between charity and justice, or in the words of the *Lectures* (p. 191) 'duties of good-will, or benevolence' versus 'duties of indebtedness or justice'. Although the two seem to be distinguished from each other in terms of the existence or absence of corresponding rights, as well as in terms of the distinction between needs and rights, they are gradually 'assimilated', mainly by reducing the former to the latter. This is based on the following line of argument (*Lectures*, pp. 194–5; cf. pp. 235–6): if everybody in the world acted according to the principles of justice without exception, there would be no misery (except for sickness and misfortune). In such an ideal world there would be no need for benevolence, charity (or any other supererogatory acts). But as human nature is such that the violation of justice is inevitable, 'Providence has implanted in our bosoms the instinct of benevolence to be the source of actions by which we restore what we have unrighteously procured.' Everyone is personally responsible for injustice, either by directly violating other people's rights or by one's very membership in a morally im-

perfect society. The inevitable conclusion is that charity (and beneficence) is 'a duty we owe to mankind and that in the last analysis it is
a question of right'. From an intuitively correct distinction between
justice and charity (supererogation) Kant leads us to the final step of
the reduction: 'Even charity . . . is an act of duty imposed upon us
by the rights of others and the debt we owe to them.'

Justifying charity and supererogatory action in general on the
grounds of one's membership in an unjust social order is an interesting suggestion. We are reminded of Aristotle's explanation of the
corrective function of equity (2.3). For in both cases there seems to
be an inevitable injustice in the law which can never be totally elim-
inated by modifying the law itself (e.g. by adding new principles of
distribution or other duties). Such a law can therefore be corrected
only by an element that is external to it (equity in Aristotle, benevolence in Kant). Yet though this equitable or charitable action can
never be formulated as a definite duty, it ought nevertheless to be
treated as obligatory in the sense that those who suffer injustice have
a right to be 'compensated' for it by those who (inevitably) stand to
gain from the moral defects of our social organizations. Kant
himself describes equity as 'a form of right which does not carry
with it the authority to enforce it' (*Lectures*, p. 212). This means that
although it is not a juridical duty, one has a right to be treated equitably.[3]

Nevertheless I think that Kant is mistaken in this reduction of
(supererogatory) benevolence to (obligatory) justice. First, the need
for charity and benevolence quite often arises in circumstances of
'sickness and misfortune', which Kant admits are wholly independent of the injustice of our social organizations. In that respect
supererogatory behaviour cannot even be considered an indirect
duty. Secondly, Kant's assumption that in an ideally just society
there would be no need for charity and benevolence can in no way
be justified. For even in a world in which everyone gets his share
and is happy with it, there are often good reasons for people to sacrifice part of their own good for the sake of others (friends, family,
leaders and even strangers who happen to have less). For those
people, generosity in itself is a value that must be expressed in
action. There is, of course, a certain element of moral gratuitous-

[3] And compare this to the passage on equity in the Introduction to The Doctrine of
Justice (the first part of the *Metaphysic*), in which it is described as a just claim
although not legally enforceable.

ness in such acts which for Kant is a reason for either denying their moral value or for reducing them to duty. But I find it hard either to deny their moral value (as they certainly bring about moral good and manifest moral strength) or to treat them as obligatory. In other words, such acts are clearly and irreducibly supererogatory.

The only way that is left open for Kant to maintain the validity of this reduction is to say that such a personal sacrifice (in an ideally just world) is a violation of one's duties *to oneself*. For Kant, this category of moral duties is no less important and binding than our duties towards others, and he can thus claim that any genuine example of supererogatory action (i.e. which cannot be reduced to any kind of other-regarding duty) is in the final analysis still contrary to duty (of the agent to himself). Such a strategy is employed by Kant in his discussion of the meritorious act of saving other people from a shipwreck at the cost of one's own life. 'Our esteem for it [the meritorious action] will be weakened very much by the concept of his duty to himself, which here seems to have been infringed' (*Critique*, p. 255). But even if we ignore the general problem of the status of self-regarding duties, we can easily imagine supererogatory actions which do not involve violation of any duty to oneself. It may be natural to criticize an extremely generous act of beneficence as a form of vice (self-indulgent prodigality) as Aristotle and Seneca do, but it can hardly be viewed as a violation of duty (except in some extreme cases).

Contrary to Kant, we believe that the pursuit of one's perfection, even if it is *morally* valuable, cannot be treated as a duty, and *ipso facto* (according to the condition of correlativity) as supererogatory. It is only the second end – the happiness of others – which logically allows for supererogation. Although this end cannot legally be enforced, some measure of concern for the happiness of others is indeed morally obligatory (but beyond that measure it is supererogatory).

It is noteworthy that Kant's two strategies and his denial of supererogation represent an approach to the nature of an ideal society which is opposite to Aristotle's view. While Aristotle regards the principles of (distributive) justice as superfluous in an ideal society which is governed by relations of friendship and generosity (both being beyond distributive justice), Kant's doctrine implies that in the perfect moral order there would be no need for those subjective, spontaneous attitudes of generosity and kindness.

For the classical philosopher, the virtuous man is one who transcends the world of claims and counter-claims, rights and duties. For the deontological theorist, he is the person who is 'conscientious and scrupulously fair' in his conduct (*Lectures*, pp. 200–3). This contrast in the view of the morally ideal world reveals the basic difference between the morality of virtue and the morality of duty.

3.4 THE LATITUDINARIAN THEORY: THE POSSIBILITY OF SUPEREROGATION

Some of the statements and distinctions in the wider theory show that Kant was less decided in his attitude towards supererogatory acts than was suggested in the previous sections. Nowhere in his theory does Kant recognize it as a distinct and valuable class of moral actions, yet he does sometimes leave room for moral acts which are not strictly obligatory. The meaning of 'duty' is extended in a way which makes the anti-supererogationist assertions seem merely to be paying lip-service to the original rigorous theory. But although my present claim is based on a debatable interpretation, no reader of Kant can fail to notice his oscillation between pure deontology and the recognition of a sphere beyond duty.

The crucial distinction for our purpose is the following: 'Ethical duties are of *wide* obligation, whereas juridical duties are of *narrow* obligation' (*Metaphysic*, p. 49). The proposed criterion for that distinction is that while the latter duties are concerned only with *actions*, the former prescribe *maxims*, a fact that explains the 'latitude for free choice': 'the law cannot specify precisely what and how much one's actions should do towards the obligatory end' (*Metaphysic*, p. 49). This distinction between ethical and juridical duties is slightly inconsistent with that presented in the Introduction to the *Metaphysic* (pp. 16–7) and with that mentioned by us in the previous section (*Metaphysic*, p. 41). In both these passages the distinction is based on the *motive* of the action (the law itself versus other motives) or on the source of its *authority* (internal versus external) rather than on the scope or degree of specificity of the obligation (wide versus narrow) as it is here. This explains why only the version of the distinction between ethical and juridical quoted above lends itself to a supererogatory interpretation.

A similar distinction between narrow (rigorous) and wider (meritorious) duty is suggested in the *Groundwork* (p. 87). The narrow duty is decided by the first sub-test of the categorical imperative, while the wider duty can only be determined on the basis of the second sub-test. The narrow type of duty is rigorous because it 'allows no exception in the interest of inclination', and hence is *perfect*. The wider duty allows for some exception, and is therefore *imperfect*. The relation between the scope of duty and its degree of perfection is explicitly expressed by the following passage: 'As the duty is wider, so man's obligation to action is more imperfect; but the closer to *narrow* duty (Law) he brings the maxim of observing this duty (in his attitude of will), so much more perfect is his virtuous action' (*Metaphysic*, p. 49). In other words, the more perfectly one fulfils one's imperfect duty, the more virtuous one is. And Kant goes a step further towards recognizing supererogation: 'Imperfect duties, accordingly, are only *duties of virtue*. To fulfill them is *merit* (= +a); but to transgress them is not so much *guilt* (= −a) as rather mere *lack* of moral *worth* (= 0), unless the agent makes it his principle not to submit to these duties' (*Metaphysic*, p. 49).

All these quotations from the *Metaphysic* (and even that from the *Groundwork*) imply at least the logical possibility of supererogation. For Kant is fully aware that the distinction between wide and narrow, imperfect and perfect duties, entails a certain latitude for free choice, a certain extent of inevitable indeterminacy in the moral law which leaves us free (in the sense of liberty) to make our moral decisions. And together with that element of option and the subjective interpretation of the imperfect moral duty, the notion of merit is introduced. This is clearly typical of supererogatory action, which is held to be meritorious and virtuous though its omission is neither wrong nor held to be a 'vice'. The symmetrical relation of commission of an obligatory action, which is right, and omission of that action, which is wrong, applies only to perfect duties. And as this criterion of symmetry serves to characterize the distinction between moral duty and supererogation, we can interpret 'imperfect duties' to be of a supererogatory nature.

Kant of course strictly qualifies this interpretation of 'imperfect duties'. First of all, the wider and imperfect duty is still a *duty*. The distinction between the strictly obligatory and the optional lies *within* the sphere of duty. Secondly, we are free to choose only the amount, extent, and circumstances in which the actions that fulfil the imperfect duty are to be performed. It is only the mode of application of the obligatory principle of action (the maxim) that is left to our free choice. Thirdly, although the way in which the imperfect duty is performed is not defined by the duty itself (indeterminacy), it is determined by other maxims (or duties). The only permission one has is to limit one obligatory maxim by another, for instance the general love of one's neighbour by the love of one's parents.

Still, even in the light of these qualifications, our interpretation cannot be wholly dismissed. Much depends on the way we understand the nature of imperfect duties.[4] If x and y are both actions which equally fulfil a certain imperfect duty D, then it is true that we may perform *either x or y*, and that this decision is itself morally indifferent. The scope for choice involved in this decision does not imply any recognition of supererogation, especially if, as Kant states, the choice of x rather than y may be guided by another maxim, or by a sub-duty of D. But although Kant says nothing about it, there is the possibility of doing *both x and y*. And doing so is clearly meritorious and praiseworthy, though by no means obligatory (cf. Hill, 1971, p. 71). To take Kant's own example, although we may limit our concern for other people if a member of our family is in urgent need of our help, it is sometimes possible to respond to both requests for help and behave supererogatorily. Despite his tendency to a reductivist elimination of supererogatory acts, Kant must admit that there are cases in which our freedom to pursue one course of action is not limited by other maxims (in the same way as our freedom to sacrifice our good for the sake of others is not *always* limited by duties to ourselves). To sum up: taken disjunctively, particular acts that fulfil an imperfect duty involve a morally neutral freedom of choice. But taken conjunctively they involve the concept of supererogation, since there is a certain extent of fulfilling an imperfect duty beyond which one's actions become supererogatory. Although there is some support for the disjunctive interpretation in Kant's writings, there is also support for the conjunctive one, especially in the use of the concept of virtue and merit in relation to imperfect duties, and in the admission of degrees of conformity with those duties.

My supererogatory interpretation of imperfect duties may be questioned by those who criticize the very validity of Kant's distinction between perfect and imperfect duties. For example, Chisholm (who refers to the disjunctive rather than the conjunctive interpretation), claims that if imperfect duties are defined in terms of the

---

[4] For an illuminating discussion of this problem, see Gregor (1963, ch. 7).

indeterminacy of 'the manner in which we fulfil them', then '*no duties are perfect*' (Chisholm, 1963, p. 4n). One can for instance return a loan either in cash or by cheque, etc. But such a broad and vague definition of the distinction should be rejected, for it fails to see that in perfect duties the freedom of choice is always disjunctive (there is no suggestion in the duty to return a loan that it should be repaid twice – once in cash and once by cheque), while imperfect duties may involve also a conjunctive freedom of choice (e.g. with the imperfect duty of benevolence, it is meritorious to help both a member of one's family and a stranger in need).

Yet in spite of the supererogatory element involved in acting in accordance with imperfect duty, Kant never adopts a fully supererogationist view. Making other people's happiness our own end is a duty, the omission of which is no less blameworthy than the breaking of a promise. In other words, there is no 'latitude' for freedom of choice with regard to taking a whole *class* of actions as our duty. If we make it 'a principle not to submit to these duties' we are guilty of a moral offence.[5] Even if Kant is justified in his belief that helping others to achieve their own ends (happiness) is our duty, we can surely think of certain *maxims* whose very adoption is supererogatory, that is to say whole classes of morally valuable acts which cannot be required. The saint is a person who not only fulfils his imperfect duties to a supererogatory degree, but also adopts certain ends (or maxims) which are altogether non-obligatory. Kant recognizes supererogation only in a secondary sense – namely the class of actions which are not in themselves perfectly (juridically) obligatory, although their omission is generally criticized (e.g. acts of help when no risk or sacrifice is involved). But saintly and heroic acts, which are perhaps the most typical examples of supererogation (being both non-obligatory and entailing no blame in the case of omission), have no place in his ethics.

In contrast with Kant's example of charity which, by being reduced to justice, served to illustrate his anti-supererogationism, the discussion of honour (versus honesty) reveals Kant's inclination to accept some sort of supererogatory action. 'Honesty is not merit', because it is the minimum of morality, the lack of which is a

---

[5] In terms of the *Groundwork*: An imperfect duty allows exceptions 'in the interest of inclination'. But such exceptions are logically limited to a few individual cases. We cannot appeal to such exceptions in every case, because then the exception would become the rule, and the imperfect duty would cease to be a duty and become a matter of inclination.

vice; whereas, 'For a man to be worthy of positive honour his actions must be *meritorious*, they must involve *more than is strictly required* of him' (*Lectures*, pp. 49–50) [my italics]. We do not deserve honour on account merely of living honestly. We are honourable only if we do more than is strictly required of us. This particular example is cited by Kant as 'a possible principle of ethics' (to be contrasted with principles of legal obligation). This is clearly the language of supererogation. The supererogatory interpretation of honour is supported by that asymmetrical relation of the positive value of action as opposed to the neutral (rather than negative) value of forbearance, which does not hold in the case of honesty. Kant also adds that 'a country where honesty is held in high regard is in a bad state', for it shows that honesty is rare there. Such a society regards the performance of strict duties as something which deserves praise although in fact it does not deserve it at all. Kant's correct perception implies that although society cannot force its members to act honourably (or supererogatorily), and although individual persons cannot be blamed for not acting so, the general absence of such actions means that such a society is morally defective (see below, 8.4). Generally the ideal of honour is significantly at variance with the 'hymn for duty' and the idealization of the sheer reverence for the moral law. Kant seems to be aware that abiding by the demands of the law is insufficient for achieving moral *worth*. The self-respect of a person is dependent on the option of acting beyond what is strictly demanded. Kant, however, clearly warns against substituting meritorious acts for strictly obligatory acts. One deserves praise only for virtuous acts which one has performed after discharging one's 'legal obligations'.

An even more striking defence of the value of supererogatory behaviour can be found in the *Metaphysic*:

> Would it not be better for the welfare of the world in general if human morality were limited to juridical duties and these were fulfilled with the utmost conscientiousness, while benevolence were considered morally indifferent? It is not so easy to see what effect this would have on man's happiness. But at least a great moral ornament, love of man, would then be missing from the world. Accordingly, benevolence is required for its own sake, in order to present the world in its full perfection as a beautiful moral whole, even if we do not take into account the advantage it brings (*Metaphysic*, pp. 126–7).

Gratitude is generally the mark of supererogation, for it means an acknowledgment of the gratuitous, supererogatory nature of the act for which one is grateful. It is therefore interesting to see how Kant is reluctantly driven to recognize the supererogatory nature of benevolence in the course of his discussion of gratitude. Although from the point of view of the agent the benevolent act should always be regarded as a duty, as something owed to the beneficiary (or to humanity as a whole), things look different from the point of view of the recipient. The *duty* of gratitude arises from the fact that 'a favour is a debt which can never be extinguished, for even if I repay my benefactor tenfold, I am still not even with him, because he has done me a kindness which he did not owe' (*Lectures*, p. 222). Kant, unlike Aquinas, does not believe that a return which is bigger than the original gift can compensate for the supererogatory element in the gift. This incongruity of the two points of view (of the benefactor and the recipient) makes Kant's position unclear. For when he says that the benefactor 'must not give the recipient the impression that [the favour] is a debt to be repaid', does he mean that acts of beneficence should be performed *as if* they were duties (*Metaphysic*, pp. 115–16), or that they really *are* – in the final analysis – obligatory? And if they are duties, or even just made to appear so, why must the beneficiary be grateful? Is it due only to the pragmatic reason that 'ingratitude decreases generosity' (*Lectures*, p. 222), or does it also represent a belief in the gratuitous (and hence meritorious) nature of the favour? Gratitude is an extraordinary type of duty. For although we, as spectators, expect the beneficiary to regard it as his perfect duty, we do not expect the benevolent agent to regard it as such. It is definitely true that we tend to praise those non-obligatory acts which are believed by their agent to be a duty. But this does not solve the problem whether the acts in question are in fact obligatory, and Kant does not seem to be fully decided on this point, although I believe he inclines towards a supererogatory interpretation of beneficence. For he treats gratitude as an opportunity to cultivate and express the 'love of man' (*Metaphysic*, p. 124).

3.5 SUPEREROGATION AS AN EDUCATIONAL IDEAL

Supererogation is usually regarded as having a special educational value. Apart from bringing about good consequences, the heroic act is valued as a model, as an example that should be imitated by everyone who is capable of doing so. And if the supererogatory act is exceptionally difficult and involves risk and sacrifice, it is set up as an idea of perfection which should regulate our moral conduct. This in effect is the idea behind military awards. They are given both as a token of appreciation and as an educational act. Publicity and ceremonial acts of recognition are therefore inseparable from society's reaction to meritorious acts. Finally, such exceptionally good acts are believed to strengthen the moral self-respect and honour of the community and to make its members proud of their society.

Kant, however, is more suspicious of the educational value of supererogation: 'The mind is disposed to nothing but blatant moral fanaticism and exaggerated self-conceit by exhortations to actions as noble, sublime, and magnanimous' (Critique, p. 191). The reason for this suspicion lies in Kant's fear of non-moral motives producing actions which appear to be highly moral. The pursuit of merit is regarded as a 'pathological' inclination. People are attracted by the fact that supererogation is not restricted by obedience to the moral law. But this is exactly the educational danger. Men should be taught that the moral worth of an action derives from a 'submissive disposition'. A duty can be traced in any noble or magnanimous act, and it is that element of the act, rather than its merit, which should be emphasized. Kant also fears that setting up supererogatory actions as an ideal may lead one to treat one's duties as petty and insignificant, and consequently to the abandonment of everyday responsibility. Furthermore, Kant believes that as a matter of empirical fact the influence of duty on our minds is more definite and penetrating than that of merit. (Critique, pp. 252–4).

Kant is unduly afraid of being forced to overstep the theoretically safe, well-defined, and determinate field of moral duty and law. Supererogation is thus connected with the notion of moral fanaticism, which means 'overstepping of limits which practical pure reason sets to mankind' (Critique, p. 192). The only legitimate moral feeling is reverence for the law. Other feelings of heroism, high-flown fantasies, and enthusiasm simply corrupt this pure moral feeling. The romantic and sentimental concepts of heroism should be replaced by sober and humbler notions of obedience, respect, and voluntary submission to the moral law. Kant rejects both Stoicism and Sentimentalism as forms of moral fanaticism (Critique, pp. 192, 252). In any case, for Kant the educational value of supererogatory acts is only marginal, because such acts can never 'wipe out . . . one act of injustice to an individual'. That is to say,

the priority of acting according to one's duty over any other meritorious acts is absolute, and should be so presented in moral education. We have already seen how Kant tries to account for the
meritorious act of saving people's lives in a shipwreck within his
anti-supererogationist theory. Kant adds to his reduction the
remark that 'the action itself does not have the full force of a model
and impulse to imitation'. We may then conclude that even if Kant
had to acknowledge the existence of some supererogatory acts, he
could never grant them the educational value of an ideal or an
example which people should be encouraged to adopt or imitate.

3.6 A POSSIBLE INTERPRETATION

This examination of Kant's view of supererogation leaves us confused. Having considered the remarks and relevant ideas in his writings, it is hard to suggest a consistent and systematic interpretation.
It seems that Kant deals with the problem of acts beyond duty once
from the point of view of his rigorous theory, elsewhere from the
point of view of his concept of virtue (the extended theory), and
sometimes from the standpoint of moral education. Though Kant is
never concerned with a *theory* of supererogation, I think that he is
aware of the problematic existence of supererogatory acts, of the
inner tension between a deontological theory and a morality of
virtue, and of his own oscillation between total rejection and full
recognition of the moral significance of such acts.

Despite the inconsistencies in Kant's attitude (which are partly
explained by the different nature of the 'preparatory' and the 'systematic' writings), a possible interpretation, i.e. a reconstruction,
which could make Kant's view more plausible, may be suggested.

Kant speaks of duty in two senses: the *formal* and the *material*.
Duty as a *form* of our behaviour (the formal principle of moral
conduct) is the motive-condition of all moral actions. All moral
conduct is based on respect for the law, the performance of duty for
duty's sake, and the doing of good in accordance with principles
rather than out of inclination. But the concept of duty is also pro-
pounded as the content of our moral acts, i.e. *what* we ought to do
(rather than how, or with what motive).

A typical example of the formal aspect of duty can be found in the
poetic passage in the *Critique* (p. 193). Duty is treated there as
freedom, as the capacity of man to act according to autonomously

legislated laws, as 'something which elevates man above himself', and as demanding submission yet not by means of threat but through reverence for the law. Principles of ethical duty (unlike those of juridical duty) tell us not only *what* to do, but also *how* to do it, namely 'from a motive of duty' (Hill, 1971, p. 65). In that sense, there is no place for supererogation. One cannot go beyond duty in that sense and still be moral. There cannot be any 'excess' in the pure moral motive of our conduct. Even benevolent action – if it is to be morally praiseworthy – must spring from 'good-will from inclination', which is love (*Lectures*, p. 192). The allegedly supererogatory acts have moral value only if they are motivated by duty, and that is why the benefactor, for example, is expected to treat his acts as duties.

On the other hand, when Kant speaks of doing more than is strictly required as a condition of attaining honour and merit, he clearly refers to the material sense of 'duty'. This concept refers to *what* can be demanded of a person (mainly to be determined by other people's *rights*). This is a minimum of morality, and being so, it can, and sometimes even should, be surpassed. One can certainly do good to others beyond that which is required as one's duty. But such acts should always be tested by the formal conditions of moral acts. And that compels Kant to regard actions which surpass the minimum required as still being a kind of duty. For that purpose he extends the concept of duty to include also those supererogatory acts. Indeterminacy of (imperfect) duty is introduced as a means of subordinating supererogatory acts to the formal condition of morality.

In terms of the distinction between legality and morality, my interpretation has the following consequences: from a formal point of view the moral ('ethical') duty differs from the legal ('juridical') one in its authority (internal versus external), yet not in its content. From the material point of view they differ in their content too (maximal versus minimal amount of good required). This explains why Kantian morality can sometimes be seen as legalistic, while at other times it seems utterly opposed to the spirit and structure of legal rules.

This interpretation is supported by an important passage in the *Metaphysic*, which tries to solve the problem of the nature of the duty to adopt the 'moral point of view'. There is a distinction between a duty of virtue (which corresponds to an end) and an obligation of virtue. There are many duties of virtue but only one obligation of virtue, 'one virtuous attitude of will, as the subjective ground determining us to fulfill our duty. This ethical obligation extends over juridical duties too' (*Metaphysic*, p. 73, cf. p. 41). Thus, duties of virtue allow for supererogation because people may attempt to get closer to an (ideal) end. But the obligation of virtue is fully determined by the moral law, and is common both to juridical and to ethical duties. In this case one cannot do better than that which is required of one. One is either acting morally or non-morally.

The suggested interpretation of Kant's attitude also explains his extremely negative view of supererogation when it is used for educational purposes. For although some actions are surely meritorious by being more than the 'amount' required, they should nevertheless be represented as arising from the sense of duty. Although people may be encouraged to transcend their duty (in the material sense) they should always regard it as part of their duty (in the formal sense). This gap between the objective judgment (concerning the content of the moral act) and the subjective judgment of the agent (concerning the source of value of that same act) is partly bridged by the indeterminacy allowed within the extended scope of duty. Thus, the alleged inconsistency between the supererogationist passages in the *Metaphysic* and the anti-supererogationist comments in the *Critique* disappears.

But even if it is true that Kant leaves some room for supererogation, no theory of that concept is suggested by him, let alone criteria for distinguishing the supererogatory from the obligatory.[6] It is therefore difficult to classify his doctrine in our terminology; that is, to decide whether in his recognition of supererogation he comes nearer to a qualified or to an unqualified version. Most of his assertions concerning friendship, generosity, and beneficence suggest the latter possibility. This is also borne out by the fact that he does not seem to say that ideally duties of virtue should be exacted like juridical duties.

Finally I would like to make a few remarks on another, slightly different, interpretation of Kant's view of supererogation (Eisen-

---

[6] There is, however, a certain suggestion for such a criterion in *Metaphysic* (p. 28). There Kant says that the merit of one's action is related proportionally to the degree of risk and self-sacrifice involved, and the degree of 'moral obstacle (duty)' by which we are bound. The more of the former and the less of the latter, the greater the merit of the act.

berg, 1966). After showing that Kant allows for both morally indifferent and morally permissible acts in his theory, Eisenberg proceeds to question the status of supererogatory (and offensive) acts, and rightly holds that this depends on the way in which we understand the distinction between perfect and imperfect duty. Eisenberg interprets the distinction in terms of 'indeterminacy' and agrees with Chisholm's criticism of it (see 3.4 above). Consequently he argues that there is a *continuum* of wider and narrower duties, a continuum which extends to include what is usually called supererogation (p. 262). But having offered an alternative interpretation of the distinction between perfect and imperfect duties, I cannot in principle accept this 'continuum thesis'. Despite some flaws and inconsistencies in the formulation of the Kantian distinction, the distinction itself is basically clear-cut. I disagree with Eisenberg's contention that perfect duties allow for 'exceptions' similar to those allowed by imperfect duties (Eisenberg, 1966, p. 264). In the context of supererogation this implies that only imperfect duties can be fulfilled to a greater extent than is necessary: one can help others more than is required, but cannot repay more than one owes, since paying more than is owed is perhaps supererogatory but not by way of fulfilling *more* of the perfect duty in question. This explains why only imperfect duties admit degrees of fulfilment, and hence open the way to supererogatory conduct.

Eisenberg finds it hard to resolve the inconsistency between the point of view of the agent, who takes his act of beneficence as a duty, and the point of view of the beneficiary who, having no rights over the act, must consider it as supererogatory. But if my interpretation in terms of the formal versus the material senses of duty is accepted, then the inconsistency can be resolved. For the duty of the benefactor is duty in the formal sense, while the gratuitous element of the beneficent act (from the point of view of the beneficiary) is to be understood in material terms.

The continuum thesis leads Eisenberg to an analogy between the Kantian theory and Findlay's distinction between minatory and hortatory duties. This I find misleading, because although it is true that Findlay's distinction implies a continuum of degrees of imperative force, this is by no means true of Kant. Imperfect duties are themselves no less obligatory than perfect duties (degrees of 'moral obstacles' are allowed only within the particular actions which fulfil a certain imperfect duty). Furthermore, actions which are the minimum required in fulfilment of imperfect duties are no less binding than actions meeting a perfect obligation. And as for those actions which are beyond that minimum, they can clearly be regarded – in terms of our reconstruction – as supererogatory. They are of no imperative necessity whatsoever. Those Kantian statements which question the existence of such acts are *anti*-supererogationist, i.e. try to reduce the supererogatory to the obligatory. But in neither case does Kant seem to take the line suggested by the continuum thesis and adopted by Findlay.

So although I would not like to claim that Kant had a clear view of supererogation, I think that those texts which do recognize the possibility of virtuous acts beyond duty imply an unqualified supererogationist view. It is significant that Eisenberg's continuum thesis fails to account for those passages in which Kant speaks of the intrinsic value of moral conduct which transcends what is strictly required. Kant is closer to adopting the correlativity and continuity conditions than is implied by Eisenberg's interpretation. Although I am in full agreement with Eisenberg's own view of the nature of supererogation, I can only partly accept his reading of Kant on that subject.

4

Utilitarianism

Utilitarianism judges the moral status of actions in terms of the goodness of their consequences. Accordingly, actions can be described as obligatory only if certain conditions relating to their outcome obtain. The notion of duty is derivative, that is to say defined by the theory in terms of the concept of good. This view may be contrasted with deontological theories that see the concept of duty as primary and that of moral goodness as derivative. One implication of this basic difference is that while deontology tends to be too strict in its definition of 'moral' (considering only obligatory actions as having moral value), utilitarianism is inclined to provide a definition of 'moral' which is too wide (taking every 'useful' action as morally good). Both theories – in their pure but crude forms – are, therefore, anti-supererogationist, but for opposite reasons: in a deontological doctrine no action which is beyond duty can be morally good. In a utilitarian doctrine no action which is morally good can be non-obligatory. Although starting at opposite points both doctrines arrive at the same conclusion, which rules out the possibility of non-obligatory yet morally good actions, i.e. supererogatory actions.

For utilitarians, as for Kant, the problem of supererogation is 'internal'. In both theories the question of the limits of moral duty and what lies beyond it inevitably arises and cannot be dismissed as 'external' or irrelevant. To account for supererogation the crude version of the deontological theory must widen the scope of duty, while utilitarianism has to restrict the meaning of moral goodness, at least as a criterion of duty. Yet the wider definition of 'moral' maintained by utilitarians makes the task of explaining supererogation easier for them than for Kant. For duty is only a derivative concept in utilitarianism, and hence can be confined to certain types of utility-promoting actions (the rest being supererogatory),

73

whereas it is harder to conceive of moral acts which are beyond duty, if duty is thought to be the primary principle of the moral value of any action.

It seems, therefore, that generally speaking utilitarianism can better account for supererogation than Kantian ethics. At least it can more readily be modified so as to accommodate supererogatory acts. Being concerned with the value of the consequences of actions rather than with the formal principle of volition, utilitarianism can distinguish not only between morally good actions and better actions, but also between obligatory and non-obligatory actions (that are morally good). The tentative definition of supererogation, suggested in the Introduction, implies that an act must promote the (general) good (welfare, happiness) in some way in order to be supererogatory. It is in doing *more* in terms of goodness that the action of surpassing the requirement of duty is regarded as supererogatory. This is a consequentialist condition shared both by utilitarians and by supererogationists.

From these broad considerations we may conclude that utilitarianism comes nearer to meeting the continuity condition of supererogation (namely that the supererogatory action should achieve more – but of the same type – than that achieved by the obligatory action) than to the correlativity condition (which ascribes the value of supererogatory acts to their being beyond duty). For on the one hand, utilitarianism is based on a continuous and homogeneous scale of moral value which admits degrees, but on the other hand it does not recognize a concept of duty which is independent of the principle of utility. It is, therefore, not surprising that most versions of utilitarianism which are not anti-supererogationist are in some way reductionist, i.e. they allow only for a qualified concept of supererogation. Consequentialism can explain the value of supererogatory acts as acts that bring about better results than their obligatory alternatives, but falls short of accounting for the value of supererogatory acts as spontaneous and virtuous acts which, by being non-obligatory, express man's ideals, and as such deserve special praise. There is more in supererogation than just the maximization of happiness, and that cannot be explained in purely utilitarian terms. This limitation of consequentialism makes it hard for utilitarians to draw the line between the obligatory and the supererogatory, because the only utilitarian way of justifying the gratuitous status of supererogatory acts is to prove that making such acts obligatory would be counter-productive. Although this may sometimes be the case, it certainly is not true of many other instances of supererogation, and indeed does not capture the essential worth of this special class of actions.

The preceding remarks referred to utilitarianism in very general terms and should be taken as pointing out the characteristics of a *type* of ethical theories ranging from the pure but crude forms of utilitarianism to the more sophisticated and 'mixed' theories such as rule-utilitarianism, negative utilitarianism, and those theories which supplement the utility principle with other principles of justice and liberty. In the present chapter the various utilitarian theories will be discussed in turn, and tested in relation to the problem of supererogation. Such axiological issues, however, as the distinction between hedonistic and ideal utilitarianism may be ignored here, as they relate to the criteria used in evaluating the consequences of actions, rather than to the moral (or deontic) status of the actions themselves. From the standpoint of the problem of supererogation, it does not make any difference whether utility is interpreted as pleasure, happiness, want-satisfaction, achievement of 'refined' pleasure or ideals, or whether actions should be assessed by their actual utility value, intended value, or rationally expected value.

But it makes an important difference whether utilitarianism is conceived as a theory of what is morally good, or as a theory of what we ought to do, i.e. as a theory of value or as a theory of duty. The former is perfectly compatible with supererogation: it provides a criterion of moral approbation and praise, but does not commit itself to any normative or deontic theory. But for that same reason it has very little to say about supererogation. On the other hand, the latter version of utilitarianism provides a criterion of moral duty, but seems to be incompatible with the suggestion that moral actions may be optional or supererogatory. A third version, which historically is perhaps the prevalent one, takes utility as the principle of moral rightness (and wrongness). This is an intermediate alternative to the other two versions, since it may mean *rightness* either in the sense of what is 'fitting' and good, or in the sense of what one has to do. But following Ross, I doubt whether 'right' can mean both 'good' and 'obligatory' at the same time. 'Right' is conceptually related either to axiological (value) terms or to normative (deontic) terms. The 'good–ought tie-up', which is often invoked by the anti-supererogationist, is not analytic and requires an ethical justification (which, as I hope to show in 8.2 and 8.3, is lacking).

In what follows, we will first discuss some examples of crude utilitarianism, which is straightforwardly anti-supererogationist. Then we shall mention some more refined versions of utilitarianism, which logically leave room for supererogatory conduct – either by limiting the normative power and the scope of the principle of utility, or by introducing additional principles and tests for the obligatoriness of actions. These two methods of adapting utilitarianism to supererogation involve a qualification of utilitarianism as a normative theory, but perhaps also of utilitarianism as a theory of value.

4.2 CRUDE ANTI-SUPEREROGATIONIST VERSIONS

William Godwin, one of the eighteenth-century precursors of modern utilitarianism, holds an extreme anti-supererogationist view. From the point of view of his ethics, any action is 'either right or wrong, just or unjust' (Godwin, 1793, p. 69), and the sole test for the rightness of actions is the actual happiness they produce. And as *my* happiness counts exactly the same as any other human being's happiness, no preference whatsoever should be given to the pursuit of my own happiness. The deontic implications of the utilitarian principle are unambiguous: 'I should do all the good in my power', the only restriction being the principle that excessive philanthropy or self-sacrifice may result in an overall negative balance of happiness (Godwin, 1793, p. 74). But whenever it does not, I may be required to make any sacrifice – including my life – for the general good. According to that theory I have no right to spend my money as I please because I have a perfect duty to give it to those who are in the greatest need of it. It is consequently impossible 'to confer upon any man a favour', since the beneficiary either has a *complete right* over the 'gift' (no less complete than if he had lent me the money), or it is wrong to give it to him. The same reasoning applies to mercy, which is also treated as a duty. This is followed by the anti-supererogationist conclusion: 'Whatever deviates from the law of justice, though it should be in the too much done in favour of some individual or some part of the general whole, is so much subtracted from the general stock, so much of absolute injustice' (Godwin, *Enquiry Concerning Political Justice,* p. 75). There are no extra-just actions which are not unjust. The only difference between duty and

76

virtue according to Godwin is that while a person can be virtuous without doing the best possible thing in every particular situation, he must always do the best action in order to fulfil his duty (p. 83). Unlike our common-sense notions of virtue and duty, Godwin seems to make the latter more dependent on the promotion of the good, than the former.

Godwin suggests a very mechanical theory of justice whose sole principle is the general utility and happiness distributed between equal 'anonymous' individuals. Although individual persons are said to be the only objects of our moral efforts, each individual (as an agent) is conceived purely in terms of his capacity to promote the general good. His very right to life is dependent on that capacity. Such an extreme view is, I believe, inconsistent (besides its being absurd), and will be criticized in 8.3. Here it may suffice to note that Godwin's denial of supererogatory acts is entailed by his all-embracing concept of justice which makes it not only unjust (and wrong) to grant some priority to one's own happiness, but also to act supererogatorily and altruistically towards other individuals. For giving someone more than his share is tantamount to infringing the rights of other persons.

Godwin's anti-supererogationist attitude is based primarily on considerations of justice (the absolute equality of all human beings in their claim over the utility-promoting actions of any agent), and accordingly he regards works of supererogation as *unjust* rather than as ruled out by the principle of utility. G. E. Moore, on the other hand, bases his anti-supererogationist view on purely utilitarian considerations. His argument is surprisingly crude: 'good' is the fundamental simple concept in ethics. 'Ought'-statements (and statements of what is right and obligatory) may, and can only, be analysed in terms of 'good' (either intrinsic good or good as a means to an intrinsically good end). The judgment that a certain action is obligatory means, therefore, that performing the action in question is the best thing to do:

to assert that a certain line of conduct is, at a given time, absolutely right or obligatory, is obviously to assert that more good or less evil will exist in the world, if it be adopted than if anything else be done instead (Moore, 1948, p. 25).

The reasoning that leads Moore to that conclusion is that any action that is our absolute duty is unique in respect of value. But this uniqueness cannot be understood in the sense that the action is the sole thing of value in the world (because then *every* obligatory action would be unique, i.e. the *sole* good thing in the world which is a contradiction). Its uniqueness must therefore consist in the total goodness of its performance, that is the fact that the action 'will cause more good to exist in the Universe than any possible alternative' (Moore, 1948, pp. 147–8). And as there usually is only one action in any given situation which will cause more good than any alternative action open to the agent at a certain time, his moral duty is unique and absolutely determined. At any moment the moral agent has a duty to do the optimific action. The only qualification to that conclusion which Moore allows is the rare situation in which two (or more) alternative actions are believed to have equally good consequences. Only then can one of the alternatives be called 'morally permissible'. The only difference between 'right' (or 'morally permissible') and 'duty' is that the former means 'what will *not* cause *less* good than any possible alternative', while the latter means that 'which will cause more good . . . than any possible alternative' (Cf. Moore, 1966, pp. 14–15). So although actions may sometimes be right yet not obligatory, they can never be supererogatory, because they cannot conduce to *better* results than obligatory actions.

Moore's anti-supererogationism is less equivocal than Kant's because he defines duty in terms of good consequences. Kant was disturbed by the fact that some actions which do not fall under his non-utilitarian category of duty produce undeniably good results. But for Moore such a situation is conceptually inconceivable. His deontic scheme does not even allow for morally indifferent actions, as every action is either right (and hence in most cases obligatory), or wrong (and hence always forbidden) (Moore, 1966, p. 13). Even virtue is analysed in utilitarian terms (Moore, 1948, p. 172), which implies that we attach to supererogatory acts (which manifest the agent's noble efforts and high moral standards).

A slightly more sophisticated advocacy of anti-supererogationism based on utilitarian principles is offered by New in a recent article. New's basic argument is that if utilitarian principles (making life good and maximizing happiness) serve to justify our 'basic' duties (which make civilized life *possible*), the same principles should also be able to justify the requirement of the allegedly supererogatory acts (which make life 'richer' and *as good as possible*).

Furthermore, the difference in moral importance and urgency of our various actions cannot be utilized to distinguish between the supererogatory and the obligatory: as honesty is no less a duty than refraining from murder just because the consequences of cheating are less harmful than of killing, so should the supererogatory acts be no less binding than our basic obligations, even though they are less vital to the survival of society (New, 1974, p. 183).

From that basic argument New infers that saintly and heroic acts can be held as 'paradigms of human virtue', only if we think everyone is under an obligation at least to try to do them. Encouraging people to imitate supererogatory behaviour implies that we maintain that people *ought* to behave so, and that in turn means that it is their *duty*. Accordingly, no one can act beyond the call of duty except in the uninteresting sense of doing more than is required by one's professional duty (a fireman helping to extinguish a fire while being 'off-duty'). And thus when saints and heroes say that they were only doing their duty, they are right (New, 1974, p. 184).

New's basic argument is correct if the utilitarian principle is taken as the sole criterion for what we ought (or are under an obligation) to do. It is indeed hard to conceive of a way of distinguishing between utility-promoting actions which are obligatory and utility-promoting actions which are optional without introducing non-utilitarian principles. But unlike New, who believes that this collision between our common moral beliefs and the utilitarian theory should be solved by changing our beliefs, I would say that it is the theory that ought to be modified.

The limits of utilitarianism are revealed even in New's own argument: his suggestion that encouraging someone to do *x* implies that it is his duty to do *x* can hardly be defended. It is, I think, a plainly false implication (which misleadingly makes use of the double role of 'ought' – the commendatory and the prescriptive), because usually we encourage people to do exactly those actions which we cannot demand of them to do (being actions which are not strictly required). Encouragement implies a pro-attitude to its object, but not usually a belief that the object is obligatory. But even if New does not admit this, he cannot deny that sometimes we refrain from encouraging people to do a certain supererogatory act altogether, because we think that it involves too great a sacrifice (even when the act is in fact good from a utilitarian point of view).

The denial of supererogation pushes New towards a reductionist stand. Instead of the supererogatory–obligatory distinction, he proposes a distinction between basic and non-basic duties. This makes Good Samaritanism a moral duty. To the criticism that we cannot expect everyone to fulfil these 'non-basic duties' (and that 'ought' implies 'can'), New replies that these very demanding duties involving saintly and heroic acts are required only of saints and heroes, i.e. of those who can perform them. The rest of us are excused from doing our 'supererogatory' duty, like kleptomaniacs in the case of the duty not to steal. (I find this analogy highly dubious, both because in the case of supererogation it implies that the great majority of moral agents should be excused, and because I believe that refraining from supererogatory action does not usually require any excuse at all). Another means of reducing the supererogatory to the obligatory used by New is the interpretation of 'supererogatory' duty as applying only to the *effort* to act, e.g. heroically. We have no duty to be successful in our attempt, but we have a duty to try. But does the kleptomaniac have a duty to *try* not to steal? And what does it mean to be under an obligation to try to act supererogatorily? And do we regard the 'taming of an obstinate nature' as the mark of supererogation (New, 1974, p. 181)? By distinguishing between the duty to *act* heroically (which is only expected of heroes) and the duty to *try* to act heroically (which is required of everyone), New tries to save his anti-supererogationist view without having to contest the common belief that not every failure to *do* the good is wrong and blameworthy.

In the second part of his article (pp. 185–8), however, New becomes more cautious about the power of utilitarianism to withstand the pressure of conflicting intuitions about supererogation. If the principle of utility is formulated in terms of the *overall* good (the sum total of happiness), then New's anti-supererogationist view entails that whenever I can increase the general happiness by sacrificing some of my own, it is my *duty* to do so. But the denial of supererogation is called into question by the common moral belief that even if we grant the anti-supererogationist that any 'useful' act is obligatory, we are *entitled* to act altruistically even if this means an overall decrease in the amount of happiness. In other words, even if we believe that *no* action which promotes the general happiness is supererogatory (which, *pace* New, I think is wrong), it must be recognized that actions which sacrifice much of the happiness of the agent for the sake of a little happiness of others are not duties. Strict utilitarians, who deny the value of altruism as such, would answer that such a sacrifice is morally wrong and forbidden. But if we are not willing to go so far in denouncing altruism, we must admit that such a type of action is supererogatory, that is to say not a duty yet by no means forbidden. We may judge extreme acts of self-sacrifice irrational, but we would not call them *morally* wrong. And even if – quite artificially – some people do, then it is because they believe that a person has some duties to himself, and not because of the loss in the overall amount of happiness.

New suggests two possible modifications of strict utilitarianism, which may avoid the collision with our intuitions: (1) extreme altruistic utilitarianism (which makes it obligatory to sacrifice *any* amount of my happiness for the sake of other people's happiness, regardless of the resulting overall balance of happiness in the world; (2) optative altruistic utilitarianism (according to which we are entitled but not obliged to do so). Now (1) is surely anti-supererogationist, to an even greater extent than the original versions of classical utilitarianism. On the other hand, (2) is *compatible* with supererogation, but New is correct to point out that it does not account for the moral preference given to the altruistic option. Acting heroically is not only something which we are entitled to, but also something for which we are praised; and *that* cannot be explained by the theory.

New rejects both modified versions as inconsistent on the grounds that they entail that in certain situations of conflict we must endorse both the performance and the prevention of an altruistic act. I believe, however, that this criticism is valid only with regard to the extreme version (1) which entails that we treat both performance and prevention (e.g. of a beneficent act) as *obligatory* (and that is a contradiction). But in the case of optative altruism (2), no contradiction is involved, since we may easily 'endorse', i.e. morally approve of, both X's wanting to sacrifice his happiness for the sake of Y and of Y's wanting to prevent that (or sacrifice *his* happiness for X's sake). We may even approve of both parties acting altruistically towards each other when the consequences are eventually seen to be less useful than if only one agent had acted (e.g. two friends covering with their own bodies an exploding hand-grenade in order to save each other's life). As we have already noted, irrational actions are not necessarily wrong.

Kurt Baier rightly criticizes strict utilitarianism as leading to 'the absurd result that we are doing wrong whenever we are relaxing' (Baier, 1958, p. 203), and hence to the denial of what he calls 'rules of supererogation'. Referring to that remark Smart tries to defend the anti-supererogationist consequences of act-utilitarianism. Firstly he states that it may very well be that we are not entitled to relax as much as we think we are, and secondly that relaxation itself has a long-term utility value. And if those two replies do not suffice to resolve the conflict between utilitarianism and our intuitions, then we ought to change the latter rather than alter the former (Smart and Williams, 1973, pp. 55–6). Smart's first reply to Baier is unclear. It is certainly our duty to make more effort to help others than we usually do, but that is not a theoretical argument against supererogation as such (but just a general moral criticism of human egoism). The second reply is empirically false. The amount of relaxation that is required for efficiently promoting the general good is far smaller than what we think we are entitled to. So it seems that a utilitarian theory which makes every optimific action that is in our power a duty is plainly counterintuitive, even though it is true that being a *normative* rather than a descriptive or explanatory theory, it cannot strictly speaking be 'refuted'.

In his *Encyclopedia* article on utilitarianism, Smart makes room for supererogation by appealing to the distinction between the wrongness (and rightness) of *acts* and the badness (and goodness) of their *agents* (Smart, 1967, p. 211). This is a typically reductionist (qualified supererogationist) account. It defines supererogation as that class of actions whose omission is wrong (as it leads to undesirable consequences), yet not bad (as we do not blame the agent for that omission).[1] The abstention from blaming omissions of supererogatory acts is justified on utilitarian grounds: 'There is nothing to be gained by censuring someone for lack of extraordinary heroism, and probably much harm in doing so.' Now apart from my general objection to reductionist accounts of supererogation (see below, 5.3 and 6.2), I believe that Smart's contention is either inconsistent or false. For if the overall utility of supererogatory acts is greater than the harm involved in punishing (or 'censur-

---

[1] Smart's terminology is unfortunate, but typical of a utilitarian who analyses 'right' and 'wrong' in terms of the goodness and badness of consequences. The converse use of terms sounds more plausible and natural: 'good' and 'bad' as referring to the consequential value of the act independently of the agent; 'right' and 'wrong' as referring to the moral status of the act which depends on its consequences *and* on the agent's duties, responsibility, intentions etc.

ing') omissions of these acts, then the utility principle compels us to make these actions obligatory, and hence to deny supererogationism. And if Smart claims that the net gain of utility produced by supererogatory acts does not justify censuring their omission, then he indeed saves his argument from inconsistency but only at the price of limiting the scope of supererogation to its more trivial examples. For there are surely some highly valuable acts which we could require of people to do at a relatively low price. My criticism of Smart on that point follows the line of the criticism of pure utilitarian theories of punishment, which are said either to be inconsistent or not to correspond to the legal facts and intuitions. But that lies beyond the scope of the present discussion.

4.3 MORE COMPLEX THEORIES: MILL AND SIDGWICK

Mill and Sidgwick, who are both undeniably utilitarians, maintain a more complex view of the relation between utility and duty. By supplementing the principle of utility by independent principles of merit, virtue and liberty, they clear the ground for the recognition of the moral status of supererogatory acts.

Mill oscillates between a reductionist, essentially anti-supererogationist attitude, and a recognition of meritorious non-obligatory acts. Like Kant, he is faced by some moral beliefs that cannot be justified in the framework of his rigorous theory. But unlike Kant, Mill is surely inclined to supererogationism. In *Utilitarianism* Mill seems to be very cautious about supererogation. He adopts Kant's distinction between perfect and imperfect duties, which coincides with the distinction between justice and 'other obligations of morality' (*The Collected Works of J. S. Mill*, vol. 10, p. 247). Generosity, beneficence, and charity are all classified as imperfect duties, which 'we are not bound to practise . . . towards any given individual', but not as supererogatory. Although not every moral duty can be viewed as a debt of justice, entailing a corresponding right, it seems that no morally valuable act can be non-obligatory altogether. A milder anti-supererogationist view is implied by the passage on self-sacrifice (Mill, *The Collected Works,* vol. 10, pp. 217–18). There Mill asserts that the renunciation of one's happiness is morally praiseworthy only if its end is the promotion of other people's happiness (i.e. there is no value in self-sacrifice for its own sake), and only if the overall balance of happiness in the world is thereby increased (i.e. even altruistic 'waste of happiness' is bad). While the second condition blocks the possibility of *some* forms of supererogation that I would like to uphold, the first condition makes a plausible point: even if there is an intrinsic value in self-sacrifice (for instance in asceticism), an act of self-sacrifice can be supererogatory only if it intends to promote the *good* of others (usually the happiness, welfare, well-being etc.). This point is of great importance as it introduces utilitarian or consequentialist considerations into the definition of supererogation. But the restriction of the value of heroic self-sacrifice just to its *utilitarian* consequences misses the point of supererogation and implies that any 'optimific' self-sacrifice is a duty.

Nevertheless, *Utilitarianism* also offers some basis for a more conciliatory attitude to supererogation. The above-mentioned distinction between perfect and imperfect duties, which implies a denial of supererogatory acts, is drawn *within* the sphere of 'morality in general'. But this sphere is marked off by Mill from 'the remaining provinces of Expediency and Worthiness' (Mill, *The Collected Works*, vol. 10, p. 246). So although there is no room for supererogation beyond justice (i.e. in the realm of imperfect duty), there might be room for it 'beyond morality'. Still, such a notion of supererogation violates the condition of correlativity and perhaps that of continuity, because Mill implies that Expediency and Worthiness are not *moral* categories.

In a later essay Mill develops a strikingly supererogationist view. Comte is criticized vigorously for the Calvinist-like extreme moral constraints imposed by his theory:

between the region of duty and that of sin there is an intermediate space, the region of positive worthiness. It is not good that persons should be bound, by other people's opinions, to do everything that they would deserve praise for doing. There is a standard of altruism to which all should be required to come up, and a degree beyond it, which is not obligatory, but meritorious (Mill, 'Auguste Comte and Positivism', *The Collected Works*, vol. 10, p. 337).

This supererogatory region is, according to Mill's subsequent assertions, limitless and consists of actions which deserve gratitude, honour, and moral praise. These actions of self-sacrifice should be spontaneous and their omission should not be reproached either by other people or even by our own conscience. Nevertheless, they are objects of encouragement and cultivation by means of moral education (which includes some forms of ascetic training as well). Mill refs Comte to the Catholic doctrine of supererogation and criticizes the extreme Calvinist view which requires of everyone to be a saint and damns anyone who fails (and see Hancock, 1975).

Mill restricts the function of the morality of duty to the prevention of harmful acts (which includes the obligation to fulfil promises etc.). This is the limit of moral sanction. Beyond this lies 'an unlimited range of moral worth, up to the most exalted heroism'. And the value of this meritorious but optional behaviour consists not merely in the utility of its consequences, but also in the self-respect of its agent (Mill, *The Collected Works,* vol. 10, p. 339).

The broader justification for this supererogationist deviation from the utilitarian principle is outlined in Mill's *On Liberty,* which takes the opposite starting-point to that of *Utilitarianism.* While the principle of utility takes the point of view of the general, overall good whose promotion is the duty of every individual, the principle of liberty puts the emphasis on the rights of the individual and the limits of the legitimate subordination of his interests to the public or general good (cf. below, 8.3). Although Mill tries to reconcile these two principles by suggesting that utility should be understood 'in the largest sense' (so as to include considerations of liberty), I think that the two are ultimately incompatible, and hence that Mill cannot claim to be a pure utilitarian. The distinction between the supererogatory and obligatory as it is drawn by Mill himself can be justified in terms of utility only on the basis of a very extended sense of 'utility'.

In his discussion of the relation between the concepts of virtue and duty, Sidgwick states that in our common-sense the two do not always coincide: there are obligatory actions which are not virtuous but also virtuous actions which are not obligatory (his example of the second class is clearly supererogatory – a rich man who lives 'very plainly' and devotes his income to 'works of public beneficence') (Sidgwick, 1884, pp. 217–18). Sidgwick is fully aware of the paradox implied in the recognition of virtuous actions beyond duty. He questions the possibility that a moral man would not do what he thinks is best (assuming that it is in his power). One way of solving the paradox is by distinguishing between what a person ought to do and what other people ought to blame him for not doing. The latter standard, says Sidgwick, is much more lax: we often refrain from blaming someone for not doing something which we would certainly regard as our duty if we were in the agent's place. This is all plain common-sense, but it hardly provides a criterion for supererogation. We are looking for means of identifying those actions which go beyond what we ought to do, not just beyond what other people ought to blame us for failing to do. One can imagine various reasons for refraining from moral criticism that have nothing to do with supererogation (for example not being immune from *ad hominem* criticism, or epistemological reasons suggested by Sidgwick himself). It is, therefore, not always a duty to criticize a moral failure, even if it involves a violation of a duty. So although the concept of virtue refers to the region of morality which lies beyond the determinate rules of strict duty, it cannot be identified with supererogation. 'Virtue seems to be primarily a quality of the soul or mind' (Sidgwick, 1884, p. 219), whereas supererogation refers mainly to actions.

A more promising passage for our purposes is that in which Sidgwick distinguishes between justice and benevolence. Sidgwick expressly recognizes 'a region of performance' which is beyond duty – that is actions (a) which cannot be claimed as a debt, (b) whose non-performance cannot be blamed (p. 241). That region, which 'belongs to Benevolence', is typically supererogatory. The problem is that no 'intuitional' principles of supererogation can be found according to Sidgwick, and hence it is not clear how far it is right for us or good to sacrifice our personal worthy aims for the sake of philanthropy (p. 244). Generally, Sidgwick is more easily led to a recognition of supererogatory acts than other utilitarians because he believes in the irreducible dualism of practical reason – i.e. the reasonable claim of the individual to his own good on the one hand and the rightness of his sacrificing it for the sake of the general good on the other. Yet he admits that he cannot state a principle which will justify our common-sense belief that rich people are not obliged to give most of their money to remove all 'the misery and want that exists around us' (Sidgwick, 1884, pp. 260–1).

These attempts to analyse the status of supererogatory acts are all part of the 'second method of ethics' – that of Intuitionism. Sidgwick has however an interesting analysis of supererogation in his discussion of the 'third method' – that of Utilitarianism. His analysis is typically utilitarian and he tries to reconcile that analysis with the common-sense view expounded (but not systematically justified) in the chapters on Intuitionism. This is done by an attempt to prove that although utilitarianism *seems* to be strictly anti-supererogationist, considerations of utility justify 'this double view of felicific conduct', which is held by our common-sense (p. 488). The first reason for recognizing virtuous non-obligatory acts is that some actions which manifest 'excellence' are not voluntary, i.e. are not controlled by our will, whereas duty always implies ability and voluntariness. But the more important (yet controversial) reason is that the distinction between duty and supererogation is '*secondarily reasonable on Utilitarian principles*', because as we tend naturally to judge people's conduct according to a certain average, we find that the admiration and recognition of excellence or virtue (which transcends that average standard) is itself 'an important source of happiness'. Furthermore, making certain virtuous acts especially worthy of praise and admiration arouses in others the desire to imitate (in a more efficient way than if they were obligatory). Generally speaking, 'jural morality', i.e. that part of morality based on duty and sanction, is 'self-limiting' from the point of view of utility.

Sidgwick's utilitarian account of supererogation suffers, I think, from the following flaws. First, the argument based on the involuntariness of some supererogatory acts justifies only the excuse granted to 'normal' persons for not doing what only extremely heroic and courageous agents *can* do. But it does not justify an excuse for not doing those virtuous acts which lie within our power and will. Secondly, the argument based on the utility of the special praise and admiration of virtuous acts can justify the recognition of a region beyond duty only if it can be shown that this kind of utility outweighs that which could be gained by making these supererogatory acts obligatory. For the utility of those good actions performed by many people who can be brought to perform them only under the 'penal' threat of moral duty and sanction may be proved to be greater than that achieved by maintaining the 'double standard' (namely, the distinction between what is admirable and what is merely right). This utilitarian balance is never tested by Sidgwick, and I suspect that he viewed the kind of secondary utility of non-obligatory conduct as *intrinsically* better than the primary utility of the overall consequence of that same conduct being obligatory. But such an opinion can be supported only by a non-utilitarian argument.

4.4 RULE-UTILITARIANISM AND NEGATIVE UTILITARIANISM

There are versions of utilitarianism that modify the classical theory in order to make it more plausible to our moral intuitions. Rule-utilitarianism tries to reconcile the principle of utility with the concept of duty (and paradigm cases like promise-keeping and truth-telling). Negative utilitarianism has in mind the restriction of some deontic implications of the classical utilitarian principle. Both versions, even if they do not actually explain supererogation, leave room for it.

The innovation of rule-utilitarianism is that a particular act which in itself is not the best from a utilitarian point of view may not only be right but also obligatory – provided that it is prescribed by a rule whose general adoption promotes utility. But that very principle raises the possibility of supererogation. For if conformity to a useful rule is the only criterion of what we ought to do, then an act may be non-obligatory (not being prescribed by any rule), yet morally good (having good consequences). The same principle which serves to block the theoretical implications of classical act-utilitarianism (which amount to the sacrifice of considerations of justice, fairness, honesty etc. to the promotion of overall utility) may possibly be used to block the strict utilitarian duty always to choose the best possible course of action. Rule-utilitarianism allows both for obligatory acts which are not optimific and for optimific acts which are not obligatory. This is also illustrated by the attitude of rule-utilitarianism to punishment, which is one of the test cases by which act-utilitarianism is shown to be wrong (e.g. justifying the punishment of the innocent when it is socially useful): the same considerations which restrict the force of classical utilitarianism in applying punishment may serve to justify the supererogatory waiving of punishment, that is to say mercy and pardon. Thus, act-utilitarianism may find the notion of pardon paradoxical, but rule-utilitarianism is compatible with it.

It is perfectly conceivable (at least from the point of view of rule-utilitarianism) that some acts are supererogatory just because the adoption of a rule making them obligatory would not have good consequences, even though individual voluntary performance of these acts is of great value. This may even be part of the reasoning underlying Sidgwick's utilitarian account of the value of supererogation. This is again a typically reductionist view which tries to justify the distinction between utility of rules and that of particular acts in (utilitarian) terms of expediency. If that is the line of argument of rule-utilitarianism, then Lyons's thesis of the extensional equivalence of act- and rule-utilitarianism is valid (Lyons, 1965, ch. 3). But of course, as Lyons himself is aware, rule-utilitarianism may justify the appeal to rules not only on grounds of utility. In that case supererogatory action acquires an independent status within the theory.

As we have already seen in the example of the soldier throwing himself on an exploding hand-grenade, some supererogatory acts are useful only if they are not performed by *everybody*. Acts of mercy and pardon and certain acts of volunteering illustrate this condition of non-universality. Now act-utilitarianism, which makes it a universal duty to maximize utility, may prove self-defeating: not knowing how other people act, or not taking it into account, may make a universal duty to act in a certain way counter-productive (e.g. if obeyed by all the people concerned). On the other hand, rule-utilitarianism allows only for consistent rules, rules whose universal adoption is not counter-productive. But beyond the obedience to rules, rule-utilitarianism does allow for acts which are assessed directly by the principle of utility. If rule-utilitarianism allows a direct appeal to the principle of utility in the case of a conflict between two rules (that prescribe the performance and the forbearance from doing the same action), there is no reason why it should not be invoked in the case of actions which do not fall under the scope of any rule. Hence, a supererogatory act can be justified in rule-utilitarian terms.

An attempt to explain away the unintuitive deontic implications of classical utilitarianism is made much more explicitly by another modern version of the theory, *negative utilitarianism*.[2] This theory's main objective is to qualify the scope of our duty to create a positive balance of good in the world. Unlike its positive counterpart, this theory does not aim at justifying the unqualified ideal of maximizing happiness or promoting the overall good. It suggests a more reasonable criterion for duty, which is still utilitarian but leaves the positive promotion of good as a supererogatory option (which of course should be encouraged because of its utilitarian value). Most negative utilitarians justify their theory in utilitarian terms – that is to say, if we have the overall balance of happiness in mind, it is more effective to reduce pain than to try and increase pleasure.

[2] Whose first modern proponent is K. R. Popper (1966, vol. I, ch. 5 note 6; ch. 9 note 2; vol. II, p. 386). See also Acton (1963), Watkins (1963), Walker (1974) and Tranöy (1967).

The sense in which their theory is 'negative' is, however, unclear, since the duty to maximize happiness can be contrasted either with the duty to avoid causing unhappiness or with the duty to minimize unhappiness. In the first sense we are only required to avoid inflicting harm. In the second sense we are also required to relieve pain (though not to make people happier). One interpretation puts the emphasis on the distinction between acting and forbearing from action. The other stresses the distinction between happiness and suffering. In both these interpretations, which are not always clearly distinguished, negative utilitarianism is based on the *asymmetrical* relation between the positive and negative terms (action: forbearance; happiness: suffering). The second version of the theory entails the first but is not entailed by it.

The first interpretation (which restricts our duty to that of avoiding harmful action) is more negative, that is to say more minimalistic in its view of our moral duty. In the demarcation of supererogation and duty it seems, however, to go too far, since it is totally unacceptable to regard every performance of good action as supererogatory. Although it may be true that forbearance from harming the interests of other people has *priority* over helping to advance them, we do have a duty to engage in actions which contribute to the well-being of at least some people to whom we stand in special relationship, or who badly need our help. And of course sometimes we have a duty to relieve people's misery. Duties of forbearance (whose paradigm principle is 'mind your own business') are absolute, easily defined, universal, and scarcely obstructed by the 'ought'-implies-'can' principle. But this does not mean that they exhaust the whole scope of moral duty. Such a version of negative utilitarianism leaves too much room for supererogation.[3]

The second interpretation (which restricts our duty to that of relieving pain and suffering) is more plausible as a moral principle, mainly because it is more justifiable on utilitarian grounds. The scope of duty is widened, but at the same time becomes vaguer, as the asymmetry of happiness and suffering does not yield the absoluteness and universality which characterize the duties of for-

---

[3] B. Gert seems to advocate that version of negative utilitarianism (together with a form of the second version): moral ideals *encourage* us (as a matter of supererogation) to change the 'status quo' by reducing the amount of evil. The moral rules on the other hand *prohibit* us from changing the status quo by causing evil (Gert, 1966, p. 132).

bearance. Furthermore, the duty to relieve unhappiness is open to the same criticism often directed against classical utilitarianism, namely the infinite demand on our lives to work ceaselessly for the welfare of others. This version of negative utilitarianism implies a prohibition of 'moral relaxation', and thus denies supererogation. Even if the negative utilitarian believes that the promotion of happiness is good yet not obligatory, there is hardly any opportunity to act supererogatorily, as we are compelled to be continuously engaged in the elimination of evil. This is why weaker versions of negative utilitarianism fail. One cannot claim that promoting happiness is a duty, yet a less stringent one than (and overriden by) the duty to relieve pain, because there will always be a call to relieve suffering, misery, and pain. So it seems that this version of negative utilitarianism does not offer an acceptable criterion for demarcating supererogation and duty either.

Then there is the problem of identifying the difference between relieving pain and promoting happiness (which I find even harder to distinguish between than action and forbearance). Sedatives are surely intended to reduce suffering as classical music is meant to increase pleasure, but what should we say of a Christmas bonus to old age pensioners? The line seems to be drawn either arbitrarily, or according to very subjective criteria. One of the ways of overcoming that problem is to introduce the notion of 'par',[4] a normal or minimal standard of well-being which defines the limits of our duty: we ought to help those who are below par to achieve that minimal standard, but not any further (though it is debatable whether we are allowed to reduce the happiness of those who are above par, especially when it is necessary for improving the lot of those who are below par). For a theory of supererogation this is an attractive suggestion, as it does not hinge on the distinction between the promotion of good and the prevention of evil. Yet it is not a purely utilitarian theory any more, because the notion of par is defined in non-consequentialist terms of social justice, fair distribution, legitimate expectations etc.

The various arguments for negative utilitarianism are by and large based on the asymmetry of good and bad, right and wrong, happiness and suffering. And as such, they are relevant to a theory of supererogation which emphasizes the asymmetry of the optional

[4] I owe this notion to J. Griffin, who uses it as the basis of one of the versions of Negative Utilitarianism.

well-doing and the obligatory abstention from doing evil (and from wrong forbearances). One argument for negative utilitarianism which is of a quasi-utilitarian nature, is that there is more urgency in relieving pain than in increasing pleasure. Only in suffering is there a call for *help,* and only a call for help justifies a personal duty of beneficence. A second argument is psychological: we are usually more moved by the suffering of others than by their happiness. We generally identify with other people's sorrows more than with their joys. (Hence, malevolence is more deplored than envy). A third argument used to support the asymmetry in question is epistemo-logical: we know very well what pain is, but we find it difficult to agree on the nature of pleasure – pleasure being more dependent on individual idiosyncrasies. This implies that there is nothing paterna-listic or coercive in our action to relieve suffering in the world, but there may be such an element in the attempt to maximize happiness. A logical argument makes pleasure and pain generically different and incommensurable. They cannot be counted as the positive and negative values of the *same thing* in a Benthamite calculus. In other words: no trade-off is allowed between pleasure and pain. Finally there is a moral argument to the effect that fairness requires us to help those who are the worst-off so that the 'felicific gap' will be narrowed as much as possible.

Obligatory acts are sometimes described as those acts whose per-formance is necessary for the very existence of our social order. This is a minimalistic concept of moral duty, which leaves the door open for supererogatory acts whose effect is to make that social order and life better or richer. In that respect duty is more *urgent* than supererogation and there is indeed something superfluous in actions beyond duty. So the quasi-utilitarian argument for the asymmetry of the positive and negative pairs of concepts holds for supereroga-tion too. The psychological argument is empirically true but irrele-vant to a theory of supererogation. The moral hero is not necessarily driven by sympathy, and the conscientious person is not necessarily doing his duty out of motives of pity. The epistemologi-cal argument for negative utilitarianism is not applicable to the distinction between duty and supererogation, because it is a necess-ary condition that the value of the supererogatory act be continuous with – of the same kind as – that which results in consequences which we *know* are good for the beneficiary (or at least sincerely believe that the beneficiary sees them as we do). Individual or personal ideals (e.g. what is good for me) cannot therefore serve as objects of supererogatory praise (although they might be praised on other grounds). So there is usually no danger of paternalistic coercion of an idiosyncratic conception of good (what Popper calls 'benevolent dictatorship') in supererogatory conduct. The goodness of supererogatory acts is of the same kind as (but more than) the goodness which makes a certain act obligatory, and if the latter is agreed upon, so is the former. The logical argument holds for supererogation in the sense that no amount of supererogatory surplus can compensate for the violation of one's moral duties. A positive balance of utility does not serve as an excuse either for the negative utilitarians or for the supererogationists. The question of the unjust felicific gap is difficult to decide. Supererogatory action may result in the widening of that gap, but I do not think that this in itself is an argument against such action. If a concept of 'par' is adopted, then we can safely hold that a gap between people who are above par (caused by supererogatory action) is not morally wrong. Yet we are reminded of Godwin's critique of supererogation as being unjust to those who have a greater need (and, for Godwin, also greater claim) for the beneficent act in question.

To conclude: although not all the arguments for negative utilitarianism are plausible and relevant to a theory of supererogation, the basic observation of the asymmetrical relations between the performance of what is right (good, above par, etc.) and the abstention from what is morally wrong (bad, below par) is shared by any theory of supererogation (cf. 6.3). The link between the wrong and the forbidden is much stronger (indeed perhaps necessary) than that between the right and the obligatory. Nevertheless, negative utilitarianism fails to serve as a criterion for the demarcation of supererogation, because (a) there are clearly acts of relieving suffering which are supererogatory (if the suffering person is far away and unknown to us, or if the act involves considerable sacrifice on our part), (b) there are happiness-promoting actions which are clearly obligatory (e.g. with regard to our children, parents etc.). What is, I hope, clear from the above discussion is that this symmetry cannot be totally explained in utilitarian terms. Although the negative version of utilitarianism comes closest to an explanation of the idea of supererogation, other considerations such as justice and rights must be introduced, as for example in the contract theory.

Supererogation will be shown to be a class of useful actions, lying beyond the call of duty in the sense of what we ought to do as a matter of justice.

5

Beyond duty in contract theory

The final ethical theory to be investigated in relation to supererogation is the contract theory of justice. This theory will, for several reasons, prove to be the most successful of the major ethical theories in accounting for acts which go beyond the call of duty. Its basic advantage over the other theories discussed above is that it takes justice, rather than virtue, duty, or utility, as the fundamental concept of morality. The notion of moral duty suggested by this theory is a *minimalist* one, because moral requirement is linked primarily to the principles of justice as fairness, or in other words because it is restricted to what the rational self-interested contractors in the Original Position would choose to adopt as binding principles. But these principles which can be agreed upon in an ideal contract of rational self-interested agents do not exhaust the whole province of morally worthy actions. They leave ample room for optional supererogatory behaviour.

A theory of justice formulates the principles of *right* conduct rather than of virtuous, good, morally worthy, or perfect action. Unlike the utilitarian equivalence of 'right' and 'good' suggested by Moore, the theory of justice assumes that not all right actions are necessarily the best from the moral point of view. Being fair, that is taking one's fair share of primary goods (and burdens), is the basic moral requirement which can be rationally justified (and enforced), but this requirement can easily be surpassed by taking a smaller share of benefits (or a bigger share of burdens) than that prescribed by the principles of justice. Although we cannot be more just than justice requires, we can do more good than required by justice without violating it.

From the standpoint of supererogation, the contract theory of justice is, therefore, a plausible theory, as it combines deontological and axiological elements (a theory of duty and obligation together

95

with an independent theory of primary goods, i.e. of the values which are to be secured and promoted by the contract). The concept of justice has well-defined limits on the one hand (unlike that of utility), and does not exhaust the whole realm of morality on the other hand (unlike the purely deontological concept of duty). Justice in its distributive meaning tries to achieve the ideal distribution of goods (and burdens), that is to say to strike a unique balance of rights and duties of persons. Similarly, justice in its non-distributive meaning tries to specify the exact and unique due, for instance, the just punishment for a crime. In both cases the theory of justice cannot *contain* supererogation as an integral part (as attempted by reductionist views), but can point to the legitimacy of surpassing its own requirements.

Naturally, a moral theory based on justice comes closer to meeting the two conditions of continuity and correlativity (of duty and supererogation). For supererogatory acts are described in terms of transcending the demands of justice, of adhering to principles other than justice, which are highly appreciated by everyone. Supererogatory acts are defined by contract theorists in relation to justice, but their special status is ascribed to their lying beyond justice.

This chapter will discuss two different accounts of the concept of supererogation by two typical proponents of the contractarian view: Rawls and Richards. The differences between the two accounts are significant and illuminating. Rawls describes supererogation as a class of *actions* which cannot be included as part of the agreement in the ideal contract situation, whereas Richards's theory tries to formulate *principles* of supererogation which can be agreed upon by the ideal contractors. For Rawls, supererogatory behaviour is, for certain reasons, left *outside* the scope of a contract. For Richards, it is incorporated within the ideal moral agreement.

Before turning to the detailed discussion of Rawls and Richards, it should perhaps be noted that there are alternative theories of justice that do not lend themselves so easily to supererogationism. We may recall Godwin's anti-supererogationist view which was partly based on considerations of justice. In theories like Godwin's, justice means an ideal, absolute distribution of good so that any deviation from it (in the form of either malevolent injustice or benevolent supererogation) is equally blamed as being wrong and unjust. Supererogatory behaviour may indeed involve some element of favouritism and partiality.[1] If we interpret justice as a total, comprehensive, all-embracing notion (analogical to utility in Moore), then no room is left for supererogation. Any favour we do someone is necessarily at the expense of another person who has more right to the act in question than the beneficiary of the favour. (This 'other' person can, of course, be the benefactor himself, which makes every act of extreme self-sacrifice wrong). And in the case of non-distributive justice, the absolute theory of justice would also argue that any kind of giving more than is *due* (or in the case of punishment and mercy, less than is due) is unjust and wrong. The contract theory, however, presents a more intuitive, minimalist, notion of justice. It assumes that individual persons have fairly wide ranging freedom and rights to pursue their own desires and ideals regardless of the desires and ideals of other people. The principles of justice refer only to a limited area of human behaviour (mainly that governed by social institutions) which can gain the consent of rational agents who want to leave room for some inequalities arising from individual desires and ideals. Godwin's extreme and totalitarian view of justice is rejected along with his rigid utilitarian principle.

Yet even in more modest theories of justice there remains a certain conflict between supererogation and justice. Feinberg, for example, distinguishes between noncomparative and comparative principles of justice. The former determine what is due to a person independently of what other people get (e.g. just punishment). The latter determine what is due to a person only in reference to other people's share (e.g. just distribution) (Feinberg, 1974, p. 298). These two types of principles may yield conflicting judgments: an act may be condoned by the noncomparative principles and at the same time condemned by the comparative principles. Supererogatory treatment of people is a typical example of such a conflict, because granting someone more than is due to him is right (i.e. not unjust) only if we judge the action from the point of view of noncomparative justice. From a comparative point of view it may be rightly criticized as favouritist, partial, and inducing legitimate envy. The strength of this criticism of supererogatory acts lies in the fact that these acts are by definition gratuitous, and sometimes personal. The general principle 'treat like cases alike' is therefore diffi-

---

[1] For further discussion of the relation between supererogation and favouritism, see Heyd (1978).

cult to apply to supererogatory conduct. To solve this problem of conflict between the two types of principles of justice (a conflict which of course occurs in non-supererogatory contexts as well), the theory of justice should formulate some rules of priority and limit the force of the comparative principles in a way that will allow for some forms of favouritism. These, I believe (*pace* Godwin), are legitimate. After certain conditions of comparative justice have been met, not only should we allow considerations of merit (non-comparative justice) to prevail unhampered by considerations of distribution, but we should also permit supererogatory excess (like giving someone more than he deserves according to *any* principle of justice). Favouritism and partiality are wrong within the boundaries of justice, but should be immune from criticism in the realm of supererogation. Feinberg points out that discrimination as such is considered morally offensive, but does not solve the problem of conflicting judgments yielded by the two types of principles of justice. For on the other hand he says that the claims of noncomparative principles are usually thought to be superior to those of comparative justice. I believe that although feelings of being discriminated against are psychologically understandable, they should not serve as the grounds for denying the moral value of supererogatory actions (except for example in cases where the supererogatory preference of one person reflects an explicitly malevolent attitude and contempt towards another person). It is only in cases where what is due can be decided solely by appealing to comparative principles that supererogatory excess is unjust and hence wrong.

Envy (which is the emotional reaction to being treated differently from others) should be taken as a relevant moral grievance only if it can be proved that the difference in treatment is *discriminatory*. And surely there are some cases in which treating some people supererogatorily while giving others 'only' what is due to them reflects a discriminatory attitude. I suggest the following principle as a tentative criterion for distinguishing between the two sorts of supererogatory action: whenever the agent of the supererogatory act stands to its beneficiary in what may be called an *institutional* (moral, political) relationship, considerations of comparative justice are valid and give rise to legitimate claims on the part of other persons who may feel discriminated against. This may be explained as arising from the fact that the institutional relationship defines a *group*, i.e. a

98

system of rights and duties applying specifically to certain people who make up that group. Thus, a tutor who is supposed to see his students once a week cannot ask his favourite pupil to come twice a week (assuming that this is a supererogatory act) without evoking the justified criticism of the other students in terms of discrimination and violation of the comparative principles of justice. On the other hand, inviting just one student to spend the summer with him in St. Moritz may give rise to feelings of envy on the part of the uninvited students, but can hardly be criticized as a violation of the principles of justice. When surpassing the requirements of justice in our personal relations – our relations to man as man – we are not constrained by the principles of fair distribution, and in the same way as we have a right to put our own interests before those of others, so we have the full right to favour one person rather than another even if there are no morally relevant grounds for that preference.

5.2 SUPEREROGATION AS LYING BEYOND THE CONTRACT

The contract theory, as formulated by its major modern proponent, John Rawls, offers only some scattered and rather cryptic remarks on the status of supererogation in ethical theory. The contract theory of justice is primarily concerned with social institutions, and only secondarily with the moral duties of individuals which apply independently of social organizations. And as supererogatory acts are related to the principles for individuals rather than for institutions, they are mentioned only 'for the sake of completeness' (Rawls, 1972, p. 117). But it should by no means be understood that Rawls treats supererogatory acts as having marginal moral importance, in spite of the priority of principles for institutions over those of natural duty. Nevertheless, it shows that these morally significant acts cannot be fully accounted for in terms of an ideal contract. But it is important to note that Rawls classifies supererogation under the 'concept of value' or that of 'moral worth' (p. 109, diagram). This means that supererogation should be understood as being necessarily *correlated* to moral requirement (duties). Supererogatory acts are accordingly characterized as permissions (which are 'significant from a moral point of view') and not just as good or virtuous acts.

Supererogatory acts are defined by Rawls as acts which 'it is good to do . . . but it is not one's duty or obligation' (p. 117). And the justification for the permissibility of these good acts is formulated in what I should call the 'argument from exemption': 'Supererogatory acts are not required, though normally they would be were it not for the loss or risk involved for the agent himself. A person who does a supererogatory act does not invoke the exemption which the natural duties allow' (p. 117; cf. p. 439).

But the Rawlsian definition of supererogation also has a positive aspect. Supererogatory acts are benevolent acts, i.e. performed 'for the sake of another's good', or 'from the desire that the other should have this good' (pp. 438–9). It is not merely a beneficent act, an act which (actually) promotes the good of another person. Beyond the condition based on the argument from exemption there is the condition of benevolent intention.

This distinction between beneficence and benevolence relates to two types of motivation in morality: the sense of justice and the love of mankind. The latter is 'more comprehensive', and 'prompts to acts of supererogation' (p. 192). This is an important point in the psychology of supererogatory conduct. Persons who act from the motivation of love do not pursue happiness, but are happy if they succeed and feel shame (rather than guilt) in case of failure (p. 484). But again we should note that Rawls considers the morality of love (supererogation) as continuous with the morality of justice (duty) and as perfectly compatible with it. The mutual disinterestedness of the contractors is only part of the picture, although indeed it is necessary for reaching an agreement on the principles of justice. For these individuals – after concluding their agreement – must be seen as having also higher-order desires, which give rise to virtuous non-obligatory acts. And accordingly, a complete moral system must include supererogation, whose aims are continuous with those of the norms of justice, though extending beyond them.

Rawls distinguishes between two aspects of the morality of supererogation. On the one hand, the love of mankind which 'shows itself in advancing the common good in ways that go well beyond our natural duties and obligations'; on the other hand, self-command which is 'manifest in fulfilling with complete ease and grace the requirements of right and justice' (pp. 478–9). Benevolence, humility and sensitivity to the wants and needs of others are examples of the first aspect. Magnanimity, courage, and self-control exemplify the second. Elsewhere (p. 117), Rawls offers four examples of supererogatory acts: benevolence, mercy, heroism, and self-sacrifice.

Although Rawls's treatment of supererogation is not systematic, it constitutes an explicit recognition and a tentative explanation of supererogatory action within the general theory of justice and duty. Yet Rawls himself implicitly admits that supererogatory acts cannot be accounted for purely in contractarian terms in the same way as obligatory actions can. For there are no *principles* of supererogation which can be agreed upon by the rational self-interested contractors in the Original Position. Supererogation is therefore described as belonging to the category of permissions. Permissions, says Rawls, do not require an explicit acknowledgment of the contract. They cover the whole area of what is not contrary to obligation and natural duty. In that respect they are defined negatively. Being beyond duty and justice, supererogation is also beyond the authority of the ideal contract.

On the other hand, the permissions that are described as supererogatory are not morally indifferent. Their moral worth is at least partly related to the values which the contractors in the Original Position try to realize as much as they can. Supererogatory acts are beyond duty but aim at the same type of values as obligatory actions.

These relations of continuity and correlativity of supererogation with duty are most typically manifest in the way Rawls justifies the very distinction between the two, particularly in the 'argument from exemption'. Supererogatory acts are not required *only* because of the loss and risk involved in their performance. In other words, they are (ideally) requirements for which there exist certain excusing provisos that may be invoked by human beings in a non-ideal world. Natural duty would contain all supererogatory acts (or standards) were it not for the risk and loss to the agent.

The argument from exemption raises some difficulties. First, against Rawls it can be argued that most moral conduct assumes some loss to the agent (taking care of one's kin, repaying debts etc.). And if Rawls bases his argument on the *degree* of loss, it should be noted that sometimes the degree of risk or loss in fulfilling duties and obligations is no smaller than that involved in supererogatory behaviour. Secondly, even if saintly and heroic acts are correctly described in terms of risk and loss, Rawls cannot use the argument from exemption to justify the other instances of supererogation which he himself mentions (mercy, some minor acts of benevolence, and sensitivity to the needs of others). Sending flowers to an old and lonely neighbour for her birthday is a non-obligatory act which is highly praised. Yet it involves no risk and very slight loss (compared to obeying an order in the army to defuse a bomb). Being merciful may be touching and praiseworthy (owing to its supererogatory nature), but the right not to grant mercy is not derived from the risk or loss involved (for what do we exactly lose by granting mercy?).

Furthermore, it is true that natural duties allow exemptions, and the same holds for obligations. But these are usually cases in which the requirement is only a prima facie duty or obligation, overridden by another duty or right. Yet the case of supererogation is different: no duty binds us – not even a prima facie one. To go out of one's way to help someone is not a duty from which one is exempted because of the special effort required. It is true that in an ideal world like the Kantian Kingdom of Holy Wills, supererogatory acts would not be considered as involving risk or loss to the agent. But then these acts would not be required (as duties) either. For Holy Wills do not regard moral action as involving loss to themselves, and hence do not need the impetus of duty. The argument based on the exemption from duties which are valid in an ideal world may be pushed *ad absurdum*, to the elimination of the notion of duty itself. And even if that ideal world model is not what Rawls has in mind, it is implied in his argument. For when he talks of supererogatory acts, he refers to the situation in which these acts 'would be duties'.

By distinguishing between benevolence and beneficence (which apply to the motives and the content of action respectively), Rawls adds an important condition of supererogation, which is absent in most utilitarian accounts. Acts beyond duty cannot be analysed purely in terms of promoting good, though the promotion of the good of others is a necessary condition of supererogatory action. Supererogation does not consist merely of a high degree of beneficent action but also of benevolence, an intention to do something not just for the sake of duty, but out of love. Rawls, however, does not draw the conclusion that the value of supererogatory acts lies in their being optional, in their extra-just status.

Rawls talks of supererogation at one point in relation to both duties and obligations and elsewhere in relation to natural duties alone. This is a minor inconsistency which can be overcome. Obligations, according to Rawls, differ from duties in three features: they are determined by institutions (rules and practices), they arise from voluntary acts and undertakings, and they are owed to specific people. Natural duties, on the other hand, bind us independently of any specific act of ours or of any institution, and they apply to every man as man. They are divided into negative and positive, the former having priority over the latter (pp. 113–15).

If we accept these definitions it is, I believe, evident that supererogation is logically related only to natural duty and not to obligation. Further, it relates to positive rather than to negative duty. Both obligations and negative duties fully determine the acts required (a) by the institutional and social rules applying to specific acts, circumstances and persons, (b) by the negation, i.e. what we are required *not* to do. They fully determine the requirement in the sense that they fix the upper and lower limits of the value which the prescribed acts are meant to accomplish. Natural positive duties are not only easily determined and applied, but the value achieved by their fulfilment extends indefinitely beyond that degree which is fixed as a minimum by the duty itself. Hence, only positive duties can be surpassed in a supererogatory manner. We can be more generous than the duty of mutual aid requires, but we cannot fulfil our promises more than necessary, nor refrain more than we ought to from injuring innocent people. And although it is true that we can pay back more than we owe as a debt (which is determined by an obligation), it is not doing more *by way of repaying a debt*. For Rawls, obligations are generally concerned with being fair, but we cannot be more fair than is required. Fairness consists of a certain ideal *balance* which may be legitimately surpassed only with reference to values other than fairness. But to justify doing more than our duty we do not need to appeal to values other than those aimed at by the duties in question. It should therefore be concluded that supererogation is related to duties (natural or 'conventional') rather than to obligations and negative duties. Although we may act supererogatorily by discharging an obligation from which we are for some reason exempted, the supererogatory act relates to the duty to discharge obligations rather than to the obligation itself (see below, 6.4). My conclusion seems to be compatible with Rawls's ideas, since the proviso 'provided that one can do so without excessive risk or loss to oneself' is applied by Rawls only to positive duties (p. 114). And so if the argument from exemption defines supererogation as action which disregards that proviso, then it must be related to positive duty.

Rawls says that negative duties have priority over positive ones. This priority order can be extended to include supererogation, which would be the least weighty. The priority order is based on the binding force of these requirements, and may serve as a guiding principle in resolving conflicts (we ought to do our duty before engaging in heroic acts). Rawls, however, seems to reject such an extension of the priority ordering. He refuses to say 'that duties are lexically prior with respect to supererogatory actions' (p. 339), but I fail to see why. Richards, as we shall see, grants the principles of duty a clear priority over those of supererogation. Perhaps Rawls cannot do so because he does not treat supererogation as being part of the principles which are agreed upon in the Original Position.

By distinguishing between two aspects of supererogation (love of mankind and self-command) Rawls seems to imply that supererogation characterizes both actions (the first aspect) and agents or traits of character (the second). Thus, the second aspect of the morality of supererogation refers to the *manner* in which an (obligatory) act is performed rather than to the content of the act (which is beyond duty). But Rawls's distinction is vague, because the virtue of humility, which is given as an example of the first aspect, suits the second better. On the other hand, although the second aspect is described as the fulfilment of 'the requirement of right and justice' with complete ease and grace, Rawls also includes under it 'seeking superior ends', which seems more relevant to the first aspect (that of 'love of human kind'). Irrespective of the above I think that self-command cannot be considered as supererogatory, as there is no duty applying to the *manner* in which (obligatory) actions should be carried out. It is nevertheless true that virtues like courage and self-command are morally valuable partly because they make supererogatory actions possible (as well as securing the fulfilment of duty under difficult conditions).

So although Rawls's remarks on supererogation come close to a plausible account of that category of moral actions (being based on a theory of justice), it falls short of what I call a full *un*qualified supererogationist view. The reason for the weakness in Rawls's position lies mainly in his argument from exemption, which makes supererogation differ from duty only on grounds of there being an *excuse* not to act, and which bases its moral value only on the loss and risk involved in the act.

5.3 SUPEREROGATORY PRINCIPLES AS FORMING PART OF THE CONTRACT

David Richards, who follows Rawls in developing the contract theory, offers a more extensive and systematic interpretation of supererogation. The most striking difference between his theory and Rawls's is that Richards formulates *principles* of supererogation to which the contractors in the Original Position consent in the same way as to other principles of justice duty and obligation. Richards's analysis is superior to the Rawlsian one in that it supplies clearer criteria both for the classification of various types of supererogatory principles and for the demarcation of duty and what lies beyond it. Richards's theory of supererogation is more contractarian in nature than Rawls's, and hence more reductionist.

Richards's analysis may be viewed as more reductionist in the sense that he treats supererogatory principles as requirements (Richards, 1971, p. 196). In that respect he differs radically from Rawls, who emphasizes the optional character of supererogation by subsuming it under the general heading of permissions (reserving the title 'requirements' for duties and obligations alone). This definitional starting point enables Richards to include supererogation among the principles agreed upon by the ideal contractors (who decide on principles which specify what we *ought* to do). It now becomes clear why Richards defines supererogatory actions as good actions which are not obligatory, rather than good actions whose omission is not wrong and reprehensible. The latter definition covers only the purely optional actions, while Richards would also like to label as 'supererogatory' certain non-obligatory acts whose omission entails legitimate reproof.

The contractors in the Original Position reach an agreement concerning both the vital requirements necessary for the existence of society as such and the more marginal ones. Principles of duty and supererogation are derived from this model of an ideal contract. The defining characteristic of principles of supererogation is the disutility of making them compulsory under a threat of direct and institutionalized sanction. The pain involved in punishing those who fail to act on the principles of supererogation is greater than the

105

benefit to the recipients of the supererogatory acts (Richards, 1971, pp. 103, 198, 200, 203).

So the reason why supererogatory standards are not considered obligatory is that this would place too great a burden on persons. The justification for distinguishing between principles of duty and supererogation rests entirely on utilitarian considerations, mainly the efficacy of enforcing the standards in question. Omission of some supererogatory acts is wrong, yet should not be punished (unlike omission of obligatory actions which should be). It should not be punished only because of the disproportion between the small benefit involved in the performance of the act, and the great burden and pain involved in punishment in case of failure to act. This being the criterion of delineating supererogation, it is not surprising that Richards considers as fully justifiable *other* forms of putting pressure on people to comply with the supererogatory moral requirements, such as commendation and praise (in the case of beneficent acts) or condemnation and blame (in the case of failure to perform certain acts). These are 'forms of informal criticism'. The maximin principle guides the contractors in their abstention from attaching sanction to omission of supererogatory acts in the same way as it guides them in their agreement on punishment of violations of duties.

It is interesting to compare at this point Richards's and Rawls's justification for the non-enforcement of supererogatory acts. For while Rawls anchors the argument for supererogation on the notion of exemption from doing things which involve high risk and loss to the agent, he does not say – like Richards – that this exemption is derived from the disutility of enforcement. His account leaves the door open to other ways of justifying the liberty not to sacrifice personal good beyond the requirements of justice. Although Richards expressly rejects a 'reduction' of supererogation to duty (on the lines of Kant, Price, Sidgwick, Ross and Findlay), and clearly distinguishes between the duty of mutual aid and the supererogatory requirement of beneficence (pp. 95, 186), he should nevertheless be classed as a *qualified* supererogationist. For he regards the justification of supererogation as a function of the expediency of its coercion, and pictures the ideal moral world as that in which duty and supererogation are assimilated under the concept of 'ought' (requirement). The distinction between supererogation and duty is due to the necessity of reacting in different ways to 'the frailty of the human will in its application of principles that often conflict with self-interest' (p. 104).

Richards distinguishes between two types of supererogatory principles:

(1) The principles of blame, governing cases of civility, mutual respect, mutual love, kindness, and gratitude. The omission of acts that are enjoined by those principles is blameworthy and wrong, and entails some forms of social censure and rebuke. Their performance, however, does not deserve praise.

(2) The principles of praise, applying to acts of beneficence, or saintly and heroic self-sacrifice. Failure to perform these acts does not justify any form of moral criticism or blame, but their performance is highly praiseworthy and usually wins admiration.

Observing the requirement of civility, i.e. being polite to other people (even if that demands containing one's moodiness or annoyance) is only of minor cost to the individual, but also brings only a marginal social benefit which is much smaller than that of non-maleficence and mutual aid. Therefore, the maximin principle justifies treating impoliteness as wrong and deserving criticism, but does not justify punishment or coercion. The same reasoning applies to the requirement of mutual respect (namely to suppress one's pride when it diminishes the personal worth of others) and to that of mutual love (which requires that we show affection for other persons in virtue of their character and personality rather than in virtue of their physical features). Being kind to others is a supererogatory principle of blame because it differs, on the one hand, from the duty of mutual help in bringing about only a minor benefit and, on the other hand, from the supererogatory principle of beneficence (which – unlike kindness – contains necessarily an actual desire to advance the good of others). Finally, gratitude is a principle of blame because ingratitude is always considered wrong and blameworthy, while being grateful does not seem to deserve special praise. Gratitude is seen by Richards as a sort of compensation made to the benefactor for the loss incurred by his beneficent act. Ingratitude is to be severely blamed so that people are not discouraged from doing beneficent acts.

The status of the supererogatory principle of praise (beneficence) is markedly different. Richards admits that the contractors abandon the maximin strategy when they come to decide on that principle (p. 206). For the maximin principle compels us to reject any principle which – like that of personal sacrifice – could lead to a 'lower lowest'. Supererogatory acts sometimes involve an overall loss (the sacrifice of the agent being greater than the benefit to the recipient). So the only way to make room for such supererogatory acts is to exclude them from the realm of requirements altogether. (Richards does not explicitly say that, but it is implied in his description of beneficence as a principle of liberty). This brings us right back to the Rawlsian account of supererogatory acts as permissions, involving free choice. Still, Richards has to justify the moral value and praise attached to beneficence, and he does so by adding the condition of benevolence (which again is reminiscent of Rawls): beneficent acts are praiseworthy (even if they do not conform to the maximin strategy) only if persons do them out of a 'desire for sympathetic benevolence, which they value more highly than their own interests'. Interestingly, this condition reverts to the notion of requirement. For Richards's argument in a way makes supererogatory behaviour *required* (in his word, 'incumbent') of people who have the capacity of benevolent sympathy. In Rawlsian terms, it is a requirement from which most of us are exempted because of the lack of that capacity to value benevolence more highly than self-interest. We might then say that the very fact that a person does not act on the 'principle of praise' indicates that he cannot, or does not wish to, pursue altruistic ideals, and hence that he should not be held as deserving blame.

Richards rightly observes that for Utilitarians the idea of beneficence and 'love' is much more central than for the ideal contract theory, because they consider it a duty. On the other hand, I think Richards is wrong in ascribing the importance of the 'principle of praise' in Christian ethics to the same kind of reason (viz. 'the failure of such love may define damnation') (p. 208), because by doing that he ignores the whole Catholic tradition which (like himself) holds a clear distinction between duty and supererogation.

The main weakness of Richards's account lies in his broad definition of supererogation, which not only allows for the principles of blame, but makes them the central cases of acts beyond duty. Surely, they fit more neatly into the contractarian scheme than saintly and heroic acts do, for the latter may be only indirectly explained in terms of an agreement in the Original Position. Acts of beneficence are, however, the paradigm cases of supererogatory behaviour, and have a positive value which cannot be expressed in contractarian terms. This value is connected with their being optional, i.e. irreducible to any principle which can be decided upon in advance by rational agents who are in the Original Position ignorant of their personal ideals. And, as we shall see, supererogation essentially involves such personal ideals which transcend the rationality of justice as fairness. Of course the contractors can decide not to decide on principles of supererogation (which in effect is what Richards says of the principles of praise), but that leaves the special value of supererogation unexplained.

Then it is not clear whether the maximin principle in itself suffices to justify the non-coercion of supererogatory principles. For sometimes Richards's cost–benefit analysis would, I suspect, yield a different result, that is to say make coercion of beneficence justified from the point of view of the highest lowest. I have in mind cases in which the relatively well-off person could make a personal sacrifice which, although painful to himself, would yield extremely beneficial results to those who are worse off. So, although it is true that supererogatory acts should not be made obligatory because this would 'frustrate people's pursuit of their basic interests for the sake of advancing the interests of others', it is not always true that such a frustration is 'contrary to maximining' (p. 196). This criticism is similar to my argument against utilitarian attempts to justify supererogation in terms of the counter-productiveness of making it obligatory.

By basing the justification of supererogation on the disutility of its *coercion*, Richards seems to confuse reasons for refraining from punishment with reasons for refraining from making an act a *moral* duty. The reasons for deciding not to punish (by legal, institutionalized sanctions) a wrong action may be of many different kinds, and therefore such a decision does not necessarily reflect a belief in the 'weakness' of the disobeyed requirement. The case of gratitude may illustrate my point: the reason why we do not *force* people to show gratitude (i.e. have a law against ingratitude) is that (a) we would find it hard to apply such a law, formulate criteria etc., and (b) we want gratitude to be a *free* expression of thankfulness.

But this does not mean that the requirement of gratitude is weaker than other requirements (which are compulsory). On the contrary, gratitude is – pace Richards – considered a very strong moral *duty*, and by no means a supererogatory counsel. It is a duty to acknowledge the supererogatory element of an act of beneficence, and thus, unlike Richards's view, it demands of persons to show a certain *attitude* rather than to do something to advance the benefactor's interests. The duty of gratitude has some characteristics of obligation, since it is related to the voluntary acceptance of a benefit (cf. below 7.1).

The same argument applies to mutual respect, which in Richards's theory is a supererogatory principle because of the disutility of its enforcement. Like Rawls (1972, pp. 178–9, 377–8), however, I think that mutual respect is a moral *duty*, even if there are good reasons (not dissimilar to those in the case of gratitude) for leaving it outside the scope of legal intervention. Mutual respect cannot be treated as having the same status as mutual love (which *is* supererogatory). On the other hand, Richards presents powerful and convincing arguments for making the principles of mutual aid not only morally obligatory (which no one contests), but also legally binding (which is controversial) (see Richards, 1971, p. 189).

Finally, civility, which for Richards is a supererogatory principle, is in my opinion hardly a case of supererogation, since it is not optional in the same way as kindness (doing favours) is. Richards treats the two as belonging to the same category (supererogatory principles of blame), but I think that only the latter is a case of doing something beyond one's duty. The former principle, prescribing polite behaviour, is a matter of etiquette rather than of morality (see below, 6.3).

Discussing supererogation as a distinct moral category, which is logically related to the concept of duty, is the main improvement of the contract theory over the attempts to account for it by previous ethical theories. What is, however, missing in the analyses of Rawls and Richards is an explanation of the moral value of supererogation beyond the utilitarian and (negative) terms of the maximin strategy.

110

PART II

Outlines of
a theory of supererogation

6

The definition of supererogation

The problem of supererogation can be tackled from two different angles. It can be investigated in the light of general moral theories, in the manner of our inquiry in the first part of this book, but it can also be analysed as a separate concept and explained independently of any particular ethical theory. This is what will be undertaken in the second part – that is, an attempt to suggest the general lines of a theory of supererogation. As we have already seen, the major ethical theories were not specifically concerned with the status of supererogatory acts, and the discussion from that angle rested inevitably on a great deal of reconstruction. Recent literature on the subject, however, concentrates on the characterization of supererogatory acts as such, irrespective of any particular general theory of moral duty and goodness. So while previous chapters tried to test the adequacy of traditional ethical systems in accounting for supererogation, the aim of the following chapters is to define, classify, and justify this category of moral actions.

Since the publication of J. O. Urmson's article 'Saints and Heroes' in 1958, many analytic philosophers have addressed themselves to the problem of supererogation. Typically they have been more interested in providing a conceptual analysis than in constructing a wider systematic theory. Many of these philosophers have been driven to a discussion of supererogation by their interest in deontic logic, in reasons for action, or in the role of rules in morality. Many discussions on the subject, therefore, assume – either dogmatically or hypothetically – the existence of supererogatory acts and confine their aim to the definition of these acts and to suggestions of ways of enriching the all too poor conceptual framework of deontic logic, of the crude theories of reasons for action, and of morality as governed by universal rules. So although analytic moral philosophy recognizes supererogation as a concept worthy of exploration, it has hardly supplied a theory of the types of supererogatory acts, their value, and their place in morality.

Generally speaking, the definition of supererogation cuts across the three cardinal groups of concepts that, according to von Wright, are relevant to ethics.[1] It refers to *value* concepts, since supererogatory acts are necessarily good; it comprises *normative* concepts, since supererogation is logically related to the concept of duty; and finally, the definition contains *anthropological* (or 'psychological') elements, being concerned – as we shall see – with benevolent intentions, voluntariness, and merit. Unlike duty, which can be logically analysed only on the normativt level, supererogation must refer to concepts belonging to the other two levels as well, since it is more than just a permission, namely something which is neither obligatory nor prohibited. Yet a definition of supererogation is not necessarily committed to any particular axiological, deontological, or 'anthropological' view, although, as the first part of the work has tried to show, there are some types of theories which lend themselves more easily to the idea of action beyond the call of duty.

One problem with the definition of supererogation is that the concept is a quasi-technical one. The word 'supererogation' is rarely used in ordinary language today, although the concept denoted by that term is easily understood by non-philosophers. The adjective 'supererogatory' has some connotations which the moral philosopher would wish to exclude from his definition (like 'superfluous', that is – over and above what is required, but containing no special value). On the other hand, the original meaning of the philosophical concept in Roman Catholic theology contains some metaphysical presuppositions which are unacceptable to secular morality. It is, therefore, not surprising that the problem was hardly ever discussed in moral philosophy using that term until very recently (even Urmson's article does not mention the word 'supererogation'). The quasi-technical nature of the concept of supererogatory acts rules out the possibility both of a purely conventional definition, and of a purely formal (theory-dependent) definition. The definition must take into account our ordinary intuitions of what is included in the notion of supererogatory behaviour, but it can delineate the definiendum only by linking it to a certain theory. The relation between the definition of supererogation and the examples suggested to illu-

---

[1] G. H. von Wright, *The Varieties of Goodness*, Routledge & Kegan Paul, 1963, pp. 6–7.

strate the concept is, therefore, circular, since the definition both determines the type of acts which are to be called 'supererogatory', and is also formed in the light of them so as to cover what we intuitively believe are the paradigm cases of supererogatory behaviour. But although we approach the definition of supererogation bearing in mind what we believe to be its paradigm cases, the full analysis of the examples must be postponed to the next chapter, and conducted in the light of the definition and the theoretical assumptions contained in it.

I suggest the following as a definition of supererogatory acts:
An act is supererogatory if and only if
(1) It is neither obligatory nor forbidden.
(2) Its omission is not wrong, and does not deserve sanction or criticism – either formal or informal.
(3) It is morally good, both by virtue of its (intended) consequences and by virtue of its intrinsic value (being beyond duty).
(4) It is done voluntarily for the sake of someone else's good, and is thus meritorious.

The rest of this chapter is devoted to the explanation and elaboration of this definition and to critical comments on alternative definitions. But before taking each of the four conditions and discussing it separately, a few general remarks may be appropriate. As already mentioned in the Introduction, supererogation is primarily an attribute of acts or actions (rather than persons, traits of character, emotions, intentions, or states of affairs). It is, therefore, natural to define the concept in relation to acts, and to treat other uses of the term (such as 'supererogatory norms') as derivative. A definition of supererogation in terms of action implies also a rejection of theories which analyse it in terms of states of affairs that ought to exist (although bringing them about is not obligatory), or in terms of traits of character or virtues that a person ought to have. Supererogation in our view is related only to 'ought to do' and not to 'ought to be', because it is correlative with duty, and duty applies only to the former.

The definition itself lists four conditions which are ordered roughly according to their strength. The first two are formulated in negative (weaker) terms; the last two, in positive (stronger) terms. Condition (1) provides the genus of supererogatory acts, characterizing them as permissible. Then, in order to contrast supererogatory acts with permissible acts whose omission is wrong, condition (2) is added. This requirement of moral toleration in the case of failure to act is supplemented by a further condition (3), which restricts supererogation to acts that are positively good, and excludes all permissible and right actions from the realm of supererogation unless they also have a distinctly moral value. Finally, condition (4) adds the specific requirement of altruistic intention, whose aim is to rule out accidental, unconscious, involuntary or self-regarding acts as cases of supererogation.

The suggested definition places relatively stringent conditions on supererogation. Supererogatory acts cannot be solely characterized in deontic terms – represented by the first condition – together with a weak condition of value (as in Chisholm's definition: 'non-obligatory well-doing'). The axiological condition (3) must be formulated in stronger and more specific moral terms. Finally, there is the last condition, which would be described by von Wright as 'anthropological'. Unlike the first three conditions, this requirement characterizes supererogatory acts in terms of the *agent's* intention and merit. This condition further narrows the scope of supererogation on grounds which may be irrelevant to the definition of duty and obligation.

The first condition is logically speaking superfluous, because (2) is logically stronger and entails it. Yet the definition mentions (1) for expository and polemic purposes, since there are alternative definitions that dispense with (2) altogether, being satisfied with the wider condition of non-obligatoriness. So although taken conjunctively (2), (3) and (4) are sufficient conditions of supererogation, it is methodologically convenient to add (1) as the general genus of the defined acts.

There is a difference in connotation between the first and second conditions, which may be put as follows: while according to (1) supererogatory acts are *permissible*, (2) makes them *optional*. From the point of view of deontic logic there is no relevant difference between these two attributes, but in ordinary language (which relates deontic concepts to the value of actions) there is a difference of emphasis: an act is permissible if despite its negative value (bad, wrong, undesirable) or because of its neutral value, it is not forbidden. On the other hand, an act is more naturally described as optional if despite its positive value (good, right, desirable) or because of its neutral value, it is not compulsory. The difference in the conno-

116

tation of these two adjectives implies that the freedom to choose an optional course of action is more fundamental than that associated with permissible actions, and in that sense (2) is ethically more relevant to supererogation as well as logically stronger than (1).

The relatively stringent conditions of supererogation reflect the complexity of the concept defined. Some theorists of supererogation try to formulate simpler definitions. These definitions typically try to provide an explanation of supererogation in terms of a wider theory, such as deontic logic, a general theory of duty, or a theory of reasons for action, rather than in terms of a theory of supererogation proper. This aim makes it necessary to define supererogation in a technical manner, which is tailored to the requirements of the wider theory in view. But focusing on the nature and paradigm cases of supererogation as they are intuitively conceived and on its ethical value compels us to formulate a definition which uses a much richer language than that of the theories mentioned above.

Poorness of conceptual language characterizes all those definitions of supererogation that share the following General Form:

An act is supererogatory if and only if it is ... to do, but not ... not to do. The two blanks are filled by a pair of contrary terms – positive and negative respectively – which carry a moral meaning. Definitions of the General Form describe supererogatory acts in terms of the asymmetry of commission and omission of those acts. By that they try to contrast supererogation with duty – which in deontic logic stands in a symmetrical relation to prohibition (the obligation to perform an action being equivalent to the prohibition not to perform it) – without resorting to a richer vocabulary than that of deontic logic plus the negation sign. Examples for pairs of concepts used to fill the blanks are: 'good' – 'bad', 'right' – 'wrong', 'virtuous' – 'wicked', 'praiseworthy' – 'blameworthy', 'just' – 'unjust'.

Our definition, however, implies that all these definitions of the General Form are either too wide (weak) or too narrow. Although a supererogatory act is surely good, omission may be bad – at least in the light of the utility principle (and especially when it can be performed without much effort). 'Right to do, though not wrong to refrain from doing' is closer to our conception of supererogatory acts, but the inadequacy of this definition lies in the weakness of the positive term, which fails to refer to the *value* of the acts beyond duty. The 'virtuous' – 'wicked' pair is irrelevant to the definition of supererogation, as it cannot serve to distinguish the supererogatory

117

from the obligatory: some supererogatory acts do not reflect any special virtue, while obligatory acts may, under certain conditions, be highly virtuous; moreover, omission of obligatory actions is not always wicked. Praiseworthiness is indeed often the mark of supererogatory behaviour, but not necessarily. The criteria of praise and blame (or more precisely, condemnation) are more often linked to the circumstances and nature of the motivation of the act than to its deontic status. Finally, being 'just' can serve merely as a necessary constraint on any action beyond the call of duty (as we have already shown in 5.1), and in this respect it is too weak (like being 'right').

A more complex version of definitions based on the asymmetrical relations of commission and omission mixes positive and negative terms of different pairs. A supererogatory act is sometimes described as a non-obligatory well-doing, or a praiseworthy act the omission of which is not wrong, or a virtuous act over which the beneficiary has no right or claim (i.e. whose omission is not unjust). These definitions are clearly superior to those of the simpler form, since they try to select the relevant attributes of both performance and omission of the acts defined. However, we shall see later on that even these less schematic definitions fail to capture some essential properties of the definiendum. Nevertheless, the asymmetry of commission and omission is the underlying structure also of the definition we have proposed, for it is in the nature of any *option* that failure to choose it does not incur a critical reaction, while taking the option may win merit. Defining supererogation in terms of this asymmetry serves to illustrate not only the logical difference between duty and supererogation, but also the ethical justification of the distinction, in particular, the right not to engage in some forms of morally good action. So although definitions of the General Form are conceptually poor and oversimplified, their basic structure exhibits an important element of supererogation.

Supererogatory acts are popularly called 'acts which go beyond the call of *duty*'. The theory must explain the sense of 'duty' beyond which an act becomes supererogatory. Is it duty in the narrow (and ordinary) sense connected with roles, jobs, and social status? Or is it to be understood in wider (technical, Kantian) terms, as characterizing any moral requirement? Does the concept of duty include obligations? Is supererogation related to duty in its institutional or 'natural' meaning? Is the supererogatory to be contrasted with what

118

we (morally) *ought* to do? Anti-supererogationists do not believe in the possibility of doing more than duty requires, so for them the question hardly arises. In the next section we shall see that qualified supererogationists, who opt for a reductionist theory, treat supererogatory acts as going beyond our duty but not beyond what we *ought* to do (or in weaker terms of the theory – beyond what ought to be done by *someone*). Unqualified versions, however, prefer to define supererogatory acts as transcending what we ought to do, that is to say duty in the sense of any moral requirement.

Yet when we explore the relation between supererogation and the correlative concept of duty, it becomes clear that supererogation must relate to duty only in a specific sense. As we already noted in the discussion on Rawls, a supererogatory act is associated with natural positive duties (rather than with negative duties, obligations, and duties arising from roles, jobs, etc.). For although we can surely do more than we have promised to do or more than our social position requires, it is not *by way of* keeping a promise or of fulfilling a social role that our behaviour is called supererogatory. In other words, we cannot fulfil a promise or refrain from stealing in a supererogatory way. What can be surpassed in a supererogatory way is, for example, the duty to meet our obligations or to fulfil our social duties. But that duty is of a higher order relative to both 'social' duties and obligations. And it is a kind of 'natural' moral duty, which applies to everyone irrespective of one's particular social roles or institutions. The fact that social duties are less clear-cut and more vaguely defined than obligations may mistakenly lead us to think that supererogation relates to social duties (though not to obligations). But such an 'argument from vagueness' is fallacious, since according to our theory supererogation is related to natural duty (in the Rawlsian sense), which is contrasted to institutional re-quirement – be it a social duty or an obligation.

So although it is trivially true that some supererogatory acts achieve more than is required by obligations and social duties, they are *correlated* and *continuous* with natural (positive) duties alone. A doctor who goes to a remote tribe to cure a rare disease is doing a supererogatory act. But he acts beyond his duty not in the sense that he is extending his social (professional, 'institutional') role so as to include that tribe, but rather goes beyond his natural duty, which in that case is confined to the fulfilment of his social duty as a doctor in *his* community. Furthermore, the social or institutional duty of an

Albert Schweitzer cannot be the sole criterion for judging whether an act (e.g. going to that distant place) is supererogatory or not, because even if it is agreed that the act in question lies beyond his institutional duty *as a doctor*, it may be his natural duty as a human being (who happens to have medical skill) to do so. A policeman touring a foreign country may have a duty to help overpower a violent criminal, because he happens to be trained to deal with such situations. His act is not supererogatory, even though he acts beyond his institutional duty as a policeman (which binds him only in his own country). To conclude this point I propose to interpret 'duty' (in the phrase 'beyond the call of duty') in a wide manner – roughly equivalent to 'morally ought'. More specifically, supererogation is correlated to natural, non-institutional positive duties of man qua man. This interpretation matches the unqualified version of supererogationism which treats supererogatory acts as being beyond any form of moral duty or 'ought'. Although this interpretation may seem to our common intuitions a little too restrictive, I believe it does not go against them.

Supererogation is more naturally defined as a class of actions which are beyond duty rather than beyond the claims or rights of their beneficiaries. This may be due to two reasons: (a) as many philosophers have conclusively shown, not every duty has a corresponding right, i.e. an act may be obligatory even if no one has a 'right' over it (Feinberg, 1966, Lyons, 1969); and (b) the definition tries to link supererogatory behaviour to the intention and merit of the *agent*, while rights focus on the *recipient* of the act (Wasserstrom, 1964, p. 631). The definition of supererogation in terms of duty rather than rights should not, however, lead us to the mistaken thesis which identifies supererogation with the area of duties that lack corresponding rights (cf. Ross, 1946, pp. 52–3). For there are various kinds of duties that do not correspond to rights – some of which have no relation to supererogation.

The next four sections discuss each of the four conditions of our definition in turn. The discussion takes into critical account some of the numerous alternative definitions which represent different theories and approaches to the subject.

6.2 PERMISSIBILITY

The first condition describes supererogatory acts as neither obligatory nor forbidden. The negative formulation is chosen so as to avoid the ambiguity of 'permissible', which in deontic logic may mean either 'not forbidden', or 'not forbidden and not obligatory'. In what follows 'permissible' should always be understood in the latter sense (that of 'liberty'). But being permissible is a very weak condition of supererogation, because it is morally neutral. It may refer to acts which should not or cannot be made obligatory for various reasons. The condition of permissibility provides only the *deontic genus* for the definition. Species of this genus include acts which have no moral status or value whatsoever, acts which are bad or even wrong, though not forbidden for some reason or other, acts which ought to be tolerated, acts which are good and 'ought' to be done yet are not obligatory in the strict sense of binding under a threat of sanction, and finally acts which can merely be commended – supererogatory acts in the sense of our definition.

The condition of permissibility renders any theory which maintains the possibility of duties of supererogation incompatible with the definition. The self-contradictory term 'duty of supererogation' is often used by philosophers who are more interested in making a distinction between different kinds of duties (usually according to their stringency), than in offering a theory of supererogation. The concept is also employed to bridge the conflicting views we might have regarding the deontic status for example of forgiveness or gratitude, which on the one hand are thought to be a moral duty, yet are also felt to be optional in a way other moral duties are not.

The failure to justify the notion of a 'supererogatory duty' stems from the confusion of supererogation and imperfect duty (see, for example, Forrester, 1975 and Burchill, 1965). While the former can be applied to particular actions (as well as to classes of actions), the latter has meaning only as an attribute of classes of action. Furthermore, as we have remarked in 3.4, the idea of imperfect duty implies a distinction between what is obligatory ('the minimum') and what is supererogatory ('beyond that minimum'). Burchill characterizes supererogatory acts, like those of charity, as acts 'which each agent ought to do on some occasions', and supererogatory acts of heroism and sacrifice as acts 'which some agent ought to do on some occasions'. But such a characterization means either that every particular act of charity (or heroism) is supererogatory, or that only those acts beyond what *someone, sometime* ought to do are supererogatory. The difference between imperfect duties and supererogation is that, while an imperfect duty to perform an act-

121

type A implies that it is a perfect duty to do either (act-token) a_1, or a_2..., or a_n, a supererogatory act-type B does not mean that it is our duty to perform *any* act-token of B.[2] And 'supererogatory' can of course be used to characterize the performance of all the act-tokens of an imperfectly obligatory act-type.

The first condition of permissibility places supererogation in one of the three types of actions considered from a moral standpoint: the obligatory, the permissible, and the forbidden. This tripartite classification underlies orthodox deontic logic, but its adequacy is controversial, especially in relation to supererogation. Urmson's fundamental argument for treating 'saintly and heroic acts' as a separate moral category rests on his rejection of that tripartite classification as failing to accommodate some important facts of morality (Urmson, 1958, pp. 198–9). Urmson's attack on the threefold classification has aroused criticism and attempts either to defend it, or to suggest an elaboration of it, which would accommodate supererogatory acts. Taking the first line, Chopra tries to discredit Urmson's argument by pointing to the ambiguity of his negative test of the moral worth of an act – whether its omission is wrong and blameworthy (Chopra, 1963, pp. 163–4). Chopra correctly indicates that sometimes we refrain from blaming people for not doing a certain act, not because of its supererogatory nature but because we are not *in a position* to do so. But this criticism fails to grasp Urmson's point, since Urmson wishes to test whether omission of certain acts is blameworthy, regardless of the position of any individual critic.

Some philosophers, like Chisholm, face the challenge of Urmson's attack on tripartitism by trying to extend the classification (Urmson's warning against it notwithstanding) in a way which accommodates supererogation. Although Chisholm admits that the tripartite approach of deontic logic is inadequate, he suggests a conceptual scheme, which is based on a parallel threefold classification of actions supplemented by the application of the three categories to *non*-performance as well as to performance (Chisholm, 1963, pp. 2, 10). Thus, to perform an act may be (1) a good thing, (2) a bad thing, or (3) neither a good nor a bad thing. This

---

[2] M. Stocker puts this point very similarly: if I have no opportunity to fulfil an imperfect obligation except by doing a particular act, then it becomes a perfect duty to perform that act; but this particular act is not supererogatory and cannot exemplify a supererogatory act-type (Stocker, 1968, p. 57).

basic list can be enriched so as to include the same three values of the hypothetical omission of the act in question. Using this improved machinery, Chisholm is now able to account for supererogation (as 'something which it would be good to do and neither good nor bad not to do') without altogether relinquishing the economical tripartite approach. Acts of supererogation are permissible, though not indifferent. By substituting the axiological terminology of *good, bad* and *neutral* for the deontic concepts of *obligatory, forbidden* and *permissible*, the way is opened to the characterization of supererogation in terms of the asymmetry of performance and non-performance. This strategy is ruled out by classical deontic logic, because supererogatory acts cannot be described as obligatory yet not forbidden not to do.[3]

Chisholm's definition of supererogatory acts as 'non-obligatory well-doings' (which is derived from the definition mentioned in the last paragraph) goes beyond the original tripartite classification – but not far enough. The language of 'good' and 'bad' applied to performance and omission of acts is not sufficiently rich to define supererogation. There is a sense in which failure to perform a supererogatory act *is* bad (e.g. has worse consequences than its performance, or reflects moral weakness). We usually prefer to describe such a failure as *not wrong*, even if it is bad in the above-mentioned sense. Consequently, we must resort to condition (2) of the definition. Indeed, Chisholm usually employs the terminology of 'not a bad thing not to do', which may be understood as being equivalent to 'not wrong for *an agent* not to do' (cf. Chisholm, 1964, p. 153).

There are philosophers who question the very relevance of the whole debate on whether deontic logic is adequate to account for supererogation. Schumaker, for example, holds that we must not dismiss logic for its 'failure' to accommodate supererogation, because it is only the logic of requirement and permission, and not – as Chisholm maintains – the logic of morality. Deontic logic, there-

---

[3] Of the nine types of acts derived from Chisholm's conceptual scheme, I will discuss later those described as 'offences'. I fail, however, to see the meaning of the 'totally supererogatory acts' (pp. 11–12), which are those acts that are good to do and good not to do. Chisholm's first example (an act having equally good consequences both in the case of performance and of omission) seems to me to exemplify indifference rather than supererogation. The second example is highly abstract, and I shall not discuss it here. In a later article, however, Chisholm drops this dubious category, together with its logical counterpart ('totally offensive acts'), and suggests a shortened list of seven types (Chisholm and Sosa, 1966, pp. 324–5, 329–30).

fore, cannot be expected to explain phenomena which lie beyond its proclaimed objectives. From the point of view of the deontic concept of requirement, the indifferent and the supererogatory are indistinguishable – they are both permitted (Schumaker, 1972, pp. 427–8).

Schumaker's point is important, especially as it stresses the need of a richer language than that supplied by deontic logic to explain the nature of acts beyond duty. Yet as a criticism of Chisholm (or for that matter any other theorist who follows Chisholm), Schumaker's argument is oversimplified and too sweeping. For Chisholm in both his 1963 and 1964 articles defines superogatory acts as those which bring about states of affairs that *ought* to exist, that is to say he regards supererogatory acts in deontic terms. Similarly, Richards, who basically accepts Chisholm's definition, treats supererogatory acts as kinds of *requirement*. And in that he could be understood to imply that it is the job of deontic logic to accommodate supererogation. Even a less reductionist type of supererogationist theory like that of Rawls may analyse supererogatory acts as those optional acts which would be obligatory in an ideal world (Chisholm hints at such an analysis when he says that 'a charitable lawgiver . . . fails to demand as much of us as he might'). And again, deontic logic may be justifiably expected to deal with such acts. It is only by holding an unqualified theory of supererogation that Schumaker's argument is fully warranted. And even in such a theory, it should be noted, supererogatory acts still have a *deontic status* and can be understood only in relation to duty.

As was mentioned at the beginning of this section, the self-contradictory concept of 'supererogatory duties' is sometimes used by philosophers who wish to salvage the threefold classification of moral actions by distinguishing between different types of duties, varying in degrees of stringency.[4] This strategy is 'reductionist', as it tries to account for supererogation in terms of duty and obligation.

Another reductionist strategy (which is typical of qualified supererogationists rather than of anti-supererogationists) consists

---

[4] For example Ladd (1957, p. 127) argues that a supererogatory act is 'somewhere in between being obligatory and indifferent'; it is right or 'fit', a weaker kind of duty. Grice too states that 'ultra obligations' (supererogation) differ from 'basic obligations' in being *'less* exacting in their requirement' (Grice, 1967, p. 157). See also Findlay's distinction between 'hortatory' and 'minatory' duties (1961, pp. 339–41, 353–4).

of defining supererogation as a 'personal', non-universalizable duty (Grice, 1967, pp. 36–7). Now not being universally applicable is indeed true of supererogatory 'standards', but if that is the case, then a further clarification of the concept of a *personal duty* is called for. If it is only what one *believes* is his duty, then it is not necessarily his duty. And if it is an 'objective' duty which applies only to certain people having a certain character, then it is not personal, but universally applicable to all persons who have such a character. Although Grice seems to reject the former interpretation (p. 157), his definition of 'ultra obligation' does not allow for the latter. To describe the devotion of one's life to the satisfaction of the needs of others as ultra obligation of anyone whose life can be 'fulfilled' in that way is extremely unnatural, but it is also logically a universal rather than a personal principle.

It should, therefore, be concluded that a definition of an unqualified notion of supererogation must contain the first condition of permissibility in its pure, absolute sense. Acts which go beyond the call of duty are in *no* way obligatory. They are not imperfect duties, or less stringent duties; nor are they just a type of duties entailing no corresponding rights. They cannot be described as something which *ought* to be done, or in acts whose omission is only permissible in the legal sense. To make that condition clear the definition adds the second and stronger condition of immunity from critical reaction.

6.3 IMMUNITY FROM CRITICAL REACTION

Only strict anti-supererogationists maintain that failure to act supererogatorily deserves and should entail condemnation in the same way as failure to do one's duty does. And even they may treat such failures as inherently excusable. There is, however, a disagreement concerning the justifiability of other, less formal, types of critical reaction towards the omission of such acts. The qualified supererogationist – who regards supererogatory acts as morally binding in *some* way – cannot regard omissions of these acts as being totally immune from criticism. If one *ought* to do a certain act, then failure to do it is wrong even if the act was not strictly speaking 'obligatory'. On the other hand, if supererogatory acts are not only permissible (in the legal sense), but also purely optional (as unqualified supererogationists believe), then omission is not wrong and cannot

125

warrant criticism or sanction of any kind under any circumstances.

This controversy underlies the difference between the wider and narrower types of definitions of supererogation. The wider type consists of definitions that take 'duty' and 'obligation' in a technical sense, and accordingly the notion of supererogation as well. Richards follows Chisholm in this respect, defining supererogatory acts as good to do but not obligatory (Richards, 1971, pp. 196–7). Condition (1) (together with an axiological condition) is sufficiently strong for that type of definition. On the other hand, our definition follows the narrower and less technical interpretation of Urmson, Stocker, and to some extent Feinberg, who define the acts in question in terms of condition (2). Not only is the omission of supererogatory actions permissible, but also it may not 'be justifiably reproved or blamed'. It is therefore, natural that both Richards and Chisholm should regard supererogation as a kind of requirement (and analyse the concept in terms of the contract theory or the 'ethics of requirement'). On the other hand, our definition belongs to the same type as Urmson's not only in substituting the stronger condition (2) for (1), but also in interpreting the condition of value (3) on specifically *moral* lines. Supererogatory acts are not just any 'non-obligatory well-doings'; they are *optional, morally* good actions.

The difference in logical strength between the two types of definitions corresponds to differences in the scope of the definiendum. Urmson takes saintly and heroic acts, or what Feinberg calls the 'meritorious, abnormally risky non-duty' (Feinberg, 1968, p. 400), as paradigm cases of actions which cannot be accounted for by the tripartite clssification. And obviously failure to act heroically does not justify any blame. On the other hand, Richards puts the emphasis on the 'principles of blame' (cf. above 5.3), and similarly Chisholm deliberately takes supererogation as referring also to acts of small-scale charity, kindness to animals and ordinary politeness (Chisholm, 1963, p. 3), or in Feinberg's terminology – 'simple favors'.

However, these specific examples regarding the scope of the concept of supererogation do not necessarily reflect the distinction between the wide and narrow types of definition and are presented in a misleading way by Richards, Chisholm, and Feinberg. It should first be pointed out that although Urmson refers solely to saintly and heroic acts, he does not claim that they encompass the whole realm of supererogatory behaviour. Urmson might have treated saintly and heroic acts as the most typical examples of supererogation if he had attempted a definition of *supererogation* (which he did not), and in that he would have been right. The terms 'saintly' and 'heroic', however, cut across both categories of duty and supererogation, and exhaust neither of them. Secondly, it is not only omission of saintly and heroic acts which is immune from blame and criticism, i.e. that meets condition (2). Small favours and other 'unextraordinary' examples of non-obligatory behaviour (like pardon) are perhaps trivial in relation to saintly and heroic acts, yet they are nonetheless supererogatory in the sense that their omission is not in any way *wrong*. Immunity from critical reaction is not necessarily due to the sacrifice or risk involved in the action (although it *may* be so, as it is in the failure to perform an exceedingly demanding duty). Our definition of supererogation assumes that it is not the case that we ought to do every good action which does not involve high risk or sacrifice (a claim which I shall try to support in more detail in 8.2 and 8.3). On the other hand, 'ordinary politeness' is excluded from the scope of supererogation, according to our definition, either because it is obligatory or because it is not a moral concept at all. Richards and Chisholm offer a much too broad definition which does not discriminate between politeness and kindness to animals on the one hand, and small acts of charity and personal favours on the other hand. Omission of the latter does not (usually) justify reproach, while that of the former may deserve criticism (although not necessarily moral criticism), for we ought to be polite and to treat animals kindly. (For a slightly different view, see Chisholm, 1964, p. 151).

The broader definition, which includes what Chisholm calls (after Hobbes) 'Small Moralls' and any other non-moral well-doings which we are permitted not to do, may serve to supplement classical deontic logic and make it richer, but it is hardly useful for an *ethical* theory of supererogation. The inclusion of condition (2) in our definition is logically linked to the stronger formulation of the axiological condition (3). For if the moral goodness of the defined acts partly lies in their being *beyond* duty, that is in their being completely optional, then failure to perform them cannot be regarded as wrong. This remark may clarify the distinction in ethical status between politeness and small acts of charity: only the latter have value which is derived from their optional nature. Our definition (like Urmson's) is not neutral in respect of a theory of moral value. Although it allows for non-heroic acts, it excludes the 'trivial' acts because in order to have *moral* value an act must be of more than negligible value. This is also implied by condition (4).

The difference between the broader and narrower types of definitions also underlies the issue whether supererogation has a symmetrical counterpart (a logical contrary). Chisholm suggests throughout his writings on the subject that in the same way as there are non-obligatory well-doings, so must there be 'permissive ill-doings'. He calls this category of actions *offences*. The state of affairs brought about by offensive actions ought not to exist, but the agent is permitted ('within his rights') to perform them. While supererogatory acts, according to Chisholm, are good to do but 'neutral' not to do, offensive acts are bad to do but 'neutral' not to do.

The logically neat symmetry of supererogation and offence attracted philosophers (Forrester, 1975, p. 225 and Richards, 1971). Nevertheless, it is vulnerable to criticism. Firstly, the symmetry can be maintained only as long as condition (2) of the definition is excluded in favour of the weaker (1). For offences can be described as permissible bad actions, but not as bad actions, the omission of which is 'not right'. Forbearance from doing evil is always a right thing to do. Secondly, even if we confine the definition of offences to the weaker condition (1), the symmetry is only partial. It only covers the 'trifling' cases (e.g. 'a disfavour or an act of discourtesy is trifling and offensive'). Chisholm can hardly find examples of the 'villainous' type of offences, which corresponds to the saintly and heroic type of supererogation. For how can an act be villainous, i.e. extremely bad and heinous, yet not forbidden? Chisholm's example of 'the informer' is extremely unconvincing: it is true that actions of informers are usually immune from legal sanction, but they are nevertheless morally wrong and morally forbidden. Informers can act only within their legal rights – not within their moral rights. And saying that under some circumstances the act of the informer is permissible or even obligatory, implies that the act is not 'heinous and inhuman'. A villain can never free himself from the grip of the moral law. The absence of a counterpart to heroic supererogation is indicative of the general asymmetry of doing good and refraining from evil in respect of duty or 'moral *ought*'. Doing good is an ideal which has no definite boundaries, and unlike refraining from evil, it is not always morally required.

128

Thirdly, Chisholm's thesis of symmetry can be contested even in his example of the non-villainous permissive ill-doings. 'Taking too long in the restaurant when others are known to be waiting' is indeed not a grave moral sin, can justify only mild forms of criticism, and is easily excusable. Yet it is, I believe, wrong and 'not to be done'. 'You ought not to but you may' is consistent only if the 'ought' and 'may' are interpreted on different levels – for instance the moral and the legal. There are definitely cases in which a bad act is (morally) permissible (in the same way as there are good acts which are not obligatory), but it is doubtful whether a *morally* bad act may be permitted in the same way as a morally good act is not always obligatory.[5] That is to say, condition (3) further curtails the validity of the alleged symmetry.

The qualified supererogatonist might try to reconcile condition (2) with his theory by arguing that although it is true that failure to act supererogatorily is not wrong, it would have been so under different circumstances. The difference in circumstances may be described in various ways. Following the Protestant tradition Rashdall refers to the 'internal' circumstances or conditions of actions which may vary from person to person (in a morally relevant way), no less than the 'external' circumstances (Rashdall, 1924, vol. 2, p. 135). An act which it is normally not wrong to omit may be a duty, if certain moral qualities and dispositions are present in the agent. Only people who have 'higher vocations' are expected to act in a supererogatory way. For instance, to sell all one's property and give the money to the poor is a duty, but only 'in persons endowed with a sufficient love of the poor to do this not grudgingly'. Therefore, it is not surprising that although recognizing a class of actions which meets condition (2) of our definition, Rashdall finds the idea of 'a work of supererogation' objectionable. Rashdall's mistake lies in the confusion of what we may expect certain people to do in the normative sense, and what we may expect them to do in the predictive sense. Only in the case of the former, does failure to live up to the expectation result in (moral) indignation or resentment. In the latter case failure gives rise only to disappointment. Failure to act supererogatorily can never invoke indignation.

[5] One reason for that might be that the adverb 'morally' adds to the general adjectives 'good' and 'bad' the dimension of 'agency' – i.e. what is good (or bad) *for a person* to do (or not to do). On this point I fully agree with Stocker's criticism of Chisholm's definitions of both supererogation and offence, and his call for a distinction between *wrongness* and *badness* (Stocker, 1967, p. 92).

An analogous reductionist argument can be constructed with reference to differences in strength of will: According to that argument *akrasia* is a ground for refraining from blaming the omission of supererogatory acts. The immunity from critical response in such a qualified version of supererogation is granted more as a matter of excuse (or supererogatory charity of an ideal law-giver) than as a right derived from the optional character of the act itself. And in such a qualified theory, weakness of will plays an important role because the theory presents supererogatory acts as ones which we *ought* to do (or have a conclusive reason for doing). Failing to do them, therefore, poses a problem which is solved in terms of the notion of *akrasia*.

Finally, it should be noted that immunity from critical reaction does not mean that at least some sorts of supererogatory behaviour may not be strongly encouraged and recommended. Consequently, failure to follow such a recommendation may entail a reaction of regret, which may be regarded as 'critical' in a secondary sense (not presupposing moral wrongness). Those for whom 'advisable' implies 'ought' are thus led to the rejection of condition (2) (Chisholm, 1963, p. 5; New, 1974, p. 183). But recommendation and advice in the case of encouraging people to perform supererogatory acts must be understood only as trying to influence them to adopt a noble ideal or to choose freely a good course of action. Recommendation assumes commendation – a belief that the recommended course of action is good, but does not imply prescription or an 'ought'-statement. The medieval Christian theory of supererogation understood that point, and accordingly set down the 'evangelical *counsels*' in terms of a *hypothetical* 'ought': one ought to follow the counsels only if one seeks certain goals and ideals. But these ideals, though highly praised, are not obligatory, and failure to adopt them is by no means wrong. But to remove the danger of ambiguity we should perhaps read condition (2) as precluding any kind of legitimate *moral* criticism of failures to act supererogatorily.

6.4 MORAL VALUE

The necessity of an axiological condition in our definition is obvious and beyond dispute. Yet its special nature and meaning for the theory of supererogation is highly controversial. It is universally agreed that supererogatory acts must be *good*, but beyond that, there

130

is disagreement. Should supererogation be confined to acts which are good in a distinctive moral way? Does the value of supererogatory acts consist in their actual or just their intended consequences? Are they intrinsically good (that is, independently of their consequential value)? The current literature on the subject – being more concerned with the deontic status of supererogation than with its moral value and justification – does not discuss these questions in much detail. However, being guided by the theoretical need to justify the class of supererogatory actions, our definition puts some specific ethical constraints on condition (3) which may be dispensed within a Chisholm-type definition (which is not explicitly committed even to the existence of the acts defined). The additional constraints are both analogous and linked to the stronger requirement made by condition (2) in relation to (1).

The additional requirement, namely that the value of supererogatory acts be *moral*, is explained by the dual source of value of the defined acts: their consequences and their optional nature. The first source of value is widely accepted as supplying grounds for supererogation, and this is perhaps the reason for Urmson's belief that supererogation can best be accounted for (although not exclusively) within a modified utilitarian theory (Urmson, 1958, p. 215). The second source is usually not mentioned by writers on the subject, yet I think it is this that gives supererogation its distinctive moral value – a contention best proved by our appreciation of those relatively minor acts of supererogation which have only little consequential value. The second source lends to supererogation a distinctive moral value, because it assumes the correlativity and continuity of supererogation with duty. This dual source of moral value explains why supererogation requires a theory which blends both axiological and deontological elements. Neither utilitarianism nor Kantianism alone is sufficient to account for supererogation as has been shown in Part I.

Supererogatory actions according to condition (3) must, therefore, bring about some good. They must result in the promotion of some value be it pleasure, happiness, welfare, friendship, or other values that enjoy a less wide consensus (e.g. sexual abnegation as commended by Christianity). The value promoted by acts of supererogation need not be utilitarian. It is normally the case that the good promoted is of other persons than the agent, and condition (4) of altruistic intention makes this a necessary condition. Some

Christian examples of supererogation (celibacy, 'obedience') are borderline cases, because the good they bring about is primarily that of the agent. They are, however, not completely beyond the scope of our definition, because they indirectly promote the good of others (as explained in chapter 1), and because their agent's intention may be described as altruistic.

The altruistic proviso of the axiological condition allows for cases in which an act is supererogatory, although the *overall* amount of consequential value is not increased. In other words, the agent of the act may lose more than others gain from it. There is nothing unreasonable about such instances of self-sacrifice, which may be justified by the second source of the moral goodness of supererogation. There is nevertheless a limit to the value of self-sacrifice. A great loss to the agent can be justified only if the amount of good secured to others is more than negligible, otherwise the act is foolish rather than praiseworthy. There is nothing valuable in self-sacrifice as such. The last point amounts to the general dependence of the second source of value on the first: there is nothing good in going beyond the call of duty if no one benefits from it (even if the act in itself is a manifestation of certain virtuous traits of character). On the other hand, the first source in itself does not grant supererogation any special moral value either. It is the combination of the two which makes supererogatory action meritorious and morally important.

The axiological condition requires that the moral value of a supererogatory act be (partly) consequential, a requirement that does not necessarily apply to duty-fulfilling acts. According to some ethical theories, an act can be duty-fulfilling even if no 'good' is directly promoted. Supererogatory acts, however, must necessarily have good consequences, because they lack other types of justifications that apply to duties (i.e. doing the right thing, obeying the moral law, adhering to God's commandments, being fair, etc.). It might be a duty to return borrowed money even if it is likely to be used for bad purposes; but returning a greater sum than required may hardly be called supererogatory in such a case. Similarly, punishment may be fully justified even if it is not likely to do any good in the consequential sense; but pardon cannot be praised as supererogatory if it is known that the remission of punishment will lead a convict to lapse into crime once more.

However, condition (3) of the definition contains an important qualification of the axiological requirement: the act's value is derived from its *intended* consequences. This qualification should be understood as meaning two different but equally relevant specifications: first, that the agent must have the intention of promoting good by his action (which is what condition (4) stipulates more explicitly), and secondly, that the act *may* be supererogatory even if the good consequences in fact fail to ensue – as long as they were sincerely intended. The last point means that success is not essential to supererogatory action. Killing oneself in the desert in order to leave enough water for one's thirsty companions is a supererogatory act, even if the water turns out to be poisoned or if the companions eventually die of hunger.

The 'intention clause' in both its meanings applies to supererogation in a way which does not necessarily apply to duty. At least some theories of duty maintain that a duty or an obligation can be discharged or met unintentionally, and *a fortiori* with no intention of benefiting anyone. And as for the second meaning of 'intended', some philosophers (notably Moore and Ross) would deny that mere intention (not complemented by actual success) can suffice to make an act duty-fulfilling.

The second source of the moral value of supererogatory acts (the *intrinsic* value) is not as clear as the first (the *consequential*) and calls for further explanation. Acts which we call supererogatory are valuable not only because of their consequences, but also because they go beyond duty; because their agents do something over and above what may be expected of them by choosing to transcend the required minimum. The moral status of supererogation must, therefore, be understood *in relation* to duty, as being characterized by the two features of continuity and correlativity. Given the literal meaning of 'supererogation', such insistence may appear superfluous, yet most theorists of supererogation have not incorporated these features as necessary conditions in their definition of the concept.

We are treading here on dangerous ground, because the ideas of correlativity and continuity of supererogation with duty might be thought to be suggesting a reductionist view of which I strongly disapprove. Continuity of the value of supererogation with that of duty indeed suggests the possibility of understanding supererogatory acts as duty of a higher level, a 'personal *ought*', or a special obligation which binds moral saints and heroes. But the correlativity condition makes it clear not only that duty and supererogation should be kept apart as two distinct categories, but also that part of the moral value of the latter is derived exactly from its irreducibility to the former.

Both conditions exclude certain 'moralities' that might be taken as supererogatory. The continuity requirement denies supererogatory status to a Nietzschean type of morality. For although Nietzsche emphasizes the fact that the guiding principles of the Superman are 'beyond duty' (and in a sense –as in our correlativity thesis – that is one of their sources of value), the values realized by such principles are totally alien to the values represented by the morality of duty. The correlativity condition also denies supererogatory status to an Aristotelian type of morality. For, although its values are of the same type as those sought by the 'legal' obligations (i.e. meets the continuity requirement), they are hardly appreciated for their extra-duty nature. The continuity requirement excludes any non-obligatory action which is not of a *moral* nature from the definition, like the pursuit of self-regarding ideals of certain kinds. The life of an artist who sacrifices everything for the sake of his art is accordingly not supererogatory, even though it may be held as 'good'. Nor is the life of a religious saint (a hermit) – unless we take religious principles as our *moral* principles. The continuity condition also explains why social rules of etiquette (politeness, rituals, how to dress for dinner, etc.) cannot be regarded as supererogatory. The correlativity condition, for its part, excludes from the definition acts which pertain to the sphere of natural relationship and instinctive feelings (which lies outside morality). A mother who makes a great sacrifice for her child is not strictly speaking acting supererogatorily. Our appreciation of such an act is not of a moral kind, as we do not tend to view it in relation to her *duties* as a mother (to which we usually refer only when she *fails* to fulfil them).[6]

The continuity condition is indirectly challenged by Feinberg's important article on supererogation. Feinberg follows Urmson in making a critical stand against reductionism, and in that he may be interpreted as adhering to an unqualified version of supererogationism (Feinberg, 1968, pp. 391–2). Feinberg's objective is to show

---

[6] Our definition also excludes from the realm of supererogation what Cooper calls the morality which governs the ideal Community of Holy Wills. Such an 'above rule morality' has no room for duty, and hence – according to the condition of correlativity – no room for supererogation (see Cooper, 1959, pp. 166 ff.).

that not every supererogatory act can be explained on the model of 'institutional over-subscription' (like working nine hours instead of the eight required, or going 'the second mile'). There are other typically supererogatory acts which are not 'duty-*plus*', but rather '*non*-duties' (like 'simple favours and heroic self-denials'), and these require a different analysis. It seems that the continuity of supererogation with duty cannot be retained in the latter type (although it can of course be applied to cases of 'over-subscription').

It should first be noted that Feinberg understands 'duty' and 'obligation' in their narrow sense (following Whiteley and Hart), which makes it natural for him to describe every act which goes beyond duty and obligation as 'over-subscription'. For indeed doing more than my job as a manager or than my contractual undertaking requires is supererogatory in the sense of institutional over-subscription. But if we understand 'moral duty' as including what Rawls calls 'natural duty', then it is not so clear that we have no moral duty to light another person's cigarette in the street (Feinberg's example of non-duty); and even if it is not, it may be interpreted as supererogatory in the sense of doing *more* than the natural duty of mutual help requires. A rejection of the institutional over-subscription model does not then amount to the refutation of the continuity thesis, unless 'duty' is understood solely in the narrow sense of jobs, roles and voluntary undertakings. A doctor who goes to a plague-stricken city, although it is not his duty as the doctor of a certain community, cannot be described as doing more than his duty in a 'quantitative', institutional way (here Feinberg is right), but that does not mean that his supererogatory action is a 'non-duty'. He goes beyond his natural duty, being concerned with the welfare of others to a greater degree than may be expected of him. The supererogatory element in his praiseworthy act lies not so much in his action *as a doctor*, but rather in his action *as a man* (who happens to have a highly relevant skill).

So it seems that supererogatory acts should not be treated as 'properly located on an altogether different scale than that occupied jointly by duties, derelictions, and over-subscriptions' (Feinberg, 1968, p. 397). On the contrary, they must belong to the same scale if they are to have moral value (which Feinberg presumably does not doubt). Our definition includes favours under the title of supererogation. For it allows for supererogatory acts which are neither 'duty-plus' in the quantitative sense, nor 'in excess of duty' in terms

135

of self-sacrifice and risk. Although I agree with Feinberg's point that not every act of duty involves sacrifice, I do not wish to make sacrifice a necessary condition of supererogatory behaviour, and hence 'abnormally risky, non-duty' cannot characterize supererogatory acts. The continuity thesis can be defended (against Feinberg's arguments) by showing that the alternative of duty-plus (institutional over-subscription) and meritorious, abnormally, risky, non-duty is not exhaustive of the morally good acts which are optional. Feinberg derives the moral value of supererogatory conduct from the risk and the sacrifice involved; our definition, however, derives part of this value from its being *beyond* duty. Insistence on the correlativity of duty and supererogation may suffice to counter Feinberg's criticism which argues that the over-subscription model looms over any theory that does not treat supererogation as non-duty. Supererogation can be analysed as duty-plus, not in a quantitative way, but rather as surpassing the duties of man qua man, and that does not involve – as Feinberg believes – 'blurring the distinction' between duty and beyond-duty, and cannot be treated as a reductionist device similar to that of making supererogation a kind of imperfect duty. I fully agree with the criticism against the institutionalization of 'moral worth' (as for example in Roman Catholicism), but I do not think it is implied in the requirements of continuity and correlativity, which may suggest a middle way between the two models presented by Feinberg.

Thus, to conclude, condition (3) of the definition places relatively strong constraints on the interpretation of the value of superarogatory acts, but this seems necessary for the justificatory part of the theory of supererogation, for the explanation of the special status of supererogation in morality.

6.5 ALTRUISTIC INTENTION AND PERSONAL MERIT

The final condition of our definition introduces a new dimension, that of the moral agent. The *personal* aspect of supererogation is manifest both in the requirement that the supererogatory act be performed out of altruistic and benevolent intention, and in the fact that the agent earns merit by performing the type of acts defined. Before analysing these two aspects of supererogatory behaviour, I would like to mention briefly another condition which belongs to the dimension of the agent, namely voluntariness. No act is supererogatory unless it is performed voluntarily, that is under no external pressure or threat of sanction. Supererogatory behaviour must be free in a stronger sense than the freedom of duty-fulfilling action. It is freedom in the sense of taking an optional course of action and having full personal discretion to make that choice or reject it. Voluntariness in condition (4) means more than freedom from compulsion by external forces or by inclinations. It should be viewed as closer to the notion of *liberum arbitrium* than to the Kantian obedience to the laws of Reason.

In the discussion of condition (3) we mentioned the special role of intention in supererogatory behaviour. We noted that sometimes acts may be judged as supererogatory by virtue of their agents' intention alone. We also suggested that the intention to promote 'good' is a necessary condition for an act to be supererogatory. This last point requires further elaboration because it is ignored by all theories with the exception of Schumaker's (1977, p. 10). The intention must be *altruistic* meaning that the act must be conceived as benefiting another person (or persons). Such altruistic intention may be absent in duty-fulfilling acts which are sometimes performed despite the fact that they are not going to benefit anyone (or anyone other than the agent). Altruistic intention should not, however, be confused with altruistic motive. While intention forms part of the description of the act, the motive is only the 'feeling' which moves us to do it (Mill, 1969a, pp. 219–20n). The motives for acting supererogatorily are diverse in character, and are not always virtuous. One may act heroically in order to gain fame, to soothe one's conscience (haunted by guilt feelings), or out of moral self-indulgence. High-minded motives are not a necessary condition for supererogatory action as so many theorists tend to believe (e.g. Peterfreund, 1978, p. 55). Although the *motives* of supererogatory acts may be self-regarding, the *intention* must be other-regarding. And only other-regarding duties can be surpassed supererogatorily. Anyway, the psychologist must be very careful in analysing the deep motives which prompt the extraordinary acts of moral heroism.[7]

[7] It is most typical that empirical studies which tried to trace the motives of people who saved Jews under Nazi occupation (assuming that it was a supererogatory act) discovered a wide range of motives. A systematic psychology of supererogation is in any case not yet at hand and I prefer not to add to the highly speculative suggestions found in the literature on the subject. Cf. J. Macaulay and L. Berkowitz (eds), *Altruism and Helping Behaviour*, Academic Press, 1970. A summary of theories of altruism in psychology can be found in D. Wright, *The Psychology of Moral Behaviour*, Penguin Books, 1971, ch. 6.

The intention clause of our definition should be understood to apply only to the first source of moral value (i.e. the promotion of other people's good), but not to the second (acting beyond duty). For although the definition does not cover actions which, as a matter of coincidence, turn out to be good, it does allow for actions which are done with the intention of fulfilling a duty. In other words, the fact that the agent *believes* that his action is obligatory does not in itself disqualify it from being supererogatory. This is an important caveat, as most supererogatory acts are proclaimed by their agents to be duties. It also marks a difference between duty and supererogation: in the former, acting for duty's sake is – in some theories – a necessary condition, whereas promotion of good is not; but in the latter, the reverse is true: bringing about some good is a necessary condition, but intending to act beyond duty ('acting for the sake of supererogation') is not.

It is, then, a typical feature of supererogatory acts that the agent often regards them as obligatory. This feature, which may be referred to as 'moral modesty' can be interpreted in two ways: the agent knows that he acted supererogatorily but does not say so (being shy, he wishes to avoid being praised or publicly rewarded); or the agent sincerely believes that he was only doing his duty. The second interpretation is problematic, because it may mean either that the agent mistakenly takes a supererogatory act to be obligatory (and, accordingly, expects others to do so as well), or that he takes a supererogatory action to be personally binding, that is a subjective duty (and does not consider others bound by it as well). Only the latter is a case of moral modesty, but in a different way from the modesty of the agent who knows that he acts beyond the call of duty but does not say so. For believing that a certain action is one's 'subjective duty' means rejecting the universalizability of that requirement. 'I feel I ought to do it', uttered sincerely, means that the agent does not regard his act as meritorious, although he does not expect others to do the same. Strictly speaking this attitude is inconsistent, and the subjective binding force cannot be identified with duty. Nevertheless, it is an indication of moral modesty. And if we interpret 'subjective duty' as the duty of a person who has a special 'call' or vocation, then it is universalizable, obligatory and has very little to do with modesty (see Cohen, 1967, p. 257).

Being morally modest may add to the praiseworthiness of the supererogatory action (and its agent), but it is not a defining characteristic in our definition. Acts which are publicly and vaunt-ingly declared to surpass the call of duty may still be supereroga-tory, although their agent is likely to be rebuked for his exhibitionist motives. The difference between subjective and objec-tive duty is reflected in the feeling of the agent who fails to perform the act in question. In the first case it is shame; in the second, guilt. The two, however, cannot be easily identified and distinguished from each other, as they both consist of self-reproach. The only valid criterion of distinction lies in the question asked from an *objec-tive* point of view (by an external judge): is anyone – other than the agent – in a position to reproach such a failure?

The second part of condition (4) introduces the personal dimen-sion by characterizing supererogatory acts as meritorious. An act is said to be meritorious only if it earns merit for its agent. Unlike the attributes of permissibility and moral goodness, which apply to acts independently of their agents, 'meritorious' is conceptually linked to persons (like 'intentional' and 'benevolent'). Condition (3) stresses the features of the *act* which make it morally valuable. Con-dition (4) focuses on the features which make the *agent* the subject of merit. This does not, however, mean that works of supererogation are meritorious just because of the altruistic intention of their agents. Moral goodness – in the two aspects of (3) – is responsible for the meritorious nature of the act no less than benevolent inten-tion.

Merit should be distinguished from praise and praiseworthiness. Urmson cogently argues that 'saintly' and 'heroic' may describe actions which are not supererogatory, and that actions so described deserve no less praise than saintly and heroic acts which do go beyond duty (see also Chisholm, 1963, p. 4). Praise can be acquired only through public recognition and the favourable attitude of others. Merit is acquired independently of the way in which the action is actually appraised by others. Praise is motivated by reasons of various types, which may change from time to time and from person (society) to person (society). Merit in that respect is more objective, being related to theoretical criteria of desert, rather than to contingencies like social interests of individual people's inclina-tions, which determine praise and condemnation. The principles that determine merit are also more objective than those of praise and condemnation in that they take into consideration primarily the act itself and not the agent's motives, virtues, strength of will, or the moral expectations of the society and the relative likelihood of other people performing the same kind of act. In that respect the choice of merit rather than praiseworthiness as a defining feature of supererogation is analogous to our preference of moral goodness in the objective sense of (3) to the notions of risk and degree of sacrifice (which are typically relative, and like praiseworthiness may be equally characteristic of obligatory action).

The Christian theological use of the concept of merit in the theory of supererogation can, therefore, be borrowed by our definition – without committing us to the theoretical implications of the Roman Catholic doctrine. Christ's merits are his *superabundant* good works, those which surpass the stipulated required amount of good works. Accordingly, merit is to be understood as 'credit' in contradistinction both to 'debit' and to a 'zero balance'. The model of a moral bank-account of good and bad deeds was criticized in 1.5 mainly on the grounds of the non-transferability between persons of moral 'credit' (or merit) and of the impossibility of trade-off between the agent's own supererogatory and wrong actions. Yet the model itself may serve – *mutatis mutandis* – as an illustration of what is meant by 'merit', namely, a certain surplus which is credited to the agent. This surplus may call for a reward or praise, but need not. For the surplus may be small and easily gained. Gratitude, however, is always appropriate in the case of supererogatory behaviour, and strictly speaking, is not the fitting response to a duty-fulfilling action. It is the *gratuitous* nature of the supererogatory act which makes it worthy of *gratitude*.

The advantage of describing supererogatory action in terms of merit, rather than praise, is that merit can be attached to relatively trivial and unextraordinary sorts of actions, whereas praise restricts the scope of supererogation to the unexpected, highly virtuous, modes of conduct. A small favour hardly deserves praise, let alone reward, yet it is meritorious and makes the agent deserving of gratitude. For the same reasons, reward should not be taken as a criterion for supererogation as suggested by Humberstone (1974, pp. 103–14).

Supererogation is often associated with virtue, or with a specially 'moral' personality. Indeed, some types of superarogatory behaviour manifest certain virtuous traits of character, and some virtues can be ascribed only to persons who supererogate. Yet we should take care not to treat the two as identical, because supererogation characterizes actions, while virtue is ascribed primarily to persons. And there is no necessary link between having a highly moral character and acting beyond duty. There are virtues, like wisdom, which are not related specifically to either duty or supererogation. There are virtues, like conscientiousness, which are associated particularly with obligatory action. Then there are virtues which may be causally connected with supererogation (courage and temperance), i.e. traits of character which make the transcendence of duty easier (although they may be expressed in duty-fulfilling action as well). Finally there are virtues that are logically linked with supererogation, like charity, benevolence, and more specifically mercifulness and generosity (Hart, 1961, p. 178). These are qualities which can be ascribed only to people who act in a charitable, benevolent, merciful, and generous way, that is to say beyond what is required of them as a duty. On the other hand, as Aristotle noted, not every individual act of the types mentioned is indicative of a virtuous disposition in the agent. Yet if we choose to regard 'altruistic intention' as virtuous – a manifestation of virtue – then condition (4) of our definition makes every supererogatory act by definition virtuous. The distinction between intention and motive, however, raises doubt as to the plausibility of that claim, since altruistic intention can accompany an act which is prompted by non-virtuous motives.

7

Some paradigm cases

Having discussed the definition of supererogation and its theoretical ramifications, we may now turn to the analysis of some cases which exemplify supererogatory conduct. These cases are meant to serve both as an illustration of the four conditions of supererogation discussed in the last chapter, and also as an intuitional support of the proposed definition. On the one hand, the definition places some theoretical constraints on the type of actions which may be treated as supererogatory (excluding certain examples which are given by philosophers advocating other definitions, and upholding other examples which are not counted supererogatory by alternative theories). On the other hand, it is believed that the types of action classified in this chapter as supererogatory do not basically conflict with our pre-theoretical intuitions of what in fact is supererogatory.

The paradigm cases of supererogation to be discussed here fall under the following six headings: saintliness and heroism, beneficence (charity, generosity, gifts), favours, volunteering, supererogatory forbearances, and finally pardon (forgiveness, mercy). This list is not exhaustive, nor are its items mutually exclusive, yet it covers the important cases of action beyond the call of duty and may be used to classify the main types of supererogatory conduct. Examples of these six types may be challenged on two grounds: firstly, some philosophers would wish to exclude *entire categories* from the list, either because they seem to be too trivial to be called 'supererogatory' (favours, for instance), or because they are, in their opinion, obligatory (e.g. forgiveness and charity). Secondly, some specific examples may be denied a supererogatory status because they (allegedly) do not fall into any of the supererogatory categories of action. In the latter case, what is contested is not the validity of the list, but its application to particular cases. The problem of application arises from the difficulty in formulating criteria of *demar-*

cation, most typically in the context of beneficence (see for example Singer, 1972). Even assuming that charity is supererogatory (and not for instance an imperfect duty), there is wide disagreement as to where to draw the borderline between charitable donation and obligatory giving. Kidney-donation may be supererogatory, but is blood-donation not obligatory, a moral duty? Do we have to give anything to Oxfam, and if so, how much? I must, however, avoid these substantive moral questions and confine my discussion to the supererogatory nature of the classes of actions listed above. It should, however, be noted that the problem of the demarcation of duty and supererogation underlies many of our everyday moral disputes. A common defence against moral criticism for not doing what one ought to have done in a certain case is to argue that the act in question is supererogatory (rather than to argue that it has no moral value, or that there are other overriding duties or obligations).

The following sections discuss each of the six types of supererogatory action only briefly. However, forgiveness and pardon deserve a more detailed analysis. They seem to be typically supererogatory, on the one hand, and surprisingly neglected by theorists of supererogation, on the other hand. They have the theoretical advantage of not raising the problem of demarcation (like volunteering, and in contrast with beneficence and heroism, it is not by surpassing a certain disputable degree of sacrifice, risk, or material loss that they gain their special status). They are also important to our theory of supererogation since they run counter to the natural tendency to treat only exceptional, difficult, and highly admirable acts as supererogatory. Finally, they lucidly illustrate those features of individuality and cohesive moral relationship which are essential to the justificatory part of our theory.

In the course of the critical review of other theories of supererogation in the preceding chapters various reasons have been given for the exclusion of some types of examples from the list of supererogatory acts (e.g. any positive promotion of good, etiquette, effortless performance of highly demanding duties, mutual respect, etc.). Gratitude, however, is dropped from the present list for different reasons. Gratitude is, in my view (and particularly the act of showing gratitude), definitely a duty, although – as I have already argued – it is logically related to supererogation. It is the natural duty of anyone who voluntarily accepts the benefits of a supereroga-

143

tory act. Its binding force as a duty can be shown by our intense moral disapprobation of ingratitude. Nevertheless, many theorists have been led into a position which mistakenly views gratitude as lying beyond duty. This mistaken view may be ascribed to various reasons. It is rightly felt that the agent of a supererogatory act has no right to expect (or demand) gratitude, and hence it is (falsely) inferred that the beneficiary has no corresponding duty. Secondly, the fact that people cannot be (legally) compelled to be grateful (because it involves an attitude and not merely an action) is wrongly taken to imply that gratitude is not even a moral duty. Finally, it is true that gratitude can be expressed in actions which may be called supererogatory, but that does not mean that gratitude itself is supererogatory. For the acknowledgment of the supererogatory nature of the act for which one is grateful is obligatory, irrespective of the manner in which gratitude is actually expressed (e.g. the extent of the benefit returned). So although gratitude is (in its paradigmatic meaning) a reaction to a supererogatory act, and as such is an indicator of supererogation, it is itself a duty. Accordingly, it does not deserve praise and is not meritorious. In Simmel's words, ingratitude is deplorable to the same extent that the supererogatory act is free.[1]

7.2 MORAL HEROISM

Supererogation is traditionally associated with religious saintliness and moral heroism. This is due both to the Christian origins of the concept and to those features of saintliness and heroism which make them so typically supererogatory. For saintly and heroic behaviour involves overcoming natural fears, desires, and considerations of self-interest, and also great self-sacrifice – either in terms of risk, or of actual loss to the agent. Acts of moral heroism display special moral virtues and, in most cases, deserve praise and admiration. They are extraordinary in being rarely performed, a fact which grants them an exemplary status. Unlike other types of supererogatory acts, moral heroism demands the relinquishment of the most basic goods – life itself, or one's way of life (rather than property or

[1] For a detailed discussion of the concept of gratitude, see Berger (1975, pp. 298–309). Berger, however, does not specifically link gratitude to supererogation, but more generally to benevolent actions (which include duties). According to Berger, gratitude is an obligatory acknowledgment of the *good will* of the agent rather than of the deontic status of the act.

money). All these factors make saintly and heroic acts supererogatory *par excellence*, because (a) it is indisputable that failure to do them does not deserve any blame or sanction, (b) their consequential value is relatively great, (c) they are conspicuously altruistic, and (d) they are beyond doubt meritorious. Acts of moral heroism satisfy the conditions of our definition as well as of alternative ones, and in that respect they form perhaps the most typical class of actions which go beyond the call of duty. Finally, this type of action forms the most serious obstacle for reductive and anti-supererogationist analyses, because all interpretations of heroic acts as less stringent obligations or imperfect duties run counter to our intuitions and sound even more artificial than reductive interpretations of charity, forgiveness, and favours.

Saintly and heroic acts raise once more the issue of the place of risk and sacrifice in the theory of supererogation. In chapter 6 we argued against their inclusion in the definition of supererogation. The argument did not, however, purport to exclude considerations of risk and sacrifice as altogether irrelevant to the demarcation of duty and supererogation. For the degree of risk and sacrifice involved in actions of a certain type may serve (along with other considerations) as grounds for classifying that type of actions as lying within or beyond the call of duty: saving a child from drowning in a shallow pond is, accordingly, a duty of any passer-by, whereas the behaviour of the teacher who saved many of his pupils' lives in a blaze in a hotel at the cost of his own life must be called supererogatory. Nevertheless, risk and sacrifice cannot be conditions of supererogation, because there are non-risky supererogatory acts on the one hand, and supererogatory acts which do much good at a relatively small cost to the agent on the other hand (charity and pardon respectively). There are also duties whose fulfilment is highly dangerous and heroic (consider the case of a police sapper whose job is, by definition, very risky). In the case of obligatory action risk and sacrifice may serve as grounds for excusing omission or as mitigating circumstances. In the supererogatory cases, however, they justify immunity from any critical reaction. Or in more positive terms: doing one's duty when it is especially risky entails praise but not merit (in the sense of condition (4)), whereas heroic action (in the supererogatory sense) deserves both merit and praise.

It should be noted that moral heroism is rare, not only because

145

only very few people are capable of it, but also because the *occasion* to engage in heroic action does not arise very often. Unlike other supererogatory acts, the opportunity to do a heroic act is rare. Firstly, circumstances which call for a heroic sacrifice (rescue operations, war situations, etc.) are not part of our daily life; and secondly, most people are bound by their social duties (family, work, community) and obligations to an extent which prevents them from engaging in some types of supererogatory conduct. Having the responsibility for the health of one's own community may hinder a medical doctor from volunteering to go to another community which needs help – even if he is prepared to do so. To put it crudely, not every person can afford to be an Albert Schweitzer. But although the opportunity of acting heroically does not often arise in daily life, there are extreme circumstances in which it arises in such a manner that a conscientious person is actually *compelled* to act supererogatorily. In a situation like that of a shipwreck – when most people are in complete panic – the only alternative to the return to a state-of-nature situation may be to volunteer to sacrifice one's life in order to save those of others (Lloyd Thomas, 1970, p. 134).

7.3 BENEFICENCE

Under the heading of beneficence we include mainly acts of *giving*. Saintly and heroic acts are described as typically supererogatory because they involve risk to, or sacrifice of, the agent's life, way of life, or health. Beneficence, on the other hand, consists usually in the contribution of one's material goods (giving money or property). This does not mean that beneficent acts are never heroic (consider the Evangelical Counsel of poverty), yet they are normally less worthy of praise and admiration than acts of moral heroism, because the value sacrificed is not held to be as important as that sacrificed by saints and heroes. Supererogatory acts of beneficence may take the form of a particularly generous contribution to a certain cause towards which we have only a limited responsibility, or a donation to a charity which has no claim whatsoever to our help. That is to say, a beneficent act may be an over-subscription to an existing duty (perfect or imperfect), but it can also be beyond any institutional or social duty altogether. (One may, for example, treat a friend beneficently by giving him a big present). Unlike saintly

146

and heroic acts, beneficence is not characterized in terms of the degree of personal sacrifice, but in terms of giving more than the specified amount that is required (which may be zero). Beneficence is exercised by ordinary people, because it does not require special strength of character, and sometimes incurs only minor loss to the agent.

Beneficence is associated with the etymology of the word 'supererogation' rather than with the theological origins of the concept, and it is a typical moral virtue in Greek and Roman ethics. Generosity (which is especially admired in classical morality) is illustrative of the supererogatory nature of beneficence: a generous act goes beyond what is required of the agent or what is due to the beneficiary. It disregards desert and does not necessarily coincide with the prescriptions of justice. It is normally altruistic in its intention (although it may be a self-regarding virtue). It is gratuitous and absolutely optional, and it is 'rule-free' (Hunt, 1975).

Yet when generosity is compared and contrasted with charity it seems that only the latter may be taken as a supererogatory case of beneficence. For generosity, as it is conceived for example by Nietzsche, may be altogether alien to human needs, and function as a self-regarding assertion of one's freedom and moral independence (Hunt, 1975, pp. 242-3).[2] In this respect, generosity does not satisfy the conditions of correlativity and continuity of supererogation with duty (which *is* other-regarding and concerned with other people's needs and with the interdependence of members of a moral community). Such a concept of generosity implies the rejection of deontological morality. Charity, on the other hand, emphasizes the agent's concern for others (sympathy, pity, sensitivity to other people's interests, etc.). It transcends duty without trying to replace it. Charity unlike Aristotelian generosity is not a self-regarding virtue. A supererogatory gift cannot be useless to its recipient (as it should be in Nietzsche's eyes). Therefore, although it is true that the generous man is 'characterologically' different from the just man, a charitable person is essentially a just person too, i.e. has full reverence for justice and duty.

Another form of beneficence is gift-giving. A gift is, by defi-

---

[2] Hunt, on the one hand, requires that a generous act be altruistic and beneficial (p. 239), yet, on the other hand, is inclined to accept the Greek or even the Nietzschean ideal, which is better called 'squandering' than generosity. See, *Thus Spoke Zarathustra*, 1:22, 1–2, which is misinterpreted by Hunt as commending generosity.

nition, something which no one has a right to be given. It is given with the intention of promoting the recipient's good or happiness, and if voluntarily accepted, it calls for gratitude. Gift-relationship complements economic exchange or other forms of give-and-take which are governed by duty and justice. But if gifts constitute the basic (or sole) form of exchange (e.g. between friends, parents and children on birthdays, or whole societies), then it can hardly be described as supererogatory, since it is not correlated to duty (Mauss, 1954, p. 1). Blood-donation is, on the other hand, a typical case of supererogatory giving (at least as it is organized in Britain). It is anonymous, impersonal, involves some sacrifice but no reciprocity (no return – even of gratitude), saves life, and is by no means obligatory. Blood-donation thus meets the conditions of our definition, especially the requirement of altruistic benevolence, which is most conspicuous and rarely mixed with self-regarding considerations. Blood-donation is also conditioned by the factor of opportunity. Societies which make blood supplies part of the economic system of exchange can hardly encourage supererogatory blood-donation. Some sociologists – like Titmuss (1973) – hold blood-donation to be so valuable (as an outlet of altruistic behaviour), that they believe it is a desirable social policy to make the system of blood-donation a purely voluntary one. Others, however, take a profoundly different approach to giving. In his Scale of Charity, Maimonides states that the highest degree is the provision of a source of income to the needy person so as to eliminate the need for charity – i.e. the very opportunity to act supererogatorily. This approach is reminiscent of Kant's theory which excludes supererogation from a deontically perfect world.

7.4 FAVOURS

We are naturally inclined not to refer to favours as supererogatory, probably because they promote the good only to a minor degree. They usually consist of small services performed without a great deal of sacrifice or loss to the agent. In other words, their consequential value is normally small. Yet according to our theory a favour must be classified as supererogatory, being an act 'of exceptional kindness, as opposed to one of duty or justice' (O.E.D.). They may be deserved or undeserved, done spontaneously or as a response to a request. Yet they are never deserved as a matter of right, and refusal to do a favour cannot be criticized as morally wrong. We can ask for a favour, but never claim it. Indeed, we might feel that we *owe* someone a favour, but that only means the willingness to express gratitude for previous favours done for us by returning a favour. Failure to return a favour is, however, not in itself a moral wrong (like failure to return a borrowed book). It may be condemned only if it reflects ingratitude. Unlike moral heroism and beneficence, the moral value of favours consists mainly in what was referred to in condition (3) as the second source of value, namely the extra-duty nature of the act. We are touched by the behaviour of a driver who stops on the highway in order to help us repair our car, not so much because his assistance is vital (we could wait for the break-down service), but because it shows kindness and concern beyond what could be expected. This may also explain why we normally do not disapprove of people who *ask* for a favour, whereas we criticize or feel uneasy about people who ask for big contributions of money or other services that involve considerable cost to the agent. By asking for a favour one expresses the desire to be treated not merely as a subject of rights, but also as a friend, and this implies the willingness to treat others similarly. Doing favours normally establishes a personal relationship based on reciprocity (we can return favours much more easily than acts of beneficence or of moral heroism). All these features of favours bear strong similarities to forgiveness, as will be shown in the last section of this chapter.

Yet unlike generous giving and saintly conduct, it is hard to say whether a given service is a favour or a moral requirement; is it our (natural) duty to pick up a hitch-hiker on the road, or is it only a duty when weather conditions are bad and no alternative public transportation is available? Is lighting the cigarette of a stranger in the street an optional act of kindness or a basic human requirement? I have to leave these questions unanswered, though I wish to argue that such acts cannot be both obligatory *and* favours at the same time. Our theory requires that failure to do a favour should never be criticized as morally wrong. Other theories take a different view. Feinberg, for example, excludes favours from the scope of supererogation, because they do not fit either of his two models of supererogation (over-subscription or non-duties which are abnormally risky and meritorious). Although he admits that doing a favour is never obligatory, he insists that it may be what we *ought* to do in a certain situation (Feinberg, 1968, pp. 392–6). But again, if the 'ought' means just 'the best thing to do' – an advice – then favours *are* supererogatory; and if 'ought' means a kind of requirement, how can Feinberg say that favours are never obligatory?

Finally, there is a logical connection between 'favour' in the sense of supererogatory service or an act of kindness, and 'favour' in the sense of preference or partiality. Like many other paradigm cases of supererogation, doing favours involves *favouritism* – a special concern for the good of a certain individual person. Moral heroism and beneficence can be exercised both on the personal and impersonal levels. Favours are confined to the personal level, and cannot be performed impersonally. In this respect favours again resemble acts of forgiveness and mercy. There is nothing morally wrong in the partiality involved in favours, as long as they do not violate the principles of comparative justice (cf. 5.1). On the contrary, personal preference is essentially one of the justifications of supererogation.

7.5 VOLUNTEERING

Volunteering is a paradigmatic example of supererogation. In its wider general meaning ('undertaking a service of one's own free will' according to the *O.E.D.*) it virtually characterizes any supererogatory action. Yet in its more specific meaning, volunteering refers to a special kind of supererogatory conduct. It is the offering of one's services (help, etc.) to do something which is collectively *required of a group*. Typical cases which call for volunteers are, accordingly, those in which there is a certain mission which must be carried out, or an objective which must be achieved by the group as a whole, although in fact it only requires the action of one (or a few) member(s) of the group, and does not allow for the equal distribution of the burden among the members. There may be no criteria for ascribing the duty in question to any particular member rather than another, or there may be such criteria. In the first case the volunteer is the one who voluntarily selects himself to perform the required act (this is the impersonal and primary sense of the concept); in the second case, the volunteer relieves another person of the responsibility of doing the required act by arbitrarily assuming it as his own duty (which may be interpreted as a personal favour). A third intermediate case is that in which the authority in charge of ascribing the mission to an individual shuns the responsibility involved, either because the criteria are vague and controversial, or because the sacrifice demanded is very great. The supererogatoriness of the act of volunteering consists in the *procedure* of selecting the agent of an act rather than in the content of the act. The volunteer does something which either there is no reason why *he* (rather than anyone else) should do, or there is a good reason why he is *not* the one to do (e.g. it is someone else's duty). Yet there is always a reason why *someone* should do the act which calls for volunteers. The distinction between 'collective duty' which is disjunctive and 'personal' duty may be put formally thus: in the former the 'O' operator (Ought) applies *de dicto*: O {(∃x) (x does q)}; in the latter it applies *de re*: (∃x) {O (x does q)}. On the other hand, other supererogatory acts, like those of moral heroism, cannot be regarded as being collectively required, even not of society as a whole. Such acts are performed in cases in which ∼O {(∃x) (x does q)}. Volunteering (in the strict sense) cannot, therefore, be taken as a model of all supererogatory action. There are borderline cases which *may* be analysed on the model of volunteering – like giving money to those who are in need (assuming that it is the duty of society to take care of those people).

When there are no relevant guiding principles to determine which of the members of a group ought to do the required action the just and fair procedure of selection is casting lots, which gives every member an equal chance of being selected to perform the action (and it may be the duty of anyone who is in charge of such a group to implement that selection procedure). Volunteering in such a situation goes beyond duty (that of accepting the verdict of the procedure of random selection) in a typically supererogatory way.

Although the situation which gives rise to volunteering bears some similarities to imperfect duties, the analogy should not be over-stressed. An imperfect duty requires of someone to do a certain number of actions of a certain class, but does not specify *which*. A duty which applies disjunctively to a group requires the performance of a particular action, yet fails to specify the individual agent who should undertake it. Thus, volunteering cannot be analysed on the model of over-subscription to a duty, doing more of a certain class of actions, but should rather be understood on the model of doing more than is required (i.e. by doing more than one's share according to the verdict of random selection).

As is the case with favours, the moral value of volunteering lies in its purely optional character, in the willingness of a person to do more than is demanded (although as with a favour, it can be a response to a request as well as a spontaneous decision). Volunteering is meritorious even if the mission involves only marginal loss to the agent (or indeed even if – as sometimes happens – the agent eventually benefits from it). Volunteering is intrinsically better than casting lots as a selection procedure; it is more honourable, although by no means more (or less) just and fair.

Volunteering is then a typically supererogatory act. It can only become a moral duty under circumstances in which the selection procedure of an agent is improperly applied. It is the duty of the person whose duty it is to perform the action required to offer to replace that member of the group who has been unfairly ordered to perform the act. In some cases of supererogatory volunteering the morally modest person *feels* that it is *his* duty to do the required action (even though the principles of justice place that duty on someone else).

7.6 SUPEREROGATORY FORBEARANCES

Supererogation (like obligation) may be predicated of *omissions* as well as actions. Acts of forbearance are supererogatory when a person does not do something which he is morally *entitled* to do, like demanding less than his due, or not insisting on his rights (granting 'a period of grace'). Forgiveness and mercy also involve supererogatory forbearance, since full punishment or justifiable resentment is withheld. Supererogatory forbearance must, according to our definition, be intended for the good of others. Letting others have our share, as a matter of neglect, is not supererogatory. Many omissions appear to be supererogatory though they are not so, because they do not satisfy the condition of altruistic benevolence. Forgiveness and mercy are supererogatory forbearance because they can never be unintentional. Yet they involve more than just refraining from punishment or resentment.

Applying condition (2) of our definition to supererogatory omissions yields a slightly different analysis from its analogical one for supererogatory actions. For in the case of actions beyond duty we argued that their omission is not wrong, i.e. morally permissible, whereas in the case of supererogatory omissions, it is often the case that commission is not only not wrong but indeed the right and just thing to do (e.g. punishment).

Supererogatory forbearances involve doing less of the due amount of something which is undesirable to another person. It cannot be thus interpreted on the model of over-subscription to duty or obligation. But it does not mean that the second half of condition (3) is inapplicable to omissions. On the contrary, the case of forbearances proves that the extra-duty aspect of supererogation should be analysed – as we have tried to do – as doing more than is required by the natural duties of mutual help, concern for others, friendliness, and respect. We can do more than is required, in these respects, by way of forbearance no less than by way of performance of actions. Unless we construe it in a quantitative manner, the continuity thesis can be held to be valid for supererogatory omissions as well. And these omissions should by no means be correlated to *negative* duties, which we claimed cannot be surpassed in a supererogatory way.

Moral systems that derive the moral authority of duties from the personal will of God may trace the reason for the existence of supererogatory acts to the supererogatory forbearance of the moral law-giver who demands of us less than he justifiably could have (Chisholm, 1963, p. 13). It is, however, a theoretical model which cannot be applied to secular morality, which is based on autonomy (be it Kantian, Contractarian or any other). Moreover, the idea of God forbearing supererogatorily from placing us under more demanding moral duties is inconsistent, because such a forbearance could be supererogatory only if God was *entitled* (had a right) to demand more, and not just if he *could* (had the power to) do so. But God's being the sole source of moral duty and justice is incompatible with his being subjected to moral constraints on his legislative power. More generally, the correlativity condition implies that not all forms of leniency are supererogatory. Mercy, as we shall presently see, is supererogatory only if it is related to certain norms (moral entitlements). Withholding *un*fair punishment can hardly be called supererogatory.

A borderline case of supererogatory forbearance is the performance of an act which strictly speaking is obligatory, yet is so exceptionally difficult, that failure to do it is excusable. Such an act is not supererogatory in the sense of going beyond the call of duty, but is supererogatory in the deliberate forbearance on the agent's part to appeal to the excusing provisos.

7.7 FORGIVENESS, MERCY, AND PARDON

Forgiveness and mercy have attracted in recent years much philosophical interest. Most discussions consist of analyses of the concepts and of attempts to reconcile them with various theories of punishment and justice. Little attention has, however, been paid to their supererogatory nature. For reasons briefly mentioned at the beginning of this chapter we take these concepts as being typical examples of supererogation. This by no means implies that forgiveness, pardon, and mercy are always supererogatory. The Home Secretary, who exercises the royal prerogative of mercy, may be under a *moral* duty to pardon a convict – e.g. in cases in which he is satisfied that it is another person who committed the crime, even if that cannot be proved for some reason or other in the courts (and hence does not justify the reopening of the file or a retrial). Or, consider the judge, whose moral duty it is to be merciful as a means of adjusting a malformulated law to circumstances which make the application of this law unduly harsh.[3] Mercy and pardon are obligatory when (full) punishment is undeserved or unjust. They are supererogatory when it is both legally and morally deserved. I shall argue for a supererogatory interpretation of cases of mercy, pardon, and forgiveness and claim that they do not conflict with justice. Or in Isabella's words: 'I do think that you might pardon him/And neither heaven nor man grieve at the mercy' (*Measure for Measure*, act II, scene ii).

Forgiveness, mercy, and pardon are all responses to some kind of wrongdoing (injury, offence, crime, insult, etc.), which are alternative to other, and no less just, reactions – like resentment, punishment, and retribution. Such an alternative creates a disturbing dilemma: if the latter type of response is just and deserved (which excludes cases discussed in the previous paragraph), how can the former be morally justified, let alone praised? We may reconcile

---

[3] These cases of pardon and mercy are, according to Smart, 'misnamed'. They are not the 'genuine' cases (Smart, 1969, pp. 212–7). They have what might be called a *corrective* function (cf. our discussion of equity and its relation to justice in 2.3). They only go beyond *legal* duty, and hence are not really supererogatory. An ideally just and sophisticated legal system could do without this type of mercy and pardon altogether.

these two alternative types of reactions to wrongdoing in two ways: either by treating them both as different, though compatible, kinds of duties, or – as I would like to advocate – by regarding forgiveness, mercy, and pardon as supererogatory.

The attempt to treat mercy, forgiveness, and pardon as duties exhibits the tendency to 'legalize' morality, i.e. to treat all morally appropriate reactions to a wrongdoing as part of a theory of justice and punishment (cf. Roberts, 1971, pp. 352–3). Rashdall, for example, argues that the duty to forgive contradicts the duty to punish (and resent) only if we adopt a retributivist theory of punishment. In a utilitarian theory, forgiveness can be understood as a duty, which like that of punishment is directed to the achievement of certain social ends. Whenever forgiveness can prove to be more beneficial than punishment, it *ought* to be chosen. In all other cases, it is wrong. Yet Rashdall himself is aware of the defects of the Butlerian 'cool' utilitarian account of forgiveness, and admits 'that there must be something more in forgiveness than the mere limitation of vengeance by the demands of public welfare'. Forgiveness 'touches the heart' not because it is supererogatory, but because it means 'laying aside *private* or personal resentment', which is especially difficult for the injured party. Nevertheless, according to Rashdall, if it is in any way right, then forgiveness is a duty (Rashdall, 1924, vol. 1, pp. 306–11; Ewing, 1929, pp. 115–16).

Alwynne Smart, who discusses mercy rather than forgiveness, joins Rashdall and Ewing in treating it as a *duty*, but departs from them when she argues that it is a duty which can be understood only against the background of a retributivist theory. The duty to grant mercy (or for that matter to forgive) makes sense only if the remitted punishment is appropriate, and only if the offender *deserves* punishment (regardless of its actual effects or utility) (Smart, 1969, pp. 217ff). Mercy is justified by the claims that other duties have on us (e.g. to consider the effects of the deserved punishment on the offender's family or health). Mercy, in other words, is justified as one duty among others which co-exist in a pluralistic retributivist theory (rather than in a monistic utilitarian theory, which subjects all duties to the one principle of utility).

This solution is, however, inconsistent. Smart says that mercy in the 'genuine' sense is justified 'only where we are compelled to be merciful by claims that other obligations have on us'. But what is the weight of these other obligations? Must they not be part of the considerations which determine what the appropriate and just penalty should be? In other words, if they are moral obligations, they must be part of the system of justice, and consequently Smart is willy-nilly led back to the 'corrective' sense of mercy. We must conclude, then, that if mercy is taken to be a moral duty, it must be subordinated to the wider considerations of either utility or due punishment, and hence neither utilitarian nor retributivist theories of punishment can allow for a duty to grant mercy in the genuine, non-corrective, sense.

Other theorists avoid the inconsistencies of utilitarian and retributivist reductions of mercy by insisting on placing it in a wider non-legal context (Roberts, 1971, Kleinig, 1969). For although (given the conclusion of the last paragraph) the judge – whose only job is to administer justice – cannot show mercy in the genuine sense, kings, presidents, fathers, and friends can do so. Indeed, mercy is sometimes construed as any benevolent concern for the welfare of poor and suffering people – even if they have not done anything wrong. In that broad meaning, mercy is typically supererogatory and does not involve any clash with justice. The short papers of Kleinig and Roberts contain the seeds of a supererogatory account of mercy, but neither of them makes it explicit. Roberts correctly insists (contrary to Smart) on the *gratuitous* nature of mercy, as it is the free relinquishment of rights, the giving up of something which is the due of the merciful person.

If forgiveness, mercy, and pardon can be shown to be supererogatory, the problem of reconciling them with just punishment naturally disappears. What is needed is not proof of the compatibility of the duty to forgive with the duty to administer justice, but simply an analysis which makes it plain that acting benevolently does not necessarily conflict with the requirements of justice (Seneca, On Mercy, in *Moral Essays*, pp. 435ff.).

So far we have been considering the deontic status of mercy, pardon, and forgiveness without paying attention to the differences in the logical properties of these three concepts. Recent literature abounds in discussions of these differences, which are not always easily drawn because of the ambiguity of these concepts. For our present purposes, a few remarks may suffice. Forgiveness is usually confined to personal relations. The right to pardon is basically a power conferred on some person in a special capacity or role. Thus we all have the power to forgive friends or any fellow human beings who have wronged us, while pardon is granted by judges, kings, presidents, etc. Forgiveness is the restoration of personal relations which were severed by the act of injury. Pardon involves the remission of penalty. Forgiveness is thus compatible with punishment, as it belongs to a logically different level of reaction to a wrongdoing. Forgiveness is a reaction to an insult or an injury rather than to an offence, and is the alternative to continued resentment; pardon is related to a violation of the law or the normative order, and is an alternative to (full) punishment. Forgiveness can be granted only by the injured party, but pardon is usually exercised impersonally by a third party. Forgiveness presupposes recognition by both parties of the wrongness of the action and its agent's responsibility; pardon can be granted to innocent people, and also asked for by people who know they have done nothing wrong (and this is one of the uses of the royal prerogative of free pardon). Forgiveness must be expressed in actions other than a declaration of intent; pardon on the other hand may be granted through a 'performative utterance'.[4] Forgiveness, being a matter of personal relationship, implies the equality of the forgiver and the forgiven; pardon implies a superiority–inferiority relationship, as it requires special powers to remit punishment. No reciprocity can be expected with pardon. One consequence of these differences is that forgiveness is not subject to any rules, whereas pardon is guided by certain rules (although it is debatable how specific these rules should be).

Mercy is used in various contexts – sometimes in the sense of leniency (in the courts), or in the sense of pardon (when exercised by an official), or just a benevolent concern for suffering people (i.e. when no offence has occurred). Mercy, unlike forgiveness, involves a superiority–inferiority relationship because it can be granted only by a powerful person or authority. As in the case of pardon, we can ask for mercy without acknowledging culpability. While forgiveness restores equality and reciprocity in personal relations, mercy creates a relation of dependence.

It is quite surprising that theorists of forgiveness, mercy, and pardon have not made explicit use of the idea of supererogation in their analysis. Most theorists stress the *virtuous* nature of forgiving and merciful acts. But when they come to define their deontic status, they argue that they are obligatory, or 'quasi-obligatory'

---

[4] For further discussion of some of these points, see Downie (1965), Horsbrugh (1974) and Neblett (1974).

157

(Kolnai, 1973–4, p. 105). Claudia Card holds an intermediate view of mercy, which resembles what we called qualified supererogationism. Mercy is not supererogatory, but neither is it obligatory. Yet there are conditions under which mercy *ought* to be shown. These conditions make the offender *deserve* mercy. Such desert is the only reason for *not* punishing the offender, i.e. for not acting on the principles of justice (without being unjust) (Card, 1972). I will argue, however, that (a) desert does not entail an 'ought' (except in the commendatory sense), and (b) mercy may sometimes be justified (as a supererogatory act) even when the offender does not deserve to be pardoned.

But if we take some typical examples of pardon, forgiveness, and mercy and test them in the light of our definition of supererogation, it will immediately become clear that the concepts bear the marks of supererogation. In accordance with condition (1), to forgive or to pardon is permissible, i.e. not wrong. When we say that X was wrong in forgiving Y, we usually mean that Y did not deserve to be forgiven, rather than that X did something wrong or blameworthy. Mercy too is always permissible, although it may be undeserved. Pardon, however, should be exercised with certain restrictions (e.g. of comparative justice) because of its official and social status. Pardon is wrong when used as a vehicle to realize certain objectionable goals or policies. Thus, exercising pardon only towards convicts of a certain colour or creed is not permissible. Other moral restrictions on the power to exercise pardon relate to the stage of the judiciary procedure in which pardon is granted. It is generally believed that to grant pardon prior to conviction in trial (or to proof of innocence) may be morally wrong (as in the case of the pardon given to ex-President Nixon). Otherwise, pardon conforms to the requirement of condition (1).

The application of (2) is more controversial, for it implies that forgiveness and pardon are not only permitted, but that their *omission* is not wrong. Withholding them *may* sometimes be wrong, but then it is mercy and pardon in the corrective sense which is referred to. Not showing mercy to someone who fully deserves punishment is not morally wrong. It may reflect the absence of a *virtue* (especially if mercy is consistently withheld), but that is not the same thing. Forgiveness may perhaps exhibit condition (2) more clearly. It is not wrong not to forgive an injurer, provided that resentment is justified. It is true that sometimes harbouring resentment can be justified only as a short-term attitude, but not as a permanent one. In those cases we ought to forgive. Some people would wish to argue that resentment is never justified if the offender has sincerely asked to be forgiven. For such people, forgiveness is supererogatory only when granted without being asked for. In any case forgiveness is not always obligatory, although the criteria which make it obligatory vary according to one's moral views (e.g. when is resentment justified).

The purely optional character of supererogatory action is better illustrated by forgiveness than by pardon. In our personal relations, we are free to exercise mercy or to withhold resentment in an inconsistent way, i.e. without being constrained by the principle of treating like cases alike. Forbearing from being merciful is not morally wrong – neither in itself, nor because other similar cases in the past were treated mercifully. Forgiveness is based on non-universalizable considerations, and may express legitimate favouritism. As long as resentment is justified, the injurer cannot complain of not being forgiven on the ground that previous similar injuries were forgiven by the same person. It is perfectly all right to forgive someone whom we love, and to withhold forgiveness from someone whose company we just wish to avoid. Pardon (in the legal context) is, however, subject to certain general rules, guidelines, and non-personal considerations. It should never be granted as a personal favour, and it must not reflect a personal bias. In exercising pardon, like cases should be treated alike. Yet the criteria of relevant similarities, and which factors of the situation make the convict deserving of pardon are left to the personal judgment of the sovereign. This is the *discretionary* aspect of the power to grant pardon. It should be added that the very point of both forgiveness and pardon is that they are in principle unpredictable, unlike actions which fall under legal rules), i.e. they are never guaranteed. We cannot rely on the mercifulness of a judge or a sovereign (or even a friend) when we decide to engage in offensive action.[5]

This raises the question of *desert*. Philosophers who deny forgiveness and pardon a supererogatory status claim that we ought to pardon or forgive if certain conditions obtain – particularly those which make the offender deserving of remission of penalty or of the

---

[5] Twambley offers a similar account of the optional and 'gratuitous' nature of forgiveness and mercy. Yet he does not specifically refer to the supererogatory status of mercy and forgiveness and their relation to duty (Twambley, 1976, pp. 84–90).

withholding of personal resentment. The anti-supererogationist accounts go further and argue that forgiving and pardoning, when they are undeserved, are inappropriate and wrong. Mercy, pardon and forgiveness are, accordingly, treated either as obligatory or as forbidden acts, which means that they are completely reduced and incorporated into considerations of justice. That, I believe, is blatantly counterintuitive. We distinguish between what a person deserves and what is due to him (what he is entitled to). The conditions of desert are 'not specified in any regulatory or procedural rules' and it is impossible to give any *a priori* principles for resolving conflicts between what is deserved and what is due (Feinberg, 1970, pp, 58, 80). The due gives rise to rights and claims and hence to duties; desert does not entail rights and duties. If a person deserves to be pardoned, it only means that he is worthy of it, that there are good reasons which call for remission of his punishment (a certain quality of character, good behaviour in the past, repentance, etc.), but these reasons do not create an obligation to pardon, nor do they render the omission of pardon wrong. We can even say that an offender 'deserves' punishment (i.e. it is right to punish him) and deserves mercy (by virtue of his character, past deeds, etc.) at the same time. For these are two different kinds of desert, based on different grounds. And again, lumping entitlements and desert into one category makes pardon part of the machinery of justice, which it clearly is not. We may add that the distinction between what is due and what is deserved applies to other cases of supererogatory action as well. One may deserve to be treated charitably, but never claim it as one's due.

In a supererogationist view of pardon, even underserved remission of penalty may be treated as supererogatory. Here the action is clearly beyond duty, but is it good, i.e. does it satisfy condition (3)? There are moral philosophers who treat mercy as always undeserved, unjustified, and absolutely gratuitous. Such a view I think goes too far, to the opposite extreme. Although it is true that we may act mercifully towards someone who does not deserve it (provided that condition (3) is met), these are not the usual cases of forgiveness, mercy, and pardon. (Compare this with cases of doing favours for someone who was in the past ungrateful, or giving money to someone who is not really in need). Wishing to avoid an anti-supererogationist analysis of the concept of mercy, these philosophers believe it must be treated as groundless. But that wrongly

160

assumes that having good reasons for doing something creates an obligation to do it. The king, who has the legal authority to pardon, may consult his advisers and informally accept advice as to the appropriateness of an act of pardon. His resulting decision is now neither groundless, nor capricious, nor arbitrary, yet it is still discretionary and supererogatory. But it is true that there is an *ad hoc* element in the supererogatory acts of granting mercy, pardon, and forgiveness (which is logically linked to the unpredictability of these actions). Pardon is granted on an individual basis and does not require justification in terms of publicly promulgated general rules whose application can be foreknown.[6] It is exactly this *ad hoc* element which is absent from the policy of pardoning only people of certain race or religious group. For in that case the power to pardon is exercised systematically and consistently in a way which serves a morally deplorable ideology. According to the supererogatory interpretation of pardon, the phrase 'ought to pardon' means only a recommendation, a counsel directed to someone who wishes to be virtuous without, however, doing something which is undeserved by the beneficiary.

The supererogatory nature of forgiveness and pardon should be carefully tested in the light of condition (3). The moral value of forgiveness and pardon is not always clear. The utility or consequential value is not as easy to assess as that of other paradigm cases of supererogation. It is of course rightly presumed that mercy and pardon are morally good in that they reduce the suffering of the wrongdoer. But the utility value of forgiveness is not easily definable. It may be the interest of the forgiven (especially when he asks to be forgiven), but can forgiveness be said to have good consequences if the forgiven does not particularly mind whether personal relations are restored or not? This difficulty may perhaps be solved by concentrating on the *intention* behind the forgiving act rather than on the actual consequences for the forgiven. For it is the decision and intention to forgive which constitute the supererogatory act, although some other behavioural manifestations of that decision are also necessary. It may be hard to predict whether an act of forgiveness would, in fact, cause a change of attitude and behaviour

---

[6] Pardoning a convict because of a suspicion that he was a victim of misidentification does, however, require a reconsideration of the cases of other convicts who might have been misidentified as well. But here the wrongness of an *ad hoc*, individual, pardon stems from the typically corrective function of pardoning.

in the forgiven, but as long as the intention is altruistic, the act is supererogatory.

Forgiveness is considered to be morally good also because we appreciate friendly relations, respect for persons, and equality in personal relations as intrinsically good. Resentment – even if it is justified – is never a virtue; forgiveness – even if it is undeserved – is always a virtue. This brings us to the second source of moral value mentioned in condition (3) of our definition, the extra-duty nature of the supererogatory act. Forgiveness is 'touching' (as Rashdall says) because of its free, optional character, that is its being more than could be morally expected or claimed. In forgiveness, more than in other paradigm cases of supererogation, this source of moral value can be detected. For it is exactly the giving up of something which one has the full right to harbour (hostility feelings), which makes the restoration of friendship and mutual respect meaningful. Both parties are aware of the fact that, despite the right not to forgive, the wronged person did forgive, and that this reflects a decision to substitute a friendly approach for the justified hostile attitude. Such a shift from one level of relationship to another is morally permitted and valuable because it is not *un*just, because it is good and altruistic (the only possible loser being the agent of the act, although unlike other cases of sacrifice, the forgiving party cannot strictly speaking be described as losing anything).

Granting legal pardon or exercising mercy in an impersonal context is also morally good both for its consequences (reduction of suffering) and for its optional, benevolent character. Although no personal bonds between the authority having the power to pardon and the pardoned convict are created, acts of pardon may lead to the strengthening of social cohesion, to the reduction of (unjustified) resentment of the convict towards his society, and to the promotion of trust. The official who has the power to pardon is in a way representing society at large, which is prepared to exact less than it is entitled to. Besides the constraints of justice, only great social risk or actual harm to society or to the authority of the law, can justify the prohibition of exercising mercy. The effectiveness of pardon consists in its being beyond what is required, and that may be further shown by comparing it to condonation, which is ineffective and rarely wins the respect of the wrongdoer. Some pardoned criminals may reform their lives just because they are aware of the gratuitous nature of the act which has made them free.

Forgiveness, mercy, and pardon satisfy the condition of correlativity. If forgiveness and mercy were not an *alternative* to justice, but rather the standard reaction to wrongdoing, they would have meant something completely different. For then they could not have meant remission of due penalties or withholding justified punishment. Furthermore, they would hardly have been able to serve the social and personal purposes they are meant to serve.

The continuity of supererogation with duty is, however, less easily applicable to this group of concepts. Pardoning does not consist in doing more than is required, or in achieving a certain value to a greater extent than that achieved by obligatory action. In this respect it is harder to justify an act of pardon, since it does not meet a certain requirement (punishment) and then go beyond it (as in the case of over-subscription). This difficulty can be solved by classifying forgiveness, mercy, and pardon as *supererogatory forbearances* rather than as supererogatory actions. Although they certainly involve action (in contrast to condonation for instance), their analysis should follow that of forbearances: to forgive is to renounce the moral right of resentment; to pardon is to relinquish the right to punish; to grant mercy is not to insist on what is due. All these actions are, therefore, continuous with justice rather than with duty. Justice makes punishment the due reaction to an offence, but not the obligatory one. It leaves room for the wronged party to relinquish the right to punish (with criminal offences it is society at large – through an official). We can go beyond justice without violating it by giving up our share, or what is due to us. And this is the case when we act mercifully towards someone who has wronged us or owes us something.

To conclude: pardon is supererogatory both when it is deserved and when it is undeserved – as long as punishment is due. It is a moral duty only when punishment is not due, and then it is not genuine pardon, but pardon as corrective measure. Deserving genuine pardon may give rise to a recommendation for pardon, but not to an obligation. An act of pardon (mercy, forgiveness) which is undeserved may be called saintly since, as in other saintly acts of supererogation, we feel that we are not in a position even to encourage or to urge the agent to supererogate.

The application of condition (4) does not pose special problems. Acts of mercy, pardon, and forgiveness are clearly intentional, as they are not merely forbearances, but involve also an active change of attitude and behaviour, or a change of legal state. They are meritorious, and call for gratitude (less with forgiveness than with pardon and mercy). Reciprocity cannot be guaranteed, that is to say, a forgiving person cannot demand to be treated similarly when he himself is asking for forgiveness, although failure to forgive someone who has forgiven us in the past may reflect ingratitude.

Forgiveness, mercy, and pardon are important cases of supererogation because the *opportunity* to practise them is always present. Unlike other types of supererogatory behaviour which may be blocked by the existence of other duties, urgent needs, moral weakness, absence of appropriate occasions etc., forgiveness (and even mercy) can be exercised by everyone. It rarely conflicts with other duties or with the pursuit of basic goods, it involves no heroism (in most cases), and everyone very often has the opportunity to engage in this kind of action (we are all wronged or offended by someone sometime).

Finally, a brief note on divine mercy, pardon, and forgiveness may be helpful. Although God's attitude towards man has always been cited as the most typical example of forgiveness, pardon, and mercy (Grace), it has recently been seriously contested by philosophers, who argue that it is logically impossible for God to forgive, that His granting mercy can only be conceived either as Divine Justice or as illegitimate favouritism. The human features of forgiveness and mercy (i.e. being personally offended, having pity, having personal preferences, etc.) make this type of behaviour unbecoming to a perfect Being (Minas, 1975; Hughes, 1974–5). Nevertheless, we have the idea of a *personal* God together with the idea of a *non-human* perfect Being, and this is perhaps the source of confusion.

According to Protestant theology salvation is not *due* to anyone, and in that sense we may be all justifiably damned. God's pardon (Grace) is never even deserved, which makes it typically supererogatory. (This is perfectly compatible with the extreme anti-supererogationist view held by the Protestants in the human sphere). Yet strictly speaking, God's Grace cannot be called supererogatory, because it is not correlated with any duty or principles of justice which exist independently of God. In the final analysis, God as a forgiving and pardoning agent can be understood only metaphorically, as an ideal for human behaviour.

8

The limits of moral duty

This final chapter is concerned with the justification of the distinction between supererogation and duty. Such a justification may be of two types: theoretical (meta-ethical) or normative (moral). The theoretical justification aims at demonstrating the usefulness – indeed, the necessity – of the concept of supererogation for the explanation of some important 'facts' of morality (e.g. some basic intuitions, everyday practices, and social institutions). So far we have been engaged mainly in this type of justification, showing the inadequacy of reductionism and anti-supererogationism and offering a theory of unqualified supererogationism that can be applied to some important paradigm cases. Anti-supererogationists may, however, still raise objections to the soundness of the moral intuitions and social practices that are taken by the theory as widely accepted facts of morality. They may argue that charity, forgiveness, and kindness *ought* to be required as duties, even if most people do not think they should be. Against this line of attack the theory of supererogation must supply a normative justification; that is, it must define the moral grounds and value of supererogation. The following sections concentrate on this type of justification (although it should be emphasized that meta-ethical and normative considerations cannot always be totally separated from each other, and that the critique of the theory of reasons for action is fundamentally of a theoretical nature).

The normative justification, whose function in part is to confirm the validity of certain moral intuitions, cannot appeal directly to these intuitions. It must offer a wider view of the nature of duty, of the relationship between the individual and society, and of the moral good – a view entailing supererogationism. Similar to the theoretical analysis of the concept of supererogation, the normative justification aims at the rebuttal both of anti-supererogationism and of qualified versions that allow for acts beyond duty only under certain conditions. In other words, I hope to show that supererogatory behaviour has intrinsic value in some ideal-world situations too, and by that to support the unqualified theory of supererogation.

There are two aspects of the justification of supererogation: the negative and the positive. In negative terms, supererogation is justified by showing that some supererogatory acts must exist because society cannot require of the individual every act that would promote the general good, and because the individual has the right to satisfy his wants and to achieve his ends and ideals regardless of their social utility (with some obvious limitations, of course). On the positive side, supererogation can be proved to have moral value by pointing out the freedom of the individual involved in purely optional choice, the social cohesion resulting from supererogatory behaviour, and the rationality of voluntary altruistic behaviour. The justification in negative terms has a priority over the positively formulated one (hence the title of this chapter), firstly because it is easier to justify the restriction on the scope of duty than to show the value of non-obligatory well-doing as such, and secondly because the value of supererogation is partly derived from its relation to duty (the correlativity and continuity theses). Indeed, the normative justification basically amounts to the explication of the second source of moral worth mentioned in condition (3) of our definition. The correlativity thesis shows, however, that a justification of supererogation does not mean taking the idea of duty lightly; on the contrary, it makes supererogation a complementary part of a theory of duty.

Urmson mentions five grounds for the distinction between 'basic rule' (duty) and 'the higher flights of morality' (supererogation) (Urmson, 1958, pp. 211–14). Put concisely, these are: (1) the special urgency of the values secured by the morality of duty, (2) the incapacity of ordinary men to go beyond basic duty, (3) the difficulty of formulating rules of supererogatory conduct, (4) the limits of our right to demand of others to serve our interests, and (5) the superiority of action based on free choice to action under (moral) pressure. Now the first four grounds belong to the negative aspect of the justification; only the fifth refers to the intrinsic value of supererogatory behaviour. The first four grounds justify supererogation only in the sense that they point out the limits of duty, leaving room for actions beyond it. The criteria of these limits are in the first three grounds 'pragmatic' (relating to urgency, capacity, and complexity of rules), and as such they do not justify supererogation beyond what I have called the qualified version.[1] The first two seem to be valid grounds for the general distinction, even if one might still think of sorts of action we would wish to call obligatory though they are not so urgent as to be indispensable, and of sorts of action we would tend to call supererogatory though they are not beyond average human capacity (cf. Schumaker, 1977, pp. 11–12). The third ground seems to me more vulnerable to criticism, not only because it is contestable whether the morality of duty is based on rules, but also because we can easily formulate *simple* rules prescribing supererogatory behaviour (e.g. 'one always ought to forgive'). The first three grounds are more plausible if they are confined to the justification of saintliness and heroism. But Urmson mentions them as referring to 'the higher flights of morality', of which saintliness and heroism are only typical examples. Urmson's fourth argument is what we called the negative justification of supererogation, but he does not work out a full justification of the distinction between what may be demanded from others as a matter of right and what may only be hoped for and received with gratitude. I shall offer a general moral view of the relation between the individual and other persons (or society), that supports Urmson's distinction as well as the last, positive ground (5).

8.2 'GOOD', 'OUGHT', AND REASONS FOR ACTION

The justification of supererogation must answer the criticism that the first two conditions of our definition are inconsistent with the last two – either logically or morally. In other words, it must be shown that there is nothing paradoxical in a good and meritorious action being completely optional, even if it is morally better than alternative non-optional actions. Raz formulates the dilemma in the language of reasons for action:[2] if a supererogatory action is morally good (praiseworthy) there must be reasons for doing it, and these

---

[1] And indeed this is perfectly consistent in Urmson's theory, which explicitly and intentionally avoids an attempt to justify supererogation in ideal-world situations. See, ibid., p. 210. For a critical discussion of Urmson's conditions see Attfield (1979).

[2] Cf. W. D. Ross (1946, p. 3). Ross's main argument is that 'right' cannot mean both 'ought to be done' and 'morally good' at the same time.

reasons must outweigh any conflicting reasons for not doing it; as there are conclusive reasons that require the performance of the act, one ought (conclusively) to do it; but if the action ought to be done, omission must be blameworthy. It seems, therefore, that an action cannot be both morally good and optional (Raz, 1975, p. 164).

Raz offers a solution to this dilemma in terms of what he calls 'exclusionary permissions'. Although we are not permitted not to act on the balance of reasons (namely the conclusive, overriding reasons), we are sometimes permitted to exclude those reasons from our considerations. An exclusionary permission is a *second-order* permission (backed by reasons) that entitles the agent to disregard the reasons for acting supererogatorily, that is to say, not to act on the balance of reasons (p. 165). According to Raz, not taking advantage of such an exclusionary permission is the praiseworthy element of supererogatory behaviour. Raz tries to solve the (apparent) inconsistency of the notion of supererogation without discarding the model of reasons for action or the concept of overridingness. He achieves this by distinguishing between two levels of *permissions*, a distinction which runs on parallel lines to that between the two levels of *reasons* (Raz, 1974, pp. 33–5).

Raz's theory fails, however, to stipulate the nature of the relations between these two levels (or orders) of reasons and permissions, noting only that they are 'separate though partly related'. The considerations (reasons) supporting the second-order exclusionary permissions cannot, according to the theory, be balanced against first-order reasons for action. Thus, though they cannot be described as overriding, they in effect are so. The fact that there are reasons entitling us to disregard the conclusive reason for action shows that the disregarded (excluded) reason is not really conclusive, i.e. not final or based on 'everything considered'.

In Raz's theory the maximization of human well-being may form a conclusive reason for action. Yet it can be excluded because of reasons relating to the value of human autonomy. But Raz does not explain why reasons of the former type create a first-order (conclusive) 'ought', while reasons of the latter type create an exclusionary (second-order) permission. Why cannot all the relevant reasons be balanced against each other? Why do not considerations of human autonomy create an 'ought' as well? It seems that Raz is unable to answer these questions because in the language of reasons for action there is no distinction between a moral 'ought' (yielded, for example, by considerations of human welfare) and a personal (or prudential) 'ought' relating to 'the pursuit of [one's] own fundamental goals' (Raz, 1975, p. 167).

So far my criticism of Raz's theory has been directed at his *theoretical* attempts to analyse the concept of supererogation in terms of reasons for action and exclusionary permissions. But beyond these meta-ethical issues, my aim is to question the *moral* assumptions involved in his normative justification of supererogation. In one of its meanings, according to Raz, a permission is *weak* if there is no *moral* duty to perform an act though there may be reasons of a different kind that require its performance (p. 161). Notwithstanding the pains he takes to criticize the very distinction between weak and strong permissions, Raz argues that exclusionary permissions are *strong*, i.e. 'not merely the result of the absence of reasons to the contrary' (p. 163). They cannot be taken for granted and always require a justification, because they authorize the exclusion of conclusive reasons. Now I think that the permission not to act supererogatorily can be treated as a weak, first-order permission (along the lines of Raz's own interpretation mentioned above). In other words, there are no reasons compelling us to prefer other-regarding to self-regarding reasons for action in cases of supererogation.

The disagreement between Raz's view and my own on that point is basically of a moral nature, not of a theoretical one. For I believe that we do not resort to special permissions (exclusionary or other strong permissions) when we refrain from supererogatory action. An appeal to second-order permissions is not needed, because it is not the case that the rational requirement (conclusive reason) is always to work for the good of others whenever it is greater than the good of the agent resulting from an alternative course of action. The idea of human autonomy (of which I shall have more to say below) is sufficient to invalidate Raz's moral assumption 'that an agent has reason to maximize human welfare assigning equal weight to the interests of every human being including himself' (p. 167). Moreover, considerations of human autonomy need not be introduced only as grounds for the second-order permission; they can and should play their part in the balance of first-order reasons. (For similar criticism see Clarke, 1977, p. 254).

So although I am in full agreement with Raz's evaluation of the importance of human autonomy, my argument is the reversal of his. According to Raz, people ought to bring about valuable states of affairs, but sometimes there are other (higher-order) reasons permitting them to disregard this reason. I suggest a view according to which human beings are free to pursue their own life plans and ideals, although sometimes there is indeed good reason to require them to sacrifice some measure of their autonomy for the sake of others. Contrary to Raz, it seems that what demands a special justification is not the priority given by the individual to his life plans and ends, but the *requirement* to sacrifice these plans and ends for the sake of the welfare of others, or for the general good.

Although Raz strongly rejects qualified versions of supererogationism (theories that treat failure to act supererogatorily as wrong but excusable), he does not adhere to a completely unqualified version either. His view seems to lie somewhere in between, containing some reductionist elements: supererogatory acts ought to be performed (if one is to act on the balance of reasons), but there is a permission (backed by moral considerations) which entitles the agent to act contrary to the requirement of practical reason. The reversal of Raz's argument, discussed in the previous paragraph, does not recognize the *prima facie* obligation to promote the general good whenever it is possible, and hence does not require an appeal to a special permission not to do so. By that reversal a purely unqualified formulation of supererogationism is accomplished.

Towards the end of his article Raz again expounds the dilemma involved in the concept of supererogation: if the promotion of human welfare is more important than the pursuit of one's own ends, how can one be permitted not to be engaged in the former? And if the converse is true, how can the promotion of human welfare be praiseworthy (p. 168)? Raz wishes to solve that dilemma by distinguishing between two levels of reasons for action, but fails to explain the nature of the relationship between them, and to state why considerations of human autonomy rather than those of social good belong to the second-order level. An anti-supererogationist could easily argue that it is considerations of social welfare which require us to exclude the reasons of human autonomy.

It seems that the model of reasons for action is inadequate to the explanation of supererogation. Raz himself admits that in the case of supererogation the competing reasons for action cannot be compared in terms of strength, a comparison that is the basis of the theory of reasons for action. The distinction between two levels of reasons does not solve the problem, it only defers it. The language of reasons for action ought to be supplemented by a moral evaluation of the reasons on which people act. The two types of reasons cannot be compared in terms of *strength*, but one type can definitely be regarded as *morally* superior to the other. Acting for the good of others while one is entitled to pursue one's own ends (i.e. when there are no moral duties which require such altruistic concern) is morally praiseworthy and meritorious, because morality is concerned with the promotion of other people's good. But this does not imply that such an action is backed by stronger or better reasons (from the point of view of practical reason), i.e. that one *ought* to do it. The concept of supererogation implies only a permission not to act on the most praiseworthy reasons. It does not involve the notion of rationality, as both the performance of supererogatory acts and their omission may be equally rational (supported by reasons). A theory of reasons for action cannot account for the concept of supererogation, because such a theory does not refer to *moral duties*, or to moral value in general. Raz's dilemma is best solved by abandoning the language of practical reason altogether, rather than by elaborating it.

The so called 'good–ought tie-up' is invoked both by anti-supererogationists and by qualified supererogationists. Essentially it is a moral thesis which purports to show either that no (morally) good action can be completely optional, or that it can be regarded as optional only on the grounds of further mitigating or excusing conditions (psychological or moral). But this moral thesis seems to take advantage of the wide range of incompatible uses of 'ought'. In its *commendatory* use it may very well be logically tied in with 'good'; it may also be so – according to some theories – if it is understood as constituting *a* reason for action (as it is indeed rational to do the good, to promote whatever is valuable). 'Ought' is also entailed by 'good' if it is interpreted *impersonally* as 'ought to be' (i.e. if *X* is a good state of affairs, let *X* exist). But all these uses fail to support the moral position of the critics of unqualified supererogationism, because what is relevant to their critique is whether 'good' entails 'ought' in the *prescriptive*, *personal* sense. My view is that it does not.

The basic reason for the existence of a gap between judgments of what is good to do and what one ought to do is that 'good' may be used impersonally, while 'ought' involves human agency. This is a general difference between value concepts and deontic concepts.

'Good' characterizes states of affairs, motives, personality traits as well as actions, independently of the existence of agents who can bring them about or hope to. 'Ought', however, at least in its prescriptive sense, applies only in situations in which there is an *agent* of whom a certain action is required. Even the apparently impersonal phrase '*X* ought to be done' has a prescriptive force only if it applies conjunctively (or disjunctively) to members of a certain group. It cannot be the case, therefore, that any valuable state of affairs in itself constitutes a reason for action (in the sense of 'ought') for an individual person.

Moral reasons for action prescribing what one ought to do arise, then, not from the desirability of states of affairs, but from a certain *relationship* between the agent and the beneficiary of the action. In this I follow Prichard's argument, 'that in order to think of some change as one which *we* ought to cause, we must think of the change as in some special way related to ourselves...' (Prichard, 1949, p. 153). This special relationship may originate from family relations, jobs, previous undertakings, opportunities to help someone in need, justice, etc. If Prichard's view is correct, it suffices to refute Moore's claim that if my happiness is good, then everybody has an equal reason to pursue it.[3] It is not true that one ought always to do whatever is good (or best), because one's *own* good may have priority in one's practical reasoning – even if it is less good than that achieved by an alternative action. The good–ought tie-up is loosened by considerations of personal autonomy, which constitute the basis of both the negative and positive justification of supererogation.

8.3 THE AUTONOMY OF THE INDIVIDUAL

Individuals have the right to pursue their own ends, to satisfy their wants, and to try to realize their personal ideals. The fact that a certain action serves their own interests constitutes for them a good reason for doing it. Morality, as a system of duties and obligations, puts *some* constraints on that basic freedom of the individual. Yet

[3] Ross follows Prichard in criticizing Moore for ignoring the personal aspect of moral duty (Ross, 1946, pp. 19, 22), but later suggests a more qualified view according to which we have a '*prima facie* duty to produce as much that is good as we can' (p. 25).

172

like social institutions and systems of rules, morality (in the form of duty and justice) should serve the individual in his search for self-realization rather than be served by the individual for its own sake. In this sense, rights precede duties. The autonomy of the individual means that he has a special reason to fulfil his own needs before getting involved in the fulfilment of other people's needs. The general moral view of the relation between individual and society outlined here is basically equivalent to the starting point of contractarian theories on the one hand, and to Mill's approach in *On Liberty* on the other hand. To borrow Dworkin's terminology (of his classification of the basic types of political theories), our *justification* of supererogation is 'right-based' (Dworkin, 1977, pp. 171ff). Nevertheless, our *definition* of supererogation contained elements of the other types of theories – the 'duty-based' and the 'goal-based'. The three-fold classification suggested by Dworkin roughly overlaps von Wright's (the deontic, the axiological and the anthropological) and we are now in a position to see the relevance of all the three dimensions to supererogatory action. Although the concept of supererogation is logically linked to duty on the one hand and value (good) on the other, the justification for going beyond the duty to promote the good must be in terms of individual rights. In that respect I fully accept Mackie's thesis that a right-based morality is not only possible, but a necessary basis for all morality (Mackie, 1978), although the axiological condition (3) is also necessary for the moral justification of supererogation.

The negative justification of supererogation amounts to the substantiation of the view that when considerations of social good conflict with considerations of individual good it is not necessarily the case that the former have more weight – even if from the point of view of the *overall* good they are in fact weightier. In his critique of utilitarianism, Bernard Williams puts this point very forcibly: according to utilitarianism an agent should adopt 'the general project of bringing about maximally desirable outcomes', but he can carry out that project only if (other people) have 'lower-order projects' which he can help to realize. These projects are personal, and depend on individual inclinations, interests, capacities, and preferences. But 'unless there were first-order projects, the general utilitarian project would have nothing to work on, and would be vacuous' (Smart and Williams, 1973, p. 110). Williams's argument is aimed at utilitarianism, but it is no less valid as a critique of

173

extreme universal altruism or pure anti-supererogationism. For if everyone worked for the promotion of the *general* good, *whose* good would be promoted? I agree with Williams that it is the first-order life plans and projects that should be taken as the starting point, and that morality as a system of requirements 'works on' these plans and projects with the purpose of safeguarding their free pursuit and the just distribution of the means of their realization. So although from the moral point of view it is certainly good to help someone else to achieve his goals, it cannot be generally required, even if his goals are higher or more important than the agent's. Further, although within the moral system of duty or justice every individual counts the same, impartiality cannot be expected of a person when he compares the weight of his own desires with that of others. For the integrity of the individual consists exactly in the special weight he gives to his own ends. The abstract ideal of promoting the general good makes the role of the individual agent to be merely a 'locus of causal intervention in the world' towards the achievement of that ideal.

This general picture of man and the relationship between personal life plans and public (overall) welfare explains the limited role of the morality of duty. It is not a system of requirements aiming at the maximization of general good or happiness, but only a means of securing some minimal conditions of cooperation and justice. Such a minimalist concept of moral duty cannot, therefore, exhaust the whole realm of moral value, and hence leaves room for acts beyond duty that are nevertheless morally good. I have tried to argue that persons are not tools for the promotion of good, and consequently that they have the right to moral relaxation – i.e. not always to take the *needs* of others as constituting a *claim* for help, even if such a help could be lent at a reasonable price. For people are entitled to be different and to have more than others. Yet sharing one's fortune with others (when it is beyond the requirement of justice) is morally good, and supererogatory. My argument for the limitation of duty on grounds of individual autonomy is analogous to the widely accepted belief that individual persons should not be sacrificed for the promotion of overall happiness (as in the case of punishing an innocent man in order to save the lives of many others). For considerations of justice make it unacceptable to require any individual to work ceaselessly for the welfare of others (or to the point at which the marginal utility of his effort becomes zero). The non-utilitarian concept of justice serves both to counter utilitarian arguments for the punishment of an innocent individual and to support the distinction between duty and supererogation.

It should be noted that the proposed negative justification for holding a distinction between supererogation and duty applies to the unqualified version of supererogationism. It implies that we need no excuse for not acting beyond the call of duty, and that even if we are capable of acting heroically (and it suits our character and inclinations), we are still free not to do so.

The positive aspect of the justification of supererogation is concerned with the value of supererogatory action itself rather than with the grounds for limiting the scope of duty. Individual autonomy does not only yield a right not to be compelled to act for other people's good, but is also of intrinsic value itself. The morality of supererogation is based on freedom and voluntariness in a more radical sense than that of freedom and voluntariness in the morality of duty. The decision to act beyond what is required is free not only from legal or physical compulsion, but also from informal pressure, the threat of moral sanctions, or inner feelings of guilt. It is purely optional.

Such a freedom allows for the exercise of individual traits of character and for the expression of one's personal values and standards of moral behaviour. Being purely optional, the supererogatory act is spontaneous and based on the agent's own initiative. Not being universally required (of everyone in a similar situation), supererogatory action breaks out of the impersonal and egalitarian framework of the morality of duty – both by displaying individual preferences and virtues, and by allowing for some forms of favouritism, partial and unilateral treatment of someone to whom the agent wishes to show special concern. This may result in friendship and in an attempt to return a supererogatory service (thus creating a higher type of reciprocity than that required by the system of mutual rights and duties). These characteristics of supererogatory behaviour are valuable partly because some types of virtuous behaviour can be realized only under conditions of complete freedom and would be stifled under a more totalitarian concept of duty. Supererogation is necessary as providing an opportunity to exercise certain virtues. It should be noted, however, that in discussing the value of supererogatory action, I am naturally restricting my attention to the more significant examples of actions beyond duty. It would of course be

175

hard to justify the special value of the relatively trivial acts of supererogation, or of those which arise from bad motives; nonetheless I have, for theoretical reasons, included them in the definition of supererogation.

John Stuart Mill presents a series of powerful arguments in support of individual freedom and autonomy. These arguments are not *directly* relevant to our present discussion, for they are put forth in the context of Mill's objection to the paternalistic interference of society in the *private* affairs of the individual (i.e. in those 'moral' actions which do not directly affect other people). It is not clear whether Mill would be willing to extend his individualistic arguments so as to protect people from social interference in some matters which do affect others (such as supererogatory behaviour). From some remarks in *On Liberty* it seems to me that Mill would be prepared to widen the scope of his argument so as to justify the limitation on the moral duty to maximize goodness (utility) in the world. For example, when speaking of those actions which 'are fit objects of moral reprobation, and in grave cases, of moral retribution and punishment', Mill lists actions injurious to others, actions violating rights, unfair and unjust actions, and forbearances from defending others against injury (Mill, 1865, p. 46). But he does *not* mention there every omission of morally valuable or altruistic action that can be said to be required by the principle of utility. It seems that Mill would classify such supererogatory forms of conduct as belonging to the same category as those actions which are strictly private, in the sense that they should all be equally protected from social intervention by the principle of individual liberty. But even if this interpretation of Mill is rejected, his arguments for individual autonomy and a pluralistic society are applicable to our justification of supererogationism.

The justification of the distinction between supererogation and duty bears some similarities to the reasoning behind the objections to Good Samaritan legislation (Ratcliffe, 1966). Good Samaritan laws make certain morally wrong actions punishable by law (e.g. the refusal to lend help to people in peril). Those who wish to restrict such legislation believe that not all moral duties should be legally binding. Similarly, supererogationists think that not all morally valuable acts should be considered as (morally) obligatory. Both parties hold that compulsion (legal and moral respectively) is in itself bad, and cannot be justified simply by proving the desirability of the enforced action. Those who oppose the attempt to legislate on moral affairs argue that it is not only self-defeating (in the sense that coercing people to comply with the moral duty of gratitude, honesty, or respect changes the very nature of the act), but that it also amounts to an illegitimate violation of individual freedom. According to this view there is a *moral* difference between the threat of physical punishment (through law) and the more informal pressure of society on the individual to comply with certain moral standards. There are areas of behaviour (often referred to as 'matters of conscience') in which moral blameworthiness does not warrant (legal) punishment. It is accordingly perfectly consistent to regard blood-donation as a moral duty (at least under some conditions), but to oppose any suggestion to make it legally binding.[4]

The argument against Good Samaritan legislation is based, therefore, not only on the self-defeating nature of such coercion, or on its impracticality (high costs, procedural problems), but also on the view that it is intrinsically better to act from a sense of duty than from fear of legal sanctions. It should be noted that the concept of individual freedom assumed by such a view is wider than that held by those who are interested in keeping the law out of the sphere of private morality (i.e. those actions which do not harm others); the present view maintains that even if they are harmful to others (mainly by not being beneficial to them) some actions should be immune from legal intervention.

The analogy between the limits of the legal enforcement of morals and the limits of moral duty relates both to the negative and to the positive justification of supererogation by means of the concept of individual autonomy. It rests on the view that both the law and the morality of duty are means of achieving certain basic aims (such as security, social interaction, and basic justice), but should be kept confined to these vital functions. This is a minimalist approach complementing the basically individualistic view of man that I offered earlier. There is no paradox in leaving man legally free to do certain morally wrong actions; similarly, people should be morally free not to be virtuous.

---

[4] The case for Good Samaritan legislation in the narrow sense (saving people's lives when no risk is involved, or reporting to the police in case of witnessing a crime) is stronger, and I personally believe that much wider legislation than that existing at the present in Western countries can be justified. But the argument against legislation in many other areas of morally wrong behaviour is not necessarily weakened by this view.

Finally, the analogy between the problem of legislation and supererogation can be extended to the reaction of the beneficiary of the act. Even the fervent objectors to Good Samaritan legislation hold that the voluntary rescuer should be immune from prosecution (by the beneficiary of his act), and in some cases should even be awarded compensation for losses incurred by his voluntary action. This corresponds to our strong condemnation of ingratitude in cases of supererogation. The fact that certain good acts should not be imposed on us as legal or moral duties does not imply the authorization of ingratitude or the treatment of gratitude as merely optional.

8.4 SOCIAL ASPECTS

There is a famous Talmudic saying: 'Jerusalem was only destroyed because judgments were given strictly upon Biblical law and did not go beyond the requirements of the law' (*Tractate Baba Mezia*, folio 30b). It expresses epigrammatically our common moral disapprobation of societies in which supererogatory behaviour is rare, societies which do not recognize the value of action beyond duty. We usually regard a social organization or a group that does not encourage supererogatory action (let alone that fails to leave room for it) as morally deficient. Such a critical judgment is perfectly compatible with a minimalist view of the scope of the morality of duty. For although social institutions (like clubs or armies) should make obligatory only those actions vital to the very existence and reasonable operation of the institution, they should be so devised as to make supererogatory conduct possible and sometimes rewardable.

Indeed, some people maintain (as does the author of the Talmudic saying) that some measure of supererogatory behaviour is necessary for the existence of society. Although, except for obligatory standards (which must apply universally), not every (or any particular) member of the group ought to do more than is strictly required, the survival of the group requires that some people surpass the minimal standards. Such a view is consistent with supererogationism, because it does not imply that supererogatory standards should be *enforced*; on the contrary, it is their voluntary (optional) character which gives them their social value. In this respect, the social gains of supererogatory conduct can serve as an additional justification to that put forth in terms of individual autonomy.

178

As in the sphere of personal relations, supererogatory action may contribute to the strengthening of social bonds and augment the feelings of a close-knit community. For by doing more than is required a member of a group shows that he has an interest in his fellow members which is deeper than his contractual commitments, or than the personal benefit he can draw from his membership in the group. Consequently, the relations between the members of the group become more friendly, personal, and based on good will. Benevolence and gratitude enhance mutual trust and confidence (since supererogatory action is usually indicative of a stronger altruistic motive than that of doing one's share or duty). Supererogatory morality adds love of one's fellow-beings to the duty of respect for persons.

So although theoretically the morality of duty is sufficient for securing basic cooperation in society, both social cohesion and dignity are conditioned by the willingness of some people to transcend justice – i.e. the relations of claims and counter-claims. In this respect the social benefit of supererogation supports only the unqualified versions of supererogationism. But even if a society (or an institution) could survive if its members no more than adhered to the requirements and rules of behaviour, it would be morally deficient. Our objection to such a society is analogous to our judgment of an individual who never forgives, who is never charitable in his dealings with others, and who always and without exception insists on his rights. Although societies – unlike individuals – cannot have duties in the basic sense of the word, cannot strictly speaking be virtuous, and *ipso facto* cannot be agents of supererogatory action, they can be judged as morally worthy or deficient.

The social value of certain supererogatory forms of behaviour has been recently discussed and debated in the context of charity and blood-donation. In his controversial comparative study of systems of blood-supply, Richard Titmuss tries to prove in much detail the advantages of a voluntary system (such as the one existing in Britain) – in economic, medical, social, and ethical respects. His argument is highly relevant to our purposes, for he claims that even if cost-benefit analysis showed that commercialization of the system of blood-supply was not economically inferior in terms of efficiency and cost, ethical considerations would still make the voluntary system more desirable (Titmuss, 1973, pp. 84–5, 101–2). In other words, economic considerations do not cover all the relevant

179

reasons in making social choices. The ethical justification of the voluntary system is that 'no money values can be attached to the presence or absence of a spirit of altruism in a society', and that altruistic behaviour 'may touch every aspect of life and affect the whole fabric of values'. It is the role of a voluntary system of blood-donation to satisfy the 'biological need to help' (p. 223, but cf. Arrow, 1972, pp. 350–1). I tend to agree with Titmuss that it is highly probable that a decline in the spirit of altruism (or volunteering) will be accompanied by deep changes in other spheres of human relationship.

Titmuss's thesis may be extended so as to coincide with our view of the value of supererogation in general. The incommensurability of economic and what Titmuss calls social considerations is parallel to our criticism of utilitarianism (in its anti-supererogationist versions). According to both my view and Titmuss's, efficiency in achieving desirable ends (for instance public welfare or maximum happiness) may be outweighed by considerations of individual autonomy and values that cannot be measured in economic terms. Furthermore, society ought (by means of social policy) to enable men to exercise their freedom to give voluntarily, a freedom which is severely curtailed in a commercialized system, or in a system which makes giving obligatory. Social institutions must provide the opportunity to practise altruism.

More recently Titmuss's study has been fiercely attacked by economists, who contest both his empirical findings and his general approach to economics and its role in social policy-making.[5] They claim that commercial systems of blood-donation have not proved to be either less efficient or to endanger social stability. To investigate the merits of these criticisms would carry us beyond the scope of the present topic. I think, however, that part of the criticism is unfair to Titmuss and wrongly attributes to him the view that altruistic giving should be preferred to commercialization even if it were to have disastrous effects on the amount of blood supplied to save lives. In general, the economic analysis of charity is irrelevant to our subject, because it does not define charity and gifts in ethical terms (viz. as something supererogatory, relative to duty and justice), but 'as an allocation at a price below the open-market price by those "giving away" the goods'. Economic analysis could accommodate charitable action if it included the moral satisfaction

---

[5] See the interesting collection of articles, Seldon (1973); particularly the article by Alchian Allen.

and value derived from the good action (the second source of value in our definition) as an economic benefit, i.e. as having a 'price'; but then such an analysis would go beyond pure commercial considerations, and furthermore it would encounter extreme difficulties in attempting to compare the values of the outcomes of actions with the ethical value of the altruistic behaviour. Nevertheless, I agree with Titmuss's critics that the *social* justification of charity (or supererogation) is dependent on highly complex empirical analysis (much more than the justification in terms of individual autonomy). Moreover, it is true that society can encourage supererogatory behaviour by means of economic policy (as in the case of income-tax reductions for gifts).

8.5 SUPEREROGATION AND IDEALS

The justification of supererogationism rests in part on the widely accepted distinction between duties and ideals. For supererogatory action may surely be considered as a moral ideal of a certain kind. Supererogatory conduct is guided by a regulative principle specifying what one ought to do if one desires to achieve moral perfection or merit (as in the case of the hypothetical 'ought' of the Evangelical Counsels). But as we shall presently see, the distinction between supererogation and duty does not wholly coincide with that between ideals and duties.

Many ethical theorists believe in the dual nature of morality: on the one hand, there is the morality of duty, obligation, and justice, which is essentially social and formulated in universal principles; its standards are strictly binding as they constitute the minimum required for the preservation of society. On the other hand, there is ideal morality, the morality of love, virtue, and aspiration, which is not formulated in universalizable principles; it is related to the diversity of values of individual persons; it is 'open-ended', in the sense that there is always more to be done in a way which can be recommended by the ideal standards; the morality of ideals is sometimes said to be similar to religion or aesthetics, whereas the morality of duty is often compared to legal systems (Strawson, 1961; Fuller, 1969, ch. 1; Bergson, 1956, part 1).

Some aspects of this vague and general distinction are irrelevant to our purposes. For according to our theory the supererogatory is related to the obligatory in very specific ways, i.e. can be under-

181

stood only as a sort of extension of the morality of duty. In this respect supererogation is not part of 'ideal' morality; it is not merely an individual ideal or an 'ethical picture of life'. It lies somewhere between social morality and individual ideals and aspirations. It is social in the sense that a supererogatory act must be other-regarding and promote the same *kind* of good that is recognized by other people to be good. It is individual in the sense that the source of authority is the individual rather than society (social rules, a contract, or a socially conditioned conscience). Being continuous with duty, supererogatory standards – though being left wholly optional – may be publicly recommended. In other words, they are not necessarily only privately pursued as are some individual ideals of the Strawsonian type. The special relation of supererogation to duty renders it easier to justify supererogatory ideals, since they realize the same kind of value as duties do. Supererogation, therefore, belongs to the 'moral' rather than to the 'ethical' (in the Strawsonian meanings).

Still, supererogatory standards of behaviour share with ideals the *exemplary* status, and hence an important role in moral education. A person performing a supererogatory action is often presented as a model to be imitated. The observers of his action are taught that it should be praised. Praise serves both as an encouragement and as a source of pride (Brandt, 1979, p. 289). Moral education tries to inculcate on the one hand conscientiousness, responsibility, obedience to the law, and fairness, but on the other hand points out the possibilities and the opportunities to act beyond duty and to exercise individual freedom in a virtuous way. Some theorists blur the distinction between these two educational functions of supererogation. They believe that the inculcation of supererogatory standards is valuable because it *guarantees* the adoption of moral principles of duty and justice (Gewirth, 1978, p. 330), or the fulfilment of imperfect duty (Schumaker, 1977, p. 43). But, as we have shown, the justification of supererogation consists of more than 'being on the safe side' (of imperfect duty or justice versus wrongdoing and violation of rights). It is good in itself. Although we may not put pressure on people to act supererogatorily, we may expose them by various means to some standards of moral excellence which would make them try to emulate those who live up to such standards.

The force of my justification of supererogation must, however, be qualified. I have attempted to outline a broad view of the value of individual autonomy and its priority over considerations of overall good and utility. But it must be admitted that such a picture of man and of the nature of morality cannot be 'proved'. Here lie the limits of a normative justification. Those who support an alternative moral view may claim that respect for the moral law, or action according to universalizable principles, is good in itself. They may argue that the value of individual autonomy cannot outweigh the value of a system of requirements covering all morally good ends. As in many other fundamental issues in philosophy, the basic divergence in views is expressed in the methodological argument on the *onus probandi*: according to my minimalist theory of moral duty the burden of proof lies on those who wish to make a certain action, rule, or standard obligatory. But for the anti-supererogationist it seems only natural to lay that burden on those who wish to excuse people from doing the most desirable action. I doubt whether such a basic disagreement in moral outlook can be resolved by rational argument, and it has not been the pretence of this book to offer such an argument.

Bibliography

Acton, H. B. 1963. Negative utilitarianism, *Aristotelian Society* Supplementary Volume **37**, 83–94.

Ambrose, St. *Concerning Widows*, New York: The Fathers of the Church.

Aquinas, St Thomas, 1928. *Summa Contra Gentiles*, London: Burns Oates & Washbourne. First published 1259–1264.

1947–8, *Summa Theologica*, New York: Benziger Brothers. First published 1265–1273.

Aristotle, 1925a. *Ethica Nicomachea* (trans. W. D. Ross), London: Oxford University Press.

1925b. *Ethica Eudemia* (trans. J. Solomon), London: Oxford University Press.

Arrow, K. J. 1972. Gifts and exchanges, *Philosophy and Public Affairs* **1**, 343–62.

Attfield, R. 1979. Supererogation and double standards, *Mind* **88**, 481–99.

Augustine, St (n.d.) *Holy Virginity*, New York: The Fathers of the Church. *Letters*, New York: The Fathers of the Church.

Baier, K. 1958. *The Moral Point of View*, Ithaca, N.Y.: Cornell University Press.

Berger, F. R. 1975. Gratitude, *Ethics* **85**, 298–309.

Bergson, H. 1956. *The Two Sources of Morality and Religion*, Garden City, New York: Doubleday.

Brandt, R. B. 1979. *A Theory of the Right and the Good*, London: Oxford University Press.

Burchill, L. M. 1965. In defence of saints and heroes, *Philosophy* **40**, 152–7.

Calvin, J. 1863. *Institutes of the Christian Religion* (trans. H. Beveridge), Edinburgh: T. & T. Clark. First published 1536.

Card, C. 1972. On mercy, *Philosophical Review* **81**, 182–207.

Chisholm, R. M. 1963. Supererogation and offence: a conceptual scheme for ethics, *Ratio* **5**, 1–14.

1964. The ethics of requirement, *American Philosophical Quarterly* **1**, 147–53.

Chisholm, R. M. and Sosa, E. 1966. Intrinsic preferability and the problem of supererogation, *Synthese* **16**, 321–31.

Chopra, Y. 1963. Professor Urmson on 'saints and heroes', *Philosophy* **38**, 160–6.

Clarke, D. S. 1977. Exclusionary reasons, *Mind* **86**, 252–5.

Cohen, B. 1967. An ethical paradox, *Mind* **76**, 250–9.

Cooper, N. 1959. Rules and morality, *Aristotelian Society* Supplementary Volume **33**, 159–72.

Downie, R. S. 1965. Forgiveness, *Philosophical Quarterly* **15**, 128–34.

Dworkin, R. 1977. *Taking Rights Seriously*, Cambridge, Mass.: Harvard University Press.

Eisenberg, P. D. 1966. From the forbidden to the supererogatory: the basic ethical categories in Kant's 'Tugendlehre', *American Philosophical Quarterly* **3**, 255–69.

Ewing, A. C. 1929. *The Morality of Punishment*, London: Kegan Paul, Trench, Trubner and Co.

Feinberg, J. 1966. Duties, rights, and claims, *American Philosophical Quarterly* **3**, 137–44.

1968. Supererogation and rules. In *Ethics*, ed. J. J. Thomson and G. Dworkin, New York: Harper & Row.

1970. Justice and personal desert. In *Doing and Deserving*, ed. J. Feinberg, Princeton: Princeton University Press.

1974. Noncomparative justice, *Philosophical Review* **83**, 297–338.

Findlay, J. N. 1961. *Values and Intentions*, London: George Allen & Unwin.

Forrester, M. 1975. Some remarks on obligation, permission, and supererogation, *Ethics* **85**, 219–26.

Fuller, L. L. 1969. *The Morality of Law*, New Haven: Yale University Press.

Gert, B. 1966. *The Moral Rules*, New York: Harper & Row.

Gewirth, A. 1978. *Reason and Morality*, Chicago: The University of Chicago Press.

Gibson, E. C. S. 1898. *The Thirty Nine Articles*, London: Methuen.

Glaser, J. W. 1970. Commands-counsels: a Pauline teaching?, *Theological Studies* **31**, 275–87.

Godwin, W. 1971. *Enquiry Concerning Political Justice*, Oxford: Clarendon Press. First published 1793.

Gregor, M. J. 1963. *Laws of Freedom*, Oxford: Basil Blackwell.

Grice, G. R. 1967. *The Grounds of Moral Judgement*, Cambridge: Cambridge University Press.

Hancock, R. 1975. Mill, saints and heroes, *The Mill News Letter* **10**, 13–15.

Hands, A. R. 1968. *Charities and Social Aid in Greece and Rome*, London: Thames and Hudson.

Hart, H. L. A. 1961. *The Concept of Law*, Oxford: Clarendon Press.

Heyd, D. 1978. Ethical universalism, justice, and favouritism, *Australasian Journal of Philosophy* **56**, 25–31.

1980. Beyond the call of duty in Kant's ethics, *Kant-Studien* **71**, 308–24.

Hill, Th. E. 1971. Kant on imperfect duty and supererogation, *Kant-Studien* **62**, 55–76.

Horsbrugh, H. J. N. 1974. Forgiveness, *Canadian Journal of Philosophy* **4**, 269–82.

Hughes, M. 1974–5. Forgiveness, *Analysis* **33**, 113–17.

Humberstone, I. L. 1974. Logic for saints and heroes, *Ratio* **16**, 103–14.

Hunt, L. H. 1975. Generosity, *American Philosophical Quarterly* **12**, 235–44.

Kant, I. 1948. *Fundamental Principles of the Metaphysic of Morals*, ed. J. Paton, London: Hutchinson. First published 1785.

1949. *Critique of Practical Reason*, trans. L. W. Beck, Chicago: The University of Chicago Press. First published 1788.

185

1963. *Lectures on Ethics*, trans. L. Infield, New York: Harper & Row. First translation published 1924.

1964. The Doctrine of Virtue: Part II of 'The Metaphysic of Morals', translated by M. J. Gregor, New York: Harper & Row. First published 1797.

Kleinig, J. 1969. Mercy and justice, *Philosophy* **44**, 341–2.

Kolnai, A. 1973–4. Forgiveness, *Proceedings of the Aristotelian Society* **74**, 91–106.

Ladd, J. 1957. *The Structure of a Moral Code*, Cambridge, Mass.: Harvard University Press.

Lloyd-Thomas, D. A. 1970. Why should I be moral?, *Philosophy* **45**, 128–39.

Luther, 1957. *Works*, ed. H. J. Grimm, Philadelphia: Muhlenberg Press.

Lyons, D. 1965. *Forms and Limits of Utilitarianism*, Oxford: Clarendon Press.

1969. Rights, claimants, and beneficiaries, *American Philosophical Quarterly* **6**, 173–85.

Mackie, J. L. 1978. Can there be a right-based moral theory? *Midwest Studies in Philosophy* **3**, 350–9.

Mauss, M. 1954. *The Gift*, London: Cohen & West.

McCloskey, H. J. 1969. *Meta-Ethics and Normative Ethics*, The Hague: Martinius Nijhoff.

McConnell, T. C. 1980. Utilitarianism and supererogatory acts, *Ratio* **22**, 36–8.

Mill, J. S. 1865. *On Liberty*, London: Longman. First published 1865.

1969a. *Utilitarianism*. In *The Collected Works of J. S. Mill*, Vol. 10, Toronto: University of Toronto Press. First published 1861.

1969b. Auguste Comte and positivism. In *The Collected Works of J. S. Mill*, vol. 10, Toronto: University of Toronto Press. First published 1865.

Minas, A. C. 1975. God and forgiveness, *Philosophical Quarterly* **25**, 138–50.

Moore, G. E. 1948. *Principia Ethica*, Cambridge: Cambridge University Press. First published 1903.

1966. *Ethics*, London: Oxford University Press. First published 1912.

Neblett, W. K. 1974. Forgiveness and ideals, *Mind* **83**, 269–75.

New, C. 1974. Saints, heroes and utilitarians, *Philosophy* **49**, 179–89.

Peterfreund, S. P. 1975. Supererogation and obligation, *The Personalist* **56**, 151–4.

1976. A note on supererogation and utilitarianism, *The Personalist* **57**, 290–1.

1978. On the relationship between supererogation and basic duty, *The Personalist* **59**, 53–7.

Popper, K. R. 1966. *The Open Society and Its Enemies*, London: Routledge & Kegan Paul.

Price, R. 1948. *A Review of the Principal Questions in Morals*, Oxford: Clarendon Press.

Prichard, H. A. 1949. *Moral Obligation*, Oxford: Clarendon Press.

Rashdall, H. 1924. *A Theory of Good and Evil*, London: Oxford University Press.

Ratcliffe, J. M. (ed.). 1966. *The Good Samaritan and the Law*, Garden City, N.Y.: Doubleday.

Rawls, J. 1972. *A Theory of Justice*, Oxford: Clarendon Press.

Raz, J. 1974. Reasons, requirements and practical conflicts. In *Practical Reason*, ed. S. Körner, Oxford: Basil Blackwell.

1975. Permissions and supererogation, *American Philosophical Quarterly* **12**, 161–8.

Richards, D. A. J. 1971. *A Theory of Reasons for Action*, Oxford: Clarendon Press.

Roberts, H. R. T. 1971. Mercy, *Philosophy* **46**, 352–3.

Ross, W. D. 1946. *The Right and the Good*, Oxford: Clarendon Press.

Schüller, B. 1966. *Gesetz und Freiheit*, Düsseldorf: Patmos.

Schumaker, M. 1972. Deontic morality and the problem of supererogation, *Philosophical Studies* **23**, 427–8.

1977. *Supererogation: An Analysis and Bibliography*, Edmonton: St Stephen's College.

Seldon, A. (ed.) 1973. *The Economics of Charity*, The Institute of Economic Affairs.

Seneca, 1953. *Ad Lucilium: Epistulae Morales*, vol. 2, London: Heinemann.

1958a. De beneficiis. In *Moral Essays*, vol. 3, London: Heinemann.

1958b. On mercy. In *Moral Essays*, vol. 1, London: Heinemann.

Sidgwick, H. 1884. *The Methods of Ethics*, London: Macmillan.

Sikora, R. I. 1979. Utilitarianism, supererogation, and future generations, *Canadian Journal of Philosophy* **9**, 461–6.

Singer, P. 1972. Famine, affluence, and morality, *Philosophy and Public Affairs* **1**, 229–43.

Smart, A. 1969. Mercy. In *The Philosophy of Punishment*, ed. H. B. Acton, London: Macmillan.

Smart, J. J. C. 1967. Utilitarianism. In *The Encyclopedia of Philosophy*, ed. P. Edwards, vol. 8, London: Macmillan.

Smart, J. J. C. and Williams, B. 1973. *Utilitarianism*, Cambridge: Cambridge University Press.

Smith, A. 1948. *The Theory of Moral Sentiments*, New York: Hafner.

Stocker, M. 1967. Professor Chisholm on supererogation and offence, *Philosophical Studies* **18**, 87–93.

1968. Supererogation and duties. In *Studies in Moral Philosophy*, ed. N. Rescher, American Philosophical Quarterly Monograph Series.

Strawson, P. F. 1961. Social morality and individual ideal, *Philosophy* **36**, 1–17.

Taylor, C. 1906. *The Shepherd of Hermas*, London: Society for Promoting Christian Knowledge.

Tertullian, *On Exhortation to Chastity*, New York: The Fathers of the Church.

Tillich, P. 1954. *Love, Power, and Justice*, London: Oxford University Press.

Titmuss, R. M. 1973. *The Gift Relationship*, Harmondsworth: Penguin Books.

Tranöy, K. E. 1967. Asymmetries in ethics, *Inquiry* **10**, 351–72.

Twambley, P. 1976. Mercy and forgiveness, *Analysis* **36**, 84–90.

Urmson, J. O. 1958. Saints and heroes. In *Essays in Moral Philosophy*, ed. A. I. Melden, Seattle: University of Washington Press.

Walker, A. D. M. 1974. Negative utilitarianism, *Mind* **83**, 424–8.

Wasserstrom, R. 1964. Rights, human rights, and racial discrimination, *Journal of Philosophy* **61**, 628–41.

Watkins, J. W. N. 1963. Negative utilitarianism, *Aristotelian Society* Supplementary Volume **37**, 95–114.

Index